Dr. Erich Gershon Steiner

the story of the
Patria

HOLOCAUST LIBRARY
NEW YORK

STATEMENT OF PURPOSE

The *Holocaust Library* was created and is managed by survivors. Its purpose is to offer to the reading public authentic material, not readily available, and to preserve the memory of our martyrs and heroes untainted by arbitrary or inadvertent distortions.

With each passing day the memory of the tragedy of European Jews, the greatest crime in the annals of mankind, recedes into history. The witnesses and survivors of the holocaust are still alive, their memories remain vivid; yet, a malicious myth about their experience keeps rising before our eyes, distorting and misinterpreting evidence, perverting history.

As new generations arise, so grows the incredible ignorance about our tragedy. Millions of men and women, Jews and Gentiles, are unaware of the basic facts of the tragedy, many have never even heard the word "holocaust." This is a seed of a new disaster.

The holocaust story should be untiringly told and retold making the world aware of its lessons. This can contribute to that moral reconstruction which alone may prevent a repetition of the catastrophe in our hate- and violence-stricken world.

ERICH GERSHON STEINER

THE STORY OF THE "PATRIA"

Translated by Dinah Cohen

Copyright©1982 by Behira Steiner
Library of Congress Catalog Card No. 81-85302
ISBN: 0-89604-035-6   cloth
       0-89604-036-4   paper

Printed in the USA

Dr. Erich Gershon Steiner, the Author

The events described in this book are based upon historical occurrences.

The characters, except for historical personalities, are the author's own creation and are therefore fictitious.

FOREWORD

After perilous journeys under inhuman conditions on ships which were barely seaworthy, convoys of illegal immigrants who had been outlawed, deprived of their rights and exposed to every sort of chicanery and indignity finally reached the shores of the Holy Land after travelling in constant peril for their lives.

With desperate courage, they tried to save themselves from the Nazis. Behind them, their synagogues went up in flames and the mob of murderers, whose aim it was to bring about the Final Solution, lay in wait. Before them stood the gates of their national homeland, barred by decree of the British White Paper on Palestine.

In March 1939, the "Artemisia" brought illegal refugees from Czechoslovakia. Seventeen of its passengers were caught by the British.

In the same month, the "Sando" arrived with 269 people on board.

In April 1939, the "Estia," with 699 Czechoslovakian refugees was caught off the coast of Herzliya. Among the passengers were fifty children.

A few days later, two hundred passengers from the "Asimi" landed at the old Roman port of Caesaria. Immediately afterwards, 170 refugees went ashore near Ashkelon.

In May 1939, 522 Jews from Austria passed the Greek islands. One hundred fifty of them had visas for Shanghai. The rest reached the coast of Palestine on board the "Agius Nikolas."

During the same month, the British caught the "Atrata," weighing only 234 tons, which was carrying four hundred Polish refugees. The ship was flying the Panamanian flag.

On June 2, a British warship escorted the "Lisel," weighing 572 register-tons and which was also flying the Panamanian flag, and 920 illegal immigrants from Austria and Czechoslovakia into the port of Haifa.

Only six days later, the Palestine Police caught 240 people near Acco who had risked the journey in five boats.

On June 30, the "Aster" landed on the south coast of Palestine with 624 passengers from Danzig.

Three days later, the police caught the 370 passengers on board the "Las-Parlos" steamer near Netanya.

The "Rim" steamer, with over four hundred people on board, caught fire near Rhodes. An Italian ship, the "Fiume," came to its assistance and brought the passengers to Rhodes. Some of the survivors possessed entry visas, but 115 passengers had no passes.

On July 14, the "Frossula" landed, flying the Panamanian flag. Among the 649 passengers were 394 men. Three hundred of them, former soldiers in the Czechoslovakian army, presented themselves unanimously at the Czechoslovakian military mission in Palestine in order to fight side by side with the British against Hitler. There were seventy children included in the convoy.

On July 30, the "Colorado," flying the Panamanian flag, landed in Haifa with 373 passengers on board.

On August 22, 1939, the "Parita" docked with 850 refugees from Central Europe.

The "Tiger-Hill," weighing 1,500 register-tons, had 1,400 persons on board.

At almost the same time, five boats with 297 refugees from Austria, Czechoslovakia and Germany were caught. Among the passengers were twenty-six children.

A month later, another five boats arrived with 364 refugees from the Bohemian and Moravian Protectorate, Slovakia and Hungary. They had three rifles, eighteen revolvers and twenty bayonets.

In September 1939, the "Nomi-Julia," under the command of a Jewish captain, brought 1,200 refugees to Palestine.

In January 1940, the "Orion" brought five hundred people.

In the same month, the "Hilda" arrived with eight hundred illegal immigrants and four calves on board.

On February 15, 1940, the "Sakaria" reached Palestine with over two thousand people on board. The convoy was interned by the British for six months in the Atlit detention camp.

In June 1940, the "Libertad," weighing only ninety tons, arrived with 380 passengers who were interned for months in Atlit.

The last of this wave of refugees were some four thousand people on the "Atlantic," "Milos" and "Pacific."

The illegal immigrants on these three ships were to have been deported on the steamer "Patria" to Mauritius.

The following story deals primarily with the fate of the groups on the "Milos." The historical background is the period between March 12, 1938, (the "Anschluss") and November 25, 1940, the day on which the "Patria" sank.

Chapter One

The last heavy snowfall was over. Sparkling icicles, from which the drops fell with a uniformly monotonous sound in the midday sun, hung from the roofs. When they became elongated and weighted down by the snow which slid from them, the dripping stopped for a moment and they broke off from the painted green gutters and shattered with a clink on the pavement from which the snow had been shovelled clear. Swarms of crows who had flown towards the city that morning, now returned. They wheeled, croaking hoarsely, over the market place, and made for the small wood nearby.

Towards evening, the dripping stopped. The roads became slippery again and the ashes strewn by the peasants, which were supposed to stop people from losing their footing, lay under a film of ice. Next morning, the snow no longer crunched underfoot. It lost its white color, and gradually became a brown pulp, turning the village street into a hopeless morass. A few snowflakes still fell from time to time, but they did not settle, their chaste purity was engulfed by the brown pulp.

It was early spring at the Obrawa Bridge. The layer of ice on the stream was cracked. The gently splashing water licked at the sloping banks. The feathers of the rooks were iridescent in the sunshine.

Small avalanches slid off the steep roof of an inn which stood just beside the bridge, and covered its worn stone steps. The Reichsstrasse, which was flanked by tall lime trees, and ran almost completely straight from Brünn, now began to climb. It reached the top of the slope parallel with its younger sister, the railroad track, and from there it commanded an unobstructed view of the Raigern monastery. To the right and left of this street, which was still embedded in snow, lay the villages and townlets of prosperous Southern Moravia. In the distance, the Pollauer mountains loomed hazily, their vine-covered slopes still snuggled under the white blanket. Behind the mountains, which projected from the plain

11

like camels' humps, lay the little town of Nikolsburg, aloof and dreamy, and almost medieval in character. The Reichsstrasse crossed the main square and after a few hundred meters reached Austrian territory at Drasenhofen. Here it reassumed its old name, and continued on to Vienna as the Kaiserstrasse.

Empress Maria Theresa had renovated this road, once the trade route to Moravia. Her son and successor, Joseph II, travelled it in order to take stock of county affairs. He had himself locked up for an hour in the gun turrets on "Spielberg," the Brünn fortress, so that he could leave the cells with the words, "I am the last man to have sat here." Napoleon used the road, and the oak table where he had sat was still in the inn by the Obrawa Bridge. Here the Prussians marched against Vienna in 1866, after the Battle of Königgrätz, and it was by this road that Bismarck had travelled in order to sign the armistice after Nikolsburg. Here the children cheered the venerable philosopher, T. G. Masaryk, the first President of the Czechoslovakian Republic, every year as he made his way to Seelowitz Castle.

A petrol lamp still hung from a huge oak beam in the inn by Obrawa Bridge. Its smoke had blackened a spot on the whitewashed ceiling. A few wooden tables stood inside the inn, together with some hard, heavy benches. Behind the brown-stained wooden partition, old Müllan bustled about, half peasant, half innkeeper. His peasant stock had already lived in the village for close to three hundred years, tilling the fields which bordered the street as far as the railroad embankment. For nearly three hundred years, the Müllans' horses had drawn cumbersome carriages up the Raigern mountains, and for as long, no doubt, feeding troughs for passing carriage teams had stood opposite the gateway in the yard. A wooden signboard with the words "Inn-lodgings available" written in half-faded Gothic lettering, hung over the wide open door. A long covered passage led inside the courtyard to the stables. Every Saturday, it was swept clean, and its worn bricks were given a fresh coat of red paint every year for Corpus Christi day. Many years earlier, travellers' cart horses had been stabled there. Now, however, greatly to old Müllan's annoyance, they had been supplanted by cars, which used the open space in front of the inn as a parking lot. The Müllans had also furnished a guest room with another petrol lamp and a clothes hook. A charming oleograph with the inscription, "Holy Florian!

12

Save us from fire!" hung above the bed whose red-checked pillows reached nearly to the ceiling.

A narrow passage led from the kitchen to the oven, where large loaves for the peasants were baked from home-grown wheat. A wooden staircase led from there up to the attic, which housed chests of flour. Sacks of goose feathers swung near the ceiling from short lengths of rope, and further inside, home-made smoked meat and pressed salami dangled from long poles. The salami was rather too strongly spiced and its consumption left one somewhat thirsty. In the midst of all these delicacies hung the Kaiser's picture. The Müllans had been forced to store it there in October, 1918, after the establishment of the Czechoslovakian Republic. Flowers were laid in front of the picture every year on the Kaiser's birthday, and left there to wither. The national holiday on October 28 was spent by the Müllans in spreading dung over their fields, until they were beaten by angry Czech peasants from Raigern.

***

A somewhat hoarse flourish of trumpets broke the early May stillness. Glaring red flags billowed in the morning breeze; in the center of each one was a white shield with the inscription SDP (Sudeten-German Party). Row upon row of flagpoles lined the village streets. From the market-place down to the festive field at Mühlgraben — which only a few months earlier had still been a pigsty — there was a bright fluttering sea of red. The peasants had received their flags directly from the Party and the latter were thus all the same length, with the white SDP shield only loosely sewn on. The latter could be replaced with another, as yet forbidden shield, which was already awaiting its day hidden in the peasants' chests of drawers. Only from the roof of the town hall did the Czechoslovakian flag hang, according to the law. It looked tired and did not billow out, having become entangled somewhere around the flagpole. It did not even reach past the gutter. Perhaps the consumptive municipal employee, Johannes, had not had enough strength to push the pole further out through the dormer window. Perhaps the mayor had ordered him to keep this flag on a short mast. Two large SDP flags swelled out on either side of it. They looked like torturers dressed in red — coarse, impudent and vulgar.

The festive procession assembled in the fields opposite the

station, between the canned food factory and the Sauerkraut Company buildings. It was led by the village orchestra, in which Králíček, an habitual drunkard, whose parents did not understand a word of German, puffed some grunting notes out of his battered instrument. Behind the orchestra came members of the Young Gymnasts' Club, in rows of four. At their head was young Šenkiřik, who, as his name indicates, had not been rocked to sleep in his cradle by the breeze in the Teutoburger forest. The board which he carried on a short pole was crowned with oak leaves and bore the name "Mödritz." The young gymnasts were followed by squads of adult members. Instead of the usual pike-grey pants and T-shirt, they wore black riding-breeches, boots and white shirts. Then came a group of motorcyclists, similarly clad, with red SDP pennants fluttering on the handlebars of their vehicles. They crowded like a pack of wolves around an open car, filled with oak branches, out of which Konrad Henlein's rather fleshy head bowed to the spectators on one side of the road, while the mayor bowed to those on the other. A stiff SDP pennant fluttered on the radiator of the car. Shouts of "Heil" drowned the noise as the hard-faced cyclists throttled their motors. The latter were followed by the Brünn gymnasts dressed in black pants, boots and white shirts marching in rows of eight. At the front of each column went the oak-wreathed board and the flag-bearers. Next came the gymnasts from the German-speaking district of Wischau. They wore peasant dress: Svonovitz girls in red woolen stockings and black plissée skirts, Rosternitz girls in high-necked jackets with starched white frills around the collar, then peasant lads from Schöllschitz with stout sticks in their hands, South Moravians from Wisternitz, Polau, Pohrlitz, Wostitz, Nikolsburg and Frain — all in white stockings. Each group marched with its orchestra and a large placard. The Modritzers' board bore the words, "South German peasant! Keep hold of your plough!"; the Wisternitzers': "Moravia! Stay German!"; and the Rosternitzers': "!The Day is Nigh!"

The Czech police, who had been gathered in from the surrounding districts in order to keep order, walked tight-lipped at the side of the procession.

The marchers passed the War Memorial Chapel. The young pipers in the procession began to play in unison, while the drummers maintained the beat. The orchestras played snappy marching tunes, even the old Austrian Radetzky march. Shouts of "Heil"

14

exploded from the loudspeakers against the whitewashed cottage walls. A train of dust swirled around the procession of ten thousand. It veiled the chapel in which an eternal light burned before a small stone altar. The light, a tiny flickering oil lamp, glimmered for those whose names were hewn in gold letters on a marble tablet. It also gave light to the old country parson, Lithuanian Church Counsellor Johann Stranetzký who, in spite of his abhorred Czechoslovakian origins, had, after more than twenty years, still not forgotten his German parishioners who had fallen in Serbia, Italy and Russia.

On marched the procession, white stockings, black boots, red stockings, all in jaunty step. The road was clear, and it slowly passed the statue of Hans Kudlich, liberator of the peasants, who had left Austria for America in 1848 and had then written a long letter to the community back home.

"We shall march on, until everything disintegrates about us, for today the homeland is ours" — they had substituted 'Czechoslovakia' for 'homeland' — "and tomorrow the whole world."

This was the refrain of their marching song. It was not the homeland of Hans Kudlich who, now long dead and the son of a peasant, had left his country with a bleeding heart in order to serve mankind as a doctor in a remote continent.

The head of the procession had already reached the carefully cleaned-out pigsty. The car stopped, and Konrad Henlein, striding through the path formed by the black boots, mounted the speaker's platform. The bright red flags fluttered, as befitted such an ascent. The horses of the peasant cavalry who closed the procession shied at the thundering, thrice-repeated "Sieg-Heil" which rent the air and Rudi Scheibl, the mayor's son, fell off his bucking farmhorse. He tried to grab hold of the green saddle cloth, but only caught the black, red and gold border. The flimsy cloth could not bear his weight and tore. He fell with a resounding thud into a ditch and a Czech policeman helped him up.

Some black-booted men had taken up positions around the speaker's platform. A threefold, blank-faced wall of men from the "Freedom Watch," as they called themselves, protected Konrad Henlein — although no one would have dreamed of attacking him.

"Fellow-countrymen!" cried Henlein. "Sieg-Heil!"

"Sieg-Heil! Sieg-Heil! Sieg-Heil!" came an answering roar from those worthies. Short and clipped. "!Sieg-Heil!"

What the speaker actually said could hardly be heard. There were, after all, ten thousand people present and even when they stood still, the wind scattered Henlein's words after a few yards. Nevertheless, every sentence was followed by a shout of "Sieg-Heil!" Henlein had imported his gestures and gesticulations from the Reich. He had certainly received the text of his speech there, and had organized the whole march based upon an approved pattern.

He called upon heaven and earth to witness the injustice which was being inflicted upon his countrymen in Czechoslovakia — an injustice that had given them full equality of rights, and had not barred them from schools and government posts. These pampered offspring of the House of Hapsburg had also been able to keep their property after the collapse of the Donau monarchy in 1918, while all around Czechoslovakia, valuables were scattered to the winds during the years of inflation. They had begotten children, nourished them on the fat of the land and infused them, while still babes-in-arms, with a hatred of the Republic. These fine German patriots had travelled to Vienna between 1919 and 1924 and, in exchange for good Czech crowns, had stripped the impoverished and starving metropolis of its loveliest possessions. They had smuggled expensive butter and ham across the border. They had sat in the Viennese bars and theaters, when the city was ruined by inflation, with the beautiful sentiment, "there is but one Mödritz and one Vienna," forever on their lips. Vienna had remained their greatest delight, although for most of them it signified the Prater pleasure-gardens with the Watschenmann who gave such a deep growl when a peasant boy gave him a whack with his fist. Vienna was now German, as it had actually always been, despite the hundred thousand Czechs who lived there. Today, however, it was part of the Reich. The ancient seat of the Kaiser was no more than a provincial town in the Austria of the Greater German Reich. Moreover, the road which led there was exceedingly short — seventy-five miles from the Obrawa Bridge. The motorcycle squad of the Gymnastic Club had once made the journey in nine hours; the "Völkische Beobachter" and the "Stürmer" now made it in fewer than two, including the illegal frontier crossing. Was this not reason enough to shout "Sieg-Heil!" and again "Sieg-Heil!"; to carry Konrad Henlein shoulder high from the platform, to shake his hand reverently — the hand that had pressed the Führer's at the National Socialist rally in Nuremberg? Was it not reason

16

enough to place young Franz Müllan, who had ridden to bring the Führer greetings from Mödritz, between Henlein and the mayor in the car?

The great speech was over and the procession formed up again. The orchestras played the Hohenfriedberger march, the pipers tooting in unison. The drummers performed like troopers — tram-tram-tram-tram — and all the red stockings, black boots, white stockings, stepped jauntily in time with them. In rows of four, in rows of eight, they marched through the village, up the Bahngasse to the Sauerkraut Company buildings. Those from Brünn continued marching the four miles back to town; those from Wischau, Rosternitz and Svonovitz, went by train. Columns of trucks took the South Moravians down the Reichsstrasse. At the Obrawa Bridge Inn, they refreshed their dry throats — these noble German throats! — with beer from the Czech Kmunicek brewery.

The glorious day was drawing to an end. Tired and sullen, the policemen left the village. The cows, who had been fed that day in the greatest haste, lowed thirstily in their stalls.

The gymnasts formed ranks once more in front of the town hall while the flags were taken down. The Czechoslovakian flag dropped quickly, and as no one moved to roll it up, fell in the dusty gateway at the feet of the laughing mayor. The SDP flags were slowly let down and ceremoniously taken in. The peasants had no more time to take down the flags on their own houses, and so they fluttered on into the darkness as night fell.

***

At the corner of the market-place near the town hall, in which Rudolf Rössler, an invalid of the First World War, and his massive wife, Marie, ran the community guest house and a butcher's shop, was a large house. A cobbled footpath turned into the Schlössl — a small, almost equilaterally-sided square, which could be reached by way of a narrow alley. The castle, after which the square was named, had been burned down by the Swedish general Torstenson during the siege of Brünn in 1645. The castle's chapel had not escaped the flames, and pious peasants had cleared the debris from the hallowed spot after the end of the Thirty Years' War, and erected their new church there. They built a clock tower as lofty and as beautiful as that of the Jakobsdom in Brünn, and dedicated the church to Saint Gotthard, who had lived in the Godesberg monastery in Germany during the thirteenth century. The church tower looked out over the walled courtyard of the big corner-house, which had been acquired more than seventy years earlier by a Jew. The church, the Jew and the peasants had always lived peaceably together. The peasants liked to buy from the Jew and the parson used to borrow a few sets of silver place-settings from him when he had several guests. On the eve of Corpus Christi, the Jew swept the narrow lane, scattered grass, like the peasants, on the path the procession would take the next day, and, as was customary in the village, placed lighted candles in his window. When old Abraham Kerner died, the house passed on to his son. Church, Jew and peasant continued to live in the greatest harmony. Julius Kerner already had Christian friends. The peasant boys sat with him on the school benches, were drafted with him into the army, and together they sang the old Mödritz recruiting song: "The Kaiser needs soldiers, so soldiers there must be!" Julius Kerner died young. His widow, who was hardly out of her teens, continued on working in the shop and looked after her only child, Erwin, industriously and economically. When she married again — a worthy man from the Nikolsburg district — she brought her husband a house and her child a father, and the good relations between the Jewish shopkeeper and the peasants continued. The latter were even more devoted to the child than to his forebears — perhaps because he had been orphaned so young, or because he went driving so happily through the fields. Erwin was, after all, a native of the village, and not a foreigner from the outside. The latter were usually shunned by the peasants, and it did not make much difference whether the outsider was a Christian, Jew, German or Czech. The peasants usually intermarried. Even during the parish fair, they preferred to remain alone on the dance floor, and no lad would have dared to bring home a girl from another village. They had already dwelt in this spot for over three hundred years. The well-cultivated cabbage fields stretched from the Obrawa brook to the Brünnel pool (these being called the "pool" fields by the natives) and then continued in a wide arc until the Schwarza Bridge. During the harvest in the late autumn, the cabbage was pickled and placed in enormous vats. For days on end, boys and girls shod in shapeless boots of sheet metal, trod the cabbage leaves after they had been chopped fine with a special plane, until the whole village smelt of sauerkraut and rotten cabbage. The odor from the huge Sauerkraut Company complex wafted as far as the neighboring village of Priesnitz, where it mingled with the invigorating vapors of the local factory, which had formerly belonged to Franz Rudoletzky, royal and imperial purveyor of sauerkraut to the Kaiser. As the country's consumption of sauerkraut increased and exports penetrated ever deeper into Italy, the peasants beçame fatter and fatter. One could give complete credence to their advertisement, "Modritzer cabbage fills you up!"

Kerner Erwin, as the peasants called him, had spent his childhood between the cabbage fields and the vat, the Obrawa Bridge and the Gerichtsberg. His friends were Drasel Hannes, Hank Alois, Scheibl Rudi, and all the boys who, according to the old village custom, bore their surnames in front and the flies of their trousers behind. For as long as he could get by with his religious instruction, which was given to him by his great-aunt, Erwin went to school with his friends. When this system was no longer practicable, he had to go to the town school. During the holidays, he came home. It was the year 1917, and all the young able-bodied men from the village were at the front. The women and old men could not manage the work in the fields by themselves, and Erwin and those of his age group had to contribute their share.

***

In October, 1918, after the fall of Austro-Hungary, the picture of the Kaiser was removed from the peasants' living-rooms to be stored in dusty attics. The church bells pealed as the peasants lifted the statue of Kaiser Joseph II off its pedestal, in order to stow it away forever in the charnel-house next to the church. Together, the peasants and the Jews dragged away the cart with the heavy bronze figure. Erwin was drafted while he was at the university, and he underwent the recruiting examination together with his village friends. They no longer sang the old song about the Kaiser who needed soldiers. There was no Kaiser now, and the Republic did not need very many soldiers. The lads were happy to return to their work. They were young and they laughed. They only pricked up their ears when the older people spoke about the Kaiser and how well the German people had fared in those days. The boys knew that there were poor Germans living in the Bohemian border-areas, in the Sudeten mountains, the Bohemian woods and in the Erz mountains. That they, too, — the "cabbage-skulls" as they were generally called — might have been labelled Sudeten Germans, would never have entered their heads.

The peasants had loved the black and yellow colors of the Hapsburg monarchy. They found the red and white national Moravian flag ridiculous, and when the Czechoslovakian flag was created by the addition of a blue wedge, they hated it. They divided the Hapsburg flag down the middle, inserted a red stripe, and called the faded old yellow cloth "gold."

The more ground the peasants sold at an inflated price to Czech settlers and artisans, the more nationalistic they became. Pupils in the agricultural school used a lighted cigarette to burn out the eyes on a portrait of Dr. T. G. Masaryk which hung over the blackboard, and thrust their penknives into his breast. The guilty parties were never found. That German Pestalozzi, Vykypil, a specialist teacher in the school, shrugged aside the deed as merely a childish prank. At the same time, Erwin Kerner loosened his ties with the village. He did not leave it, for he loved the fields too dearly, nor did he avoid Drasel Hannes and Hank Alois in order to find other friends in the town. Nevertheless, the business with the picture had agitated him considerably. How could one burn the eyes of the President's portrait, the portrait of Masaryk who had come forward courageously against the ritual murder fable at the Hilsner trial; Masaryk, who had accorded the Jews the right to declare themselves openly to be a Jewish nation. Perhaps the books of Herzl and Pinsker, Grätz and Dubnov were to blame for the fact that he suddenly felt so alien. Or perhaps it was the tiny drops of Hussite blood which flowed in his veins from his mother's side.

The relationship between the Church, Jews and peasants began to change. The clock tower of the Saint Gotthard church still looked out over the courtyard of the corner-house, and Johann Stranetzký, the Church Counsellor, still raised his hat to acknowledge the greeting of young Erwin Kerner, whom he had described in a humorous moment as his Jewish parishioner. Only the young peasants had changed. They shunned the parson as well as the Jew.

Chapter Two

The spring sowing dragged on unusually long that year. The snow had long since melted, but the work proceeded very slowly. Older peasants did not leave the house before sunrise, and their sons only arrived in the fields just before ten o'clock in the morning. The rows of tiny cabbages were not so scrupulously straight as in earlier years.

In the community inn, however, business was already lively in the early afternoon. You could have cut through the fog of cigarette smoke and beer fumes with a knife. The radio, with its funnel-shaped loudspeaker, went at full blast. The beer, which the innkeeper's wife poured directly from the barrel into the tall glasses, had a thick layer of foam on top which left the glasses no more than half full. The sourish wine was adulterated, and the buxom landlady recorded drinks in her well-thumbed ledger which were still down below in the cellar. The peasants drank their beer, wiped their mouths with the backs of their hands, and listened, enthralled, to the radio's pronouncements. The promises of the new age were received by them as promises are always received. They did not perceive that this new teaching was contradictory to their old beliefs, their experience of life until then, their very existence, and they did not grasp that they would be deceived by this bawling voice on the radio, just as they were deceived by the landlady with her half-empty glasses. Since they had taken to frequenting the inn every day in order to hear the latest news from Vienna and then held discussions about the situation, their fields remained untilled and untended.

Every evening, the peasant lads assembled in the conference hall in the gymnastic club to attend lectures on the best way to injure the enemy in the kidneys with nailed boot tips. Together, they read the "Völkische Beobachter" and the "Stürmer."

Above the entrance to the gymnasium was a big escutcheon, with four F's intertwined in a wreath of oak leaves. Only a few

21

weeks earlier, this escutcheon had been endowed with a noble meaning: "Fresh, Frolicsome, Free, Faithful." The times were past when this maxim had any relevance. The position of the wreath of F's changed: it no longer stood upright. The escutcheon on the gymnasts' buckles also changed: escutcheon and buckle became politically united. Dexterity with a dagger took the place of physical exercise with a bar.

As the young members of the club had wandered until now with mandolin and guitar through the Obrawa valley, so did the young National Socialists now march through the dusty streets to the shrilling of pipes and a trooper's drum roll. Song had been replaced by a speaking chorus. The picture of Jahn, the father of gymnastics, had been replaced by a photograph of Konrad Henlein, the new leader of the gymnastic club.

Church Counsellor Stranetzký read two masses every Sunday in the village church. The House of God was by no means fully packed. The first mass, which the parson celebrated for German peasants, was sparsely attended; the Czech workers and artisans who came to the second mass only filled the first three pews of the middle aisle.

Churchgoers became scantier each week. Only a few weather-beaten peasants, bewhiskered like the old Kaiser, still came to mass, together with some elderly ladies, bent by the weight of years and hard work, who arrived carrying their black prayer-books with a gold cross and their rosaries in their wrinkled hands. Slowly they went by the corner-house to the Schlössl.

In front of the community guest house stood the gymnasts in black boots, riding breeches and white shirts, with Schmiedt Heinrich at their head. As a visible sign of his intelligence, he wore a pair of horn-rimmed glasses — whose lenses were of the finest plate glass. He bragged and boasted, mocking the old people who were going to hear a mass read by an alien Czech parson. The peasant boys scoffed and laughed along with him.

Heinrich Schmiedt distributed a miniature edition of the "Völkische Beobachter" specially printed for illegal distribution. He gave orders, directions and information. For some of the boys he had provided motorcycles. All these various activities had been undertaken in his diplomatic capacity, for he had already worked for some years as an official in the German consulate at Brünn. He apparently enjoyed a certain immunity and found it beneath his dignity to greet anybody.

A light rain fell on the morning of Corpus Christi day. The cool, tangy scent of the meadows pervaded the village street, which was freshly strewn with grass. Schoolgirls dressed in white with little baskets of rose petals in their hands went to Church accompanied by an elderly schoolmistress. The fire-brigade, in shining polished helmets, marched from the town hall to the church to the strains of their band. Four State-Police sergeants in Sunday uniform, and peasant men and women, including some from Priesnitz, who did not have their own church and had thus been incorporated into the Saint Gotthard parish, walked past the large corner-house. Old Ponzer quickly put heavy candlesticks on his house altar which had been erected, as it was every year, under the arcade in front of his door. Seppel Müllan pulled along the Corpus Christi cannon on a long, worm-eaten pole. It looked like an elongated, funnel-shaped barrel, and its black, red and yellow paint had already suffered badly from the sun. Bartl, the wheelwright, had to hastily put two new spokes in the creaking wooden wheels on which the cannon rested, or else it would never have negotiated the journey to the school from the barn in the courtyard of the town hall.

Seppel Müllan, a Jack-of-all-trades — he was a carpenter's assistant, horn player in the fire-brigade band, night watchman, grave-digger, and field keeper — had put on a hunting jacket in order to celebrate the day and as a gesture of respect for the important functions with which he had been entrusted. His hunting rifle hung like a yoke around his neck. The cannon was placed in its firing position near the school. Seppel had already put a rifle barrel inside the cannon's narrow mouth and was waiting impatiently to fire it off. The occasion, as always, threw him into a state of considerable agitation, for this was no trivial matter: when he blasted off the cannon, the whole pious congregation sank to its knees.

Meanwhile, the procession had become more organized and slowly descended the narrow path past Kerner's house. Every window was illuminated by candles. The school children came first, the youngest in front, then the girls in white dresses with their flower-filled baskets. They were followed by a peasant boy in white gloves, who carried a banner of the Virgin Mary on a red-lacquered pole topped by a heavy golden knob. On either side of him walked an attractively, if somewhat primly-dressed peasant girl. After the fire-brigade came the gymnasts, wearing riding

23

breeches and white shirts, instead of their usual light grey outfits. The apprentices followed them, carrying their guild symbols atop red-lacquered poles. Now another group of girls in white appeared, strewing the path with flowers. Novice priests in their red and white surplices came next and finally two priests, who walked in front of the canopy swinging their censers rhythmically.

The four red-lacquered poles of the canopy were held by the mayor and three municipal counsellors. A police sergeant in festive uniform carrying a burning candle under a glass dome accompanied each of the bearers. Under the canopy walked Church Counsellor Johann Stranetzký attired in his priestly vestments, serious, dignified and aloof, holding the monstrance in front of him with both hands.

The windows of the corner house were open, and the candles flickered slightly. Erwin Kerner stood inside, keeping somewhat in the background. The heavy perfume of incense wafted to him from the street.

The procession moved towards the first house altar under Ponzer's arcade. The Corpus Christi cannon boomed and the people around the altar fell on their knees. The priest's voice rose from the silence which hovered over their bowed heads, and Erwin Kerner heard clearly and distinctly as he uttered the words: "Deus Israeli" in broad Church Latin.

Erwin lifted his head slightly and looked at the crowd kneeling near his house. Were they still the same peasants? To be sure, he saw them kneeling there every year on Corpus Christi day. But today it was quite different. A wave of unrest began to spread through the crowd from below the market-place where the gymnasts and the peasant boys stood upright while the others knelt. The prayer by the first altar was already finished, however. The church bells rang, the orchestra played a march, and the procession moved on to the second altar.

Suddenly the music stopped. Heinrich Schmiedt had approached the musicians. The procession faltered. Schmiedt, the consulate official, stretched out his arm in the Nazi greeting. "Play the Horst-Wessel Song," he commanded, and then wheeled smartly and marched back to reassume his position at the head of the gymnasts. And the orchestra played, giving everything that lungs and metal could produce. The gymnasts and the fire-brigade marched more quickly to keep time with the strains of the

24

"Horst-Wessel" song, and thus broke up the solemn procession. A few worshippers stepped out of line. Church Counsellor Stranetzký, who held the monstrance aloft in his raised hands, stopped dead. Even Mayor Scheibl could not let go of the pole of the canopy in order to applaud the gymnasts. A novice priest told the musicians that Stranetzký had ordered them not to play Nazi marching songs. Consulate official Schmiedt raised his voice peremptorily, however. "*I* decide what's to be played here!" he cried. The musicians resumed playing.

Sergeant-major Novotny gave his lighted wax candle to the station-master who was walking next to him and went to intervene with the gymnasts. The musicians stopped playing, and the fire-brigade and peasant boys, followed by the hooting gymnasts, went into the village inn.

Young Blüml, who was holding the blue silk banner of the Virgin Mary in his white-gloved hands, and the two girls on either side of him stood still, but the three were not so godforsaken as to drop the banner and run away.

The procession was breaking up. Only a few gnarled peasants with bushy eyebrows, some bent old ladies and a few Czechs who stood huddled in a small group, held out.

Stranetzký walked on imperturbably, holding the monstrance aloft. He completed the ceremony at the second altar, but the black, red and yellow wooden cannon failed to fire. The worshippers knelt when they saw Stranetzký kneel, as he intoned the words "Deus Israeli." After the prayer, the remnants of the procession moved on to the third and fourth altars. The church bells rang spasmodically, and then stopped entirely. Heinrich Schmiedt had sent someone to chase away the bell-boys from the tower. The priest, having finished the divine service at all four house altars, made his way back to the church.

Mayor Scheibl attempted to hide his triumph. The other canopy-bearers and those who belonged to the immediate entourage, were very disconcerted. The candles had been removed from the windows of houses around the market-place. Only in Erwin Kerner's house did the lights still burn.

A wizened old woman limped along at the tail-end of the procession, leaning on her stick. A dull murmur could be heard through the open windows. Crowds of gesticulating people were gathering in front of the town hall and the gymnastic club. Singly or in small groups the worshippers timidly left the church. They lingered for a few moments in the churchyard, shook their heads disapprovingly and made their way back home around the village pool. They avoided the town hall and the gymnastic club; peasant boys and gymnasts had taken up positions on either side of the Bahngasse between the parsonage and the vestry. A lane of black riding boots waited to receive the parson. On the stone steps leading to the vestry, the voice of the speaking chorus surged like a wave: "We hate Christians, yes we do, because Jesus was a filthy Jew!"

The narrow alley which led to the Schlössl was blocked by wolf cubs. The twelve-year-old hooligans crowded into Ponzer's arcade. Their loudspeaker bawled directly into Kerner's window: "The world won't be safe until we take the last priest's guts and hang up the last Jew on them!"

As Jews were mentioned last on this occasion, they had another pithy slogan: "Jews and priests to the wall!"

The youths also possessed a talent for rhyme, and had a verse ready: "Whet your knife on a black, black stone. And prick the Jew's belly till you hear him groan!"

At this, they moved their hands like barbers stropping their razors.

Old Ponzer shouted at the ruffians, who laughed in his face. "Parson's darling! Parson's darling!" they called out to him. The peasant made a move to catch one of them, but the wolf cub was too quick for him. He gave up and went hastily inside his house, banging the door behind him. The green glass pane trembled. A few half-withered leaves fell off the wreath of flowers which surrounded the tablet above the front door. The tablet, which was black and shaped like an Iron Cross, bore the inscription: "Georg Ponzer, of this house, died a hero's death for his Fatherland. Lieutenant in the Eighth Infantry Regiment. Fell at the Russian front on June 26, 1915."

Chapter Three

The old Kaiserstrasse ended only four miles north of the village. It entered the outskirts of the Moravian capital, Brünn, at the central cemetery and became the Wienergasse. The houses at the extreme end of the street still had a rural character and behind their gateways lay flower and vegetable gardens. The owners of the villas had close ties with the villages in the German-speaking area of Brünn.

In the city, there was as yet no open display of nationalist sentiments. The day had not yet arrived when twenty thousand Germans — half of them the offspring of mixed Czech and German marriages — could overthrow a Czech majority ten times their size. Nevertheless, they went to the village for the midsummer festivals and Henlein's marches with shouts of "Heil!," white stockings, rustic hats and dirndls. While in the city, they went under the guise of honest citizens, and spoke Czech as badly as German in the street. They reserved their hatred of Jews for Sunday excursions and a future date.

Until the Anschluss, this road had been much frequented by Jewish car-owners, who drove over to Vienna for a theater première, spent the evening there and usually only returned after midnight. The Anschluss had put a stop to these trips. The Wienergasse was now seldom used by Jews, as it boasted neither large shops, factories, lecture halls, nor elegant cafés. The Jews of Brünn were not interested in the many small inns and the cemetery gardens.

Brünn, the city of weavers, the Moravian Manchester, was more than a little indebted for its good name to its Jewish community of eleven thousand. Here stood cloth factories which were famous far beyond the borders of Czechoslovakia; the Stiassny brothers, Aron Löw-Beer, Neumark, Moses Löw-Beer, Samek and Hecht, weaving-mills, worsted cloth mills and the large dying plants. Here were the giant brickworks owned by Kohn, one of the richest men in the Republic. Here was the multi-story Placek textile warehouse, where one could buy anything from sewing thread to a Persian carpet. Here were the large fabric warehouses, the Jewish business houses whose representatives, mostly using their own cars, travelled the length and breadth of the Republic with their samples. In the Minoritengasse there was Stern's china house, whose fantastically arranged show windows offered everything which could be manufactured from glass and porcelain, from simple earthenware plates to the most expensive pieces of Rosenthal and Meissen. Fur and fashion shops, leather shops, fixed-price stores, the shining branches of the Opp chocolate factory — all well-established exemplary businesses — employed thousands of Christians, not only from the town but also from the surrounding area. In addition, there were gardeners, chauffeurs, cooks and maids who were employed in Jewish households.

Jewish doctors, engineers, lawyers, judges, professors, actors and journalists set the tone on their professional and social lives. The loveliest villas, the most modern apartments, the fastest cars, the most elegant evening dresses and the most expensive jewelry were as natural to them as the yearly trips abroad and the cures in Bohemia at Karlsbad, Joachimstal and Franzensbad.

In the evening, the cafés were filled to overflowing. Jewish life throbbed in the Zionist clubs and societies. The "Maccabi" gymnastic club and the organization's numerous other sections had a membership of over a thousand. "Wizo," the Jewish student union, "Blue and White," "Maccabi-Hatzair," "Hechalutz," "Hashomer Hatzair," and "Betar" were all very active in arranging meetings and lectures.

Welfare organizations and cultural societies received large donations. The German theatrical company was about to build a playhouse with the help of enormous Jewish funds. Jews had, until now, felt secure as free citizens of a well-run democratic state. They did not want to consider that for anti-Semitism, too, the distance from Vienna to Brünn was but a stone's throw. They did not yet feel the smouldering flame which was creeping ever closer down the Wienergasse from Southern Moravia.

In Vienna, conditions had become untenable for the Jews immediately after the Anschluss on March 12, 1938. They tried to escape, using all possible, as well as impossible means, and to save a pitiful remnant of their property. One man had his arm put in a plaster cast in which he had hidden some jewelry. Another had thin gold plates built into the heels of his shoes. For most people, these methods were useless. The customs officials were soon supplemented by members of the Gestapo, SS or SA, who had sufficient time to inspect every emigrant. Jewish shoemakers were scarce in Vienna, and their Czech colleagues soon lost any desire to become entangled in such matters. The "Master Race" had special methods for extracting confessions, and woe betide the poor little shoemaker whose name the victim let slip!

Well-to-do Viennese Jews tried to obtain emigration passes. They stood in line outside foreign consulates, urged every kind of protection, and gazed, trembling, at the new star which was rising on the Nazi horizon. Adolf Eichmann, an SS man who had been trained for the "Austrian Legion" at Dachau, had begun working to expel the Viennese Jews shortly after the occupation. He had introduced completely new methods in order to make the city *judenrein*. One day, for example, he had a few Jews and their families sit down on the garbage heap near Pressburg. He was totally indifferent as to what happened to the poor wretches. They could starve, drown in the Danube, or be taken by the Czechs to Pressburg. It was of no interest whatsoever to him. Those Jews who, despite having already lived for many years in Austria, held foreign citizenship or were able to obtain it, could count themselves fortunate. Many a small Moravian village community earned a nice sum by supplying the son of a former Jewish inhabitant with a certificate of domicile, thus enabling him to cross the border.

Jews who did not possess Austrian nationality wore the colors of the country of which they were, or claimed to be, citizens, in their buttonholes. For the masses, however, this was impossible. Their only refuge was to register for one of the illegal convoys to Palestine which were arranged by Jewish organizations. A few Jews, mostly those with Czechoslovakian parents or of Czechoslovakian nationality themselves, attempted to cross the Austro-Moravian border.

Until early 1938, the inhabitants of Brünn only knew of the existence of the "League for Human Rights" through Dr. Ignaz Schürf, a scholar who walked abroad with an unkempt beard and shabby clothes, and who, as could be seen from the then still liberal "Tagestoten," gave some lectures in the institution. The people of Brünn were of the opinion that the League was superfluous — the sort of occupation for a slightly eccentric private scholar.

The town had three societies for the prevention of cruelty to animals, for an animal was, after all, defenseless and needed protection. Humans, on the other hand, enjoyed their rights as a matter of course, and there was nobody, in the worthy citizens' opinion, who would have disputed a person's right to live like a human being.

The "League for Human Rights" owned three small office rooms, each furnished with a writing desk and two chairs. It would never have occurred to anyone that those desks would one day become the goal of hundreds of helpless and desperate people. Never would it have entered Dr. Ignaz Schürf's head that he would have to deal with so many people, and that instead of teaching them, he would supply them with food and a place to spend the night.

The small rooms were crowded with people waiting in line. The long wooden bench in the ante-room was packed. The air was filled with wisps of smoke from cheap cigarettes. Dr. Schürf and a few women volunteers worked in shifts. There was no break for lunch: the small office was open from early in the morning until late at night.

It was relatively simple to provide food and shelter. The telephone was in constant use. Families were asked to donate blankets, clothes and food. Women came to fetch refugee children in order to offer them a home for a few days.

A young woman, accompanied by two pretty dachshunds, requested that her pets be given a good home. They were all she had brought with her when she fled from Vienna.

The volunteer dialled 2467. "Could you possibly look after two dachshunds?"

Those waiting in the ante-room muttered impatiently about the "young lady" and her two dogs. The volunteer dialled again. 2538. "Hallo, this is the League for Human Rights. Would you be kind enough to look after two charming dachshunds?"

"No."

"Thank you." The volunteer dialled again.

"No thank you."

The Czechoslovakian Society for the Prevention of Cruelty to Animals was willing to try to find a home for the dogs within a week.

The young woman stroked the heads of her darlings alternately with a well-kept hand, and sighed.

"A week . . . yet another week."

The League for Human Rights did not give up the fight for the dogs. The secretary dialled once more.

"This is the League for Human Rights."

"Who?" asked a man's voice on the other end.

"The League for Human Rights," the secretary replied.

"This is Mr. Pirner, Director of the German Society for the Prevention of Cruelty to Animals."

"Would you be able to shelter two pure-blooded dachshunds?" asked the secretary somewhat shyly.

Her only answer was the shrill bang made by the receiver, as Director Pirner slammed it back on the rest.

The secretary did not realize, and would in any case have been unable to grasp, that the German Society for the Prevention of Cruelty to Animals was already pure-blooded, Aryan, and politically integrated.

The young woman left the office with both her dogs in tow. She was tired and dispirited. Her husband, a chemistry student, was somewhere in Vienna in the hands of the Gestapo. He had committed the crime of standing in the way of an Aryan colleague.

**

At Drasenhofen, the Hausner family was trying to cross the border into Czechoslovakia. They were accompanied by Georg Freibug, a blond, blue-eyed giant and Hausner's former company commander, whom not even the most well-trained racial fanatic would have suspected of being a Jew. Freibug had not forgotten how his sergeant had dug him out of a shell crater under a hail of bullets. Because of his Aryan appearance, Freibug was able to obtain information from the Nazis who lived near him, which enabled him to warn his friend in time about the planned "actions." As things were becoming too hot for him, he joined the Hausners. Mr. Hausner carried a briefcase, his wife a small suitcase, and the two grown-up sons a rucksack each. The clothes which they were wearing, a spirit-stove, two saucepans, cutlery, plates and a few pieces of underwear made up their entire store of worldly possessions.

Georg Freibug had a frontier-pass. He had no luggage, nor any considerable sum of money with him. His memory was so good that he could remember any piece of information, even if he had only heard it once.

31

After the collapse of the Hapsburg monarchy in October, 1918, Sergeant Adolf Hausner had made a mistake; he had been born in a South Moravian village but had chosen to live in Austria. It would never have occurred to him to do otherwise. He had grown up in Vienna and gone to school there, and after completing his studies had started a small leather factory. Three years after his marriage, in the middle of August, 1914, he had departed with his regiment for the Belgian front. While rescuing his company commander during the fighting around Lüttich, he had been shot in the leg and received a silver medal for bravery. In November, 1918, when he jumped down in the Viennese Nordbahnhof from the buffer of a goods wagon, whose sliding door bore the legend, "Six Horses or Forty-Eight Men," his Kaiser had already abdicated. Hausner consequently tore off the black and yellow cockade on his cap, and stored it in a cigarette box, together with some photographs from the front. His civilian suit had meanwhile become much too wide for him. While he had it altered, he continued to wear his field-grey uniform, from which he first removed the three stars and the yellow stripe on the collar. Later, he also cut off the silver medal for bravery. He kept these valuable souvenirs together with the photographs. Unfortunately he could not remove the wound in his leg.

As he had a wife, two small children and a working permit, he possessed everything which a man needed in order to exist in a well-run state. He was living in a metropolis which, although impoverished, still retained something of its former royal and imperial glory. So he opted for Austria, reopened his leather business and lived as a tax-paying citizen with full rights until the Kaiser's old seat on the Danube became a city in Ostmark, and SS officer Adolf Eichmann began to solve the Jewish question in Vienna.

The SA sent Hausner an Aryan apprentice leather-worker to direct his flourishing business, and his apartment in the Wallensteinstrasse was visited by the SS. On the first occasion, the new masters shouted a bit; on the second, the closets were ransacked and when the SS appeared for the third time, the Hausner family, under Freibug's guidance, had already crossed the Austro-Moravian border.

***

Since the British had sent Lord Runciman to review the grievances of the German minority, the Sudeten-German party had become quite boastful cock-a-hoop. At first, the senators and representatives of the party spoke a great deal about equal rights, and then discussed autonomy. However, when Lord Runciman actually advised the Czechoslovakian government to surrender the towns of Asch, Eger and Karlsbad, the Sudeten-Germans could no longer contain themselves. They demanded that the so-called Sudetenland be annexed by the Reich. The Czechs countered their extremely threadbare argument that Asch and Eger had once belonged to Germany with a declaration that the towns had been given to the King of Bohemia as a pledge eight hundred years earlier. Moreover, they said, the pledge had never been redeemed. They were also unable to find any international law according to which one had to return an unredeemed pledge to the former owner, when the latter had never claimed it.

In reply to Hitler's threats, the Czechs fortified the Bohemian border areas, and as Moravia, too, was threatened through the occupation of Austria, they mobilized strong security forces in Southern Moravia.

Under these tense conditions, the German-speaking colony in Brünn was naturally unable to remain silent. It was actually their political representative, Dr. Franz Beran, who then lived as a refugee in Munich who was responsible for their restlessness. Dr. Beran, the parliamentary delegate, had lost his immunity because he had thrown a stinkbomb in the parliament at Prague. The Czechs' noses were too sensitive for this type of parliamentarism, and they threw Dr. Beran out. He took flight to the Reich, from where he broadcast inflammatory speeches until the Brünn Nazis, reinforced by their colleagues from the surrounding villages, came out in full force to campaign for their rights.

They set off in groups (white-stockinged, of course) for the entrance hall of the red brick house, which they had named the "German House." There they listened to a speech by Mr. Krčal, who had tried in vain to appear more German by writing his name "Krtschal" and accompanied his revolting attacks against the Republic with shouts of "Sieg-Heil!"

The representative of the police force, who could not arrest the

33

speaker since the latter enjoyed immunity as a member of the Senate, ordered him three times to cease his attacks on the State. Being unable to gain a hearing, the only course of action left open to him was to dissolve the meeting and telephone for police reinforcement. Before they arrived, however, the "German House" had already been surrounded by Czech students and workers. The white-stockinged demonstrators were unable to leave the house, and to keep up their spirits, they sang the "Horst-Wessel" song. Outside, the Czechs unfurled the national flag and replied with the anthem of the Republic. They sang bare-headed, tightly packed together. When they reached the last words of the anthem: "to jest ta krásná zemé — zemé česká, domov muj" ("and this beautiful country, this Czech country is my homeland"), the Germans yelled "ugh!" The police then began to move — not in order to arrest the rowdy German citizens who shouted "ugh" at the singing of the national anthem, but actually to ensure that they departed safely from their beleaguered fortress.

The cries of "ugh" were greeted by a hail of stones which broke all the window panes, and the heroic mood of the white-stocking Nazis cooled off visibly — probably as a result of the draught. The previously planned march through the town center was hurriedly called off.

Mr. Krtschal had forgotten to close his address with a resounding "Sieg-Heil." He had, in fact, entirely forgotten his preachings of a few moments earlier, suddenly remembered his immunity and demanded police protection. As the reinforcements had proven too weak, the government representative asked for mounted police to be sent. The horses came riding across the Freiheitsplatz and through the Rasingasse, turned smartly into the public gardens which bordered the "German House" and went to work. The noble beasts had been especially trained to disperse crowds. They rode into the thickest crowds, danced with their hind legs once to the right and once to the left, pushed people aside with their wide croups, and made room for themselves until they could turn round completely. This technique had always been successful during the many riots which the nationalist student body had instigated for some time against the German technical high school. In this case, however, it failed.

The Czech students and workers made way for the horses and allowed them to ride into the throng, but then closed their ranks again, pressing themselves against the horses' broad hindquarters, so that the latter could not even move their docked tails. The policemen in the saddle were only armed with flimsy riding-sticks. Their real weapons were the horses, and these no longer functioned properly. The students were nice boys. One of them fondled the neck of a beautiful bay amicably and smiled at the policeman in the saddle.

"A nice horse you've got there, sergeant!"

The police were in a difficult position. They were not allowed to take any action against the Nazi rowdies, and the students and workers did not resist them — they only hindered the departure of the Nazis. The police ordered the Czechs to make room but in vain. Only after they had been promised that the beleaguered Nazis would not be allowed to march off in procession, but only to retreat silently in small groups under police supervision did the Czechs disperse. They formed ranks again a few streets farther back, so that the "German House" was still surrounded, but in a wider circle. Meanwhile, evening had fallen. There was very little traffic in the streets. Four white-stocking Nazis slipped out of the "German House" and crossed Lazansky square, creeping along by the wall of the Friedrich Irgang printing press, where the "Tagesboten" was published. For the past few weeks, the latter had existed entirely on anti-Semitic propaganda.

Another group went through the Salzamtsgasse. A few slunk away down Jodock street. The Nazis scattered silently and ingloriously in all directions, without any trumpeting choruses of "Heil." Each group was accompanied by the police, who then turned back to supervise the rest of the departures.

Behind the town hall and in every street and alley around the "German House," in the Basteigasse, Eichorn Street, near the Augarten, Czechs lay in wait. Each small group of students snapped up a Nazi, frogmarched the future Gauleiter, together with his girlfriend who was dressed to look like Krimhilde, to the nearest park bench, and painted their white stockings with a coat of ink. The struggling, shrieking Nazis were then allowed to depart!

Chapter Four

Erwin Kerner had invited Margit Heller to spend the Whitsun vacation with his parents. The two young people decided to go on excursions in the district. Erwin's mother, who looked so young that one would never have believed that her son had already taken his doctorate, was used to receiving guests in her house — relatives from Vienna, her husband's business friends, Erwin's colleagues, ladies from her circle of acquaintances in the city: they all gladly came to enjoy the peace of rural life and her excellent cooking for a few hours or days. Often, rich peasant women from the village came simply for the purpose of trying out a recipe or to be advised on the ticklish question of a well-laid table. Whenever the Kerners expected visitors, the peasant girls fought amongst themselves for the honor of being allowed to serve at the table. On such an occasion, they had the opportunity to acquire skills which they could never have learned at home or even at a school for domestic science. They were taught how to neatly fold damask napkins, to lay out silver cutlery correctly, and to polish the wine glasses until they sparkled. And if a very fragile gold-rimmed plate with a monogram did occasionally get broken, one could replace it quite easily and quickly by sending the broken pieces to the factory. Crystal bowls and valuable Rosenthal or Meissen ornaments were kept under glass and were thus in less danger.

Erwin's mother was in a state of considerable excitement over Margit's visit. It was the first time her son had brought a girl home, and she knew exactly what that meant. Her mother's heart, as she admitted to herself, was a trifle hurt. She had always been very proud of having a son, but now she observed more than once to her friends: "If you have a son, you lose a child; if you have a daughter, you gain a child."

She had been forced to become used to the idea of sharing the love of her only child with another woman, and she was shrewd and experienced enough to realize that her share would be the smaller. However, she owed it as much to the girl, who came from a most distinguished family, as to her son, whom she loved above all things, to give the former a fitting reception, and, in addition, it did give her pleasure to decorate her home for the visit.

Although the house was in perfect condition, she ordered an interior decorator from the city, as the one living in the village was too provincial for her sophisticated tastes. A carpenter, also from the city was ordered to give the furniture a new coat of polish, and the chandelier in the guest room was replaced by a lamp with a wide yellow shade. A charwoman came to help the maid, but Mrs. Hahn, Kerner's mother, herself had to deal with the silver cutlery.

The peasant girls would have willingly come to serve at the table as usual — they were plagued with curiosity, and wanted to know what this young lady from the city looked like. Kerner's mother had not invited them this time, however, and even had she asked them, none of them would have come. The gymnastic club and the young peasants had given them to understand that serving at Jew Kerner's was beneath the dignity of a German peasant girl.

So the girls only peeped surreptitiously at Margit and Erwin when a taxi drew up in front of the Schlössl corner-house towards eleven o'clock on Whit-Sunday. A wide crystal bowl with marguerites stood in front of Margit's place at the festively-laid table. The sunlight sparkled through the open window on the wine glasses and glittered on the crystal dishes and silver cutlery. Mrs. Hahn herself served.

Erwin's stepfather, a somewhat lively septuagenarian in a grey suit, talked about conditions in Vienna where his younger brother lived. He wished to help him to emigrate to Czechoslovakia, where such an Anschluss to the Reich would be impossible. Erwin disagreed, asking his father whether he had not read the notices on the doors of the peasants' houses, but Mr. Hahn snapped his fingers contemptuously and replied that that meant nothing, and was just the work of a few young scamps. The older peasants were strict Catholics and in any case this was not Austria: Czechoslovakia was a well-armed constitutional state and would soon put a stop to all this nonsense.

Erwin already knew from experience that it was pointless to warn his father about the danger which was threatening the Jews. He took out his golden cigarette case and lit a cigarette without

37

offering one to Margit. He refrained for the sake of his mother who would have regarded Margit's smoking in an unfavorable light.

***

In the afternoon, Erwin and Margit took a walk along the Schwarza dam to the mouth of the Obrawa river, and then upstream as far as the bridge. Their path took them through a field full of marguerites. Margit was entranced at the sight. Erwin told her that he had once wished to possess that field, to have his own piece of land, just so that he could feel his own earth under his feet like a true peasant.

Margit looked at him in surprise. His face had darkened, and his eyes looked beyond her to the Reichsstrasse, the escape route taken by the Viennese Jews to lead them to safety. Every day, impoverished, desperate and persecuted Jews came down that road. Chased across the border by Eichmann's order, they sought shelter in Czechoslovakia. But how long would they be able to stay, when large placards saying: "German peasant! Don't let a Jewish doctor enter your yard!" hung on the doors of the peasants' houses? How would the Czechoslovakian Jews fare? What would be his own position? The future which he had built up for himself, his house, money, possessions, social position — everything would collapse in ruins about him. A wave of bitterness rose up in him. He, who loved the woods and the land, was a stranger here — a wayfarer.

In the Klosterwald across the river, the bells were ringing for vespers. An old peasant walked through the fields towards the road. He plunged his hand into the rippling wheat, tore off an ear and put it in his mouth. He raised his hat when he heard the bells. Erwin led Margit to the road. They walked in silence, gazing at the peasant making his way through the fields which his ancestors had tilled for three hundred years. He had his roots in this ground: no one could drive him out. The young couple who walked silently through the village, however, had no ground of their own, no country, no tiny spot on earth whither they could turn. They were walking into a void.

Peasant women in Sunday dress were sitting by the road in front of their houses. Only a few replied to Erwin's "Grüss Gott."

A large board with the sign: "No entry to Jews and dogs" was attached to the garden gate of the Prochazkas inn. Erwin and Margit turned and walked on. Behind them, someone sniggered,

"Moritz and his little Sarale." Erwin gripped Margit's hand and hurried her along. "I should have spared you that," he said, but even as he said the words, he knew with certainty that he would be unable to spare her anything. In the city where she lived, anti-Semitism was not yet quite so overt. Rich Jewish factory owners had not yet been expelled from the German Theatrical Society. Their large donations to German culture were willingly received by people who pronounced themselves liberal. The Jews still had their cars, and one even had a private aeroplane. That summer, as in previous years, they visited the fashionable spas, or travelled to the blue Adriatic. The German spas on the Baltic were, however, omitted from the vacation plans. Well-paid German nannies, gardeners, servants and chauffeurs grew fat on the prosperity of their Jewish employers. The wave of hatred had not yet penetrated to the villas of the Jewish wholesale merchants and factory owners.

For decades, the Sulzer family had owned a much-frequented guest house in the popular German resort of Schöllschitz. The shady garden by the rushing Obrawa brook had always been filled to overflowing on Sundays. Now the round tables with their red-checked cloths stood neglected. Mrs. Sulzer went to and fro among them, pushing chairs straight and brushing off a few withered oak leaves. She seemed to have aged by years during the last few weeks. Her husband was almost always away from home. He was trying to sell the property in order to buy a tiny modest apartment in the city, but there was no one who was prepared to give anything for the beautiful house and well-kept garden. The German inhabitants of Schöllschitz were waiting: the Jew would run away one day in any case, and leave his property abandoned. Czechs, on the other hand, were afraid to move into a German town. Teachers who had lunched at the same table at Sulzer's for years, no longer wished to be served by the Jew. They had also talked the peasants into not going there any longer. The Sulzers, like all the rest of the Jews living scattered in the villages, still defied the boycott, but they were living on capital.

***

Franz Bednár, the postman, had discovered one day that the little stroke which softened the sound of the "r" in his name could be replaced by the letters "rz" and that his name, when pronounced, would still sound the same. His inventiveness did not

39

stop there and after changing the spelling of his name once again, he landed up in the German Gymnastic Club, which had meanwhile ennobled its title by the addition of the adjective "Aryan," as Bednarsch.

It was now naturally far beneath his dignity to allow his wife to continue working for Dr. Silberschein, although her job paid very well. Let it be said in his wife's defense, however, that she only left after energetic requests from the mayor, Mr. Scheibl. Before the elderly bachelor had recovered from his astonishment, Mrs. Rossler, the innkeeper's wife, informed him just before the church clock struck midday that she would henceforth deliver him no more meals.

Dr. Silberschein, who had a weak heart and was quite alone in the world, had no alternative but to go to Erwin Kerner's parents and beg for a meal. He ate with them as a guest for a few days, but suffered greatly as a result of the humiliation to which he had been subjected.

When Erwin came home in the evening, he was glad to talk to Dr. Silberschein, who had been the community's district doctor for many years. He often accompanied the ailing doctor home, and helped him as much as his busy timetable allowed. Sometimes, the two went for a walk around the War Memorial Chapel. However, the peasants no longer greeted them. "What have I done to them?" asked Dr. Silberschein.

One Sunday morning, Dr. Silberschein came hurrying up the market-place as fast as he could to the Schlössl. Erwin saw him approaching and went across the yard to meet him.

"They've stuck a notice on my window," the doctor said excitedly.

"Mine too," replied Kerner quietly.

Kerner's mother brought milk, tea and cakes. "You must eat," she pressed the doctor kindly, and turning to her son, said softly, "I can't get it off the window — the thing's stuck fast. I shall have to scrape it off with a knife."

A few days later, Dr. Silberschein was dead. He suffered a stroke at his brother's house in Hradisch. Church Counsellor Stranetzký learned of the death of the district doctor through the papers. When he met Erwin at the ticket office in the railway station, he remarked loudly, "What our people did to Dr. Silberschein was quite incredibly beastly." All the bystanders heard his words.

40

Chapter Five

In this period of tension and uncertainty, Erwin seldom visited Margit. However, he telephoned her twice or three times a week to find out how she was, and promised to visit her as soon as possible. When he finally came, he was tired and rather taciturn. Margit, who wanted him for herself alone, begged him not to exhaust himself so much.

He kept silent about what was happening to him in the village, and Margit discovered nothing about the warning which had been transmitted to him by his father, or the last conversation which had transpired with his former school-friend, Scheibl Rudi. "When the Germans march in, you can look for a cherry tree to hang on," Rudi had said. Erwin did not allow this to pass. "Only fools sell a bear's skin before they have it, and one can only hang someone one's already caught." Scheibl Rudi became even more incensed. He hissed like a wild cat. "Just you wait, you Jew! I'll pay you back for that!"

Erwin's worried mother urged him to leave the village, but he replied with a harsh "no."

Nevertheless, he had become more careful. If he took the train to the city in the morning, then he came back with the bus. He never travelled the same way on consecutive trips. He had given up his walks. He had no time for them in any case. His dog was always at his side — she even slept at the foot of his bed. The hunt for Erwin Kerner was on.

After the mobilization had been called off, the troops returned to their barracks. Dusty, cross and tired, the columns passed by the Obrawa inn. The Czechs who brought the soldiers refreshments looked despondent.

In the Gymnastic Club's debate room, the radio went at full blast. Heinrich Schmiedt, who had put the set on at top volume raised his voice. "Quiet!" he commanded. "Comrades, Sieg-Heil! The Führer is about to speak."

41

The agricultural experimental station where Erwin worked had been compelled to release several of its employees for army service during the mobilization, and had therefore restricted its activities to the completion of current projects. When the men returned to their jobs, they possessed no real zest for their work. Why should they do more experiments? Their future — indeed the future of the whole country — was very uncertain. Microscopes gathered dust by the large sliding windows of the laboratories. Food tests were broken off and instead of reading technical magazines, the workers gave the daily papers their deepest attention. They shook their heads and smoked cigarettes in nervous haste. As the days passed, less and less mail arrived. Farmers seemed to take no more interest in the experimental station, and there were no more inquiries even from the Provincial Culture Council. Kerner's colleagues valued his tireless zeal and organizational talent very highly, since he had, in spite of everything, kept up contact between the farmers and the experimental station. For him no road was too long, no village too remote. They invited him to spend his evenings with them, wishing to show him how little they approved of the German hate-campaign. But Kerner withdrew from them cutting himself off more and more, and at the same time reducing his work load.

***

During the early morning, the thick fog which blanketed the city prevented smoke rising from the factory chimney. On the eve of Rosh Hashanah, the Jewish New Year, the Czechoslovakian president, Dr. Benes, bade his people farewell. The Jews filled the synagogues and prayerhouses to the last seat. With trembling hearts, they sent their prayers to heaven. The Czechs clenched their teeth, and went about their daily work discouraged and resigned. The Nazis sat by loudspeakers in their taverns and rejoiced. Their newsmongers ran through the streets, extolling the new borders and the "new day." "Sieg-Heil! The day is nigh!" they called to their customers. In Godesberg, Mr. Chamberlain met Hitler for talks. Armed only with his umbrella, he approached the vicious beast of prey. The whole world held its breath. The Jews prayed.

The Czechoslovakian ambassador in Berlin, Mr. Chvalkovsky, waited for hours in the State Chancery for an audience with the Führer. He brought home to Prague nothing less than an ultimatum — an order to evacuate the border areas.

During Chamberlain's second round of talks in Munich, the Republic was dealt its death blow in order to keep peace for a short while longer. Following the Munich Agreement, the Bohemian frontier zones were to be relinquished to the thousand-year Reich. A plebiscite was to be held in Southern Moravia. No one in the world had the slightest doubt what the results of the latter would be. England expressed its gratefulness to Czechoslovakia for its sacrifice. At about the same time, Britain also announced that the Palestine White Paper immigration restrictions would remain in force. Adolf Eichmann simultaneously urged the Austrian Jews to emigrate. Illegal Jewish transports of emigrating Jews came to a standstill on their way up the Danube. No country would give them asylum. The only land which could have taken them in, and to which they had a historic right according to the Balfour Declaration of November 2, 1917, remained closed to them.

With a courage born of despair, the Austrian Jews sought a way out, an asylum somewhere in the world. A few hundred who were more fortunate than their expelled Viennese brethren managed to reach Shanghai.

During the early morning of October 10, 1938, the German army crossed the border. A few members of the National Guard had dug themselves in among the bushes on the banks of the river Taya near Znaim. In bitter desperation they opened fire. Czechoslovakian officers with raised revolvers and faces streaming with tears forced their own soldiers to evacuate their positions. A prepared and unbeaten army had to retreat without firing a shot. Southern Moravia became politically integrated. The Germans advanced to within fifteen kilometers from Brünn. Czech villages in which no German had ever lived were torn from the Republic. The railroad which ran from Pressburg through Dundenburg to Brünn and thence to Prague, the country's main artery which connected the capital with Slovakia, was cut by the German territorial gains in eight places. The Republic's fighting potential was thus paralyzed. The limbless rump did not dare to move. The Germans no longer talked of the plebiscite which should have been held in accordance with the Munich agreement. Only the

43

Czech radio exhorted Czechs and Jews to vote for the Republic. Jews fled from the provincial towns and villages in trucks, carts and on foot. The Czechoslovakians refused to allow them to use public transport for fear of German reprisals. Car owners earned a fortune in a few minutes. At the very last moment, carts piled high with luggage left for Brünn. Some of the baggage which had been packed in extreme haste fell off onto the road. No one bothered about it. Down-feathers from burst pillows were scattered by the autumn wind. They whirled in the air like snowflakes. Carts crammed with baggage were wedged in between the long lines of army trucks which were retreating in perfect order towards the capital. The landlord of the Obrawa inn stood in front of the tavern with his sons. They laughed and mocked. A notice proclaiming "The Day is Nigh!" in large letters hung on the gate.

A lieutenant rode past the inn with two NCO's. He reined in at the door, and read the notice. "Our day will also come sometime," he said, and the three cantered off without even glancing at the Müllans.

While the Czechoslovakian army retreated sadly but in perfect order, the Germans occupied city after city and village after village. In the wake of the troops came the Gestapo and Eichmann's "Judenkommando." A few Jews were unable to flee quickly enough, or, as true citizens of the Republic, wished to wait for the plebiscite. They were arrested according to a black list which was handed over by the local Nazis to the Gestapo when the latter marched in. Adolf Eichmann made short work of the rest of the Jews — he had them chased over the border into no-man's-land.

***

In the middle of the fields between Wojkowitz and Raigern, a wide strip of land a few yards long was zealously guarded by German soldiers, SS and Gestapo on one side, and Czechoslovakian frontier guards and police on the other. Day and night this piece of stubble field was watched. A cold autumn wind blew, driving grey clouds before it. Thick fog rose from the Schwarza riverbed and the narrow Obrawa valley. The earth was cold and damp. The sun only broke through towards midday, and its rays did not provide any warmth. It disappeared again behind the grey clouds from which a peaceful, persistent rain fell — a rain in which peasants delight. In the evening, the shower became heavier. The sentries in their black raincoats sought shelter behind some straw ricks. From there they observed the patch of rain-whipped ground. On these few square yards of ownerless field crouched a number of wretched people, trembling from damp, cold, fear and misery, whom no one wanted. They had been ridiculed by their fellow-citizens, with whom they had lived for decades in peace and harmony, despoiled and beaten by the SA and finally chased into no-man's-land by Eichmann's "Judenkommando." The majority of them were women, children and old people, and they were all of Czechoslovakian nationality. Their husbands, fathers or sons had not yet been demobilized, and were still with their regiments. The Republic had called them to defend their country. Now ironically Czechoslovakian sentries prevented the families of these men from crossing the border.

The policemen wore good warm coats, and warm hearts as well, but they also had strict instructions from their government. The latter no longer actually governed, but out of fear of the Nazis did anything in order not to provoke Hitler. For this reason, women and children lay out in a stubble-field in the wind and rain, and had to freeze and starve. The state which they loved and had faithfully served could give them no food or shelter. After all, they were only Jews. Who needed them anyway!

The National Jewish Council and representatives of the Jewish community negotiated with the authorities for the transfer of these unfortunate Jews to the city. The negotiations dragged on for hour after hour, one day, two days, seemingly an eternity. Finally permission was given to take blankets and food into no-man's-land. The police escort which accompanied the car had to take care that no one was smuggled into the town, and had to return that same night. After some days of lengthy negotiations, the women and children were brought out to the city. The men had to remain.

Kerner knew all the Jewish families in the district. For him and his friends, the negotiations were far too long-winded. They took the shortest way, and ran the risk of getting into trouble with the authorities, but that did not concern them very much.

When the women and children had been taken in by some of the families in the city, they stormed the officials, pleading with them to deal humanely with their husbands and fathers.

The gentlemen in the offices listened to the rain pattering

against the window-panes. The central heating gave out a cosy warmth. The officials filled their working hours faithfully. They leafed through bundles of reports, read carefully through the new orders, and did everything pertaining to their official functions. They filled out forms, each for the sphere in which he was competent to act.

They were not qualified, however, to deal with the men in no-man's-land and so they did not worry about the fate of those poor wretches. These gentlemen had their own worries and fears. Why should they bother about Jews as well? Such a delicate question would be best solved by saddling someone else with it or putting it aside and forgetting about it.

Inquiries about the matter from Prague were referred to Brünn, for the officials had a great deal of work and even more patience. Only the Jews were in a hurry. They did not want to understand what difficulties were involved in allowing them to cross a border which had never existed before.

One afternoon, a covered delivery van stopped by the pub which was situated between a mill and the entrance to the Klosterwald. The driver and his mate sat near the open door of the inn, scanning the road. They had settled the bill immediately, and they sat reading the newspapers which lay around inside. The inn was empty, as only a village inn on a weekday can be. The innkeeper worked in his front garden and having served his customers, left them alone.

Sergeant-major Hapalek patrolled the Wojkovitzer bridge. When he saw a cart laden with straw coming up the road, he leaned his hands on the bridge's wide iron supports and stared very attentively at the railroad track which ran beneath the bridge. Only after the cart had already gone quite some way up the lane did he turn his gaze from the fascinating sleepers below. He looked across the fields from his vantage point on the bridge. The cart stopped by the straw-rick near the barn. Hapalek saw that straw bales were unloaded and reloaded a few minutes later. The cart stood behind the barn and was thus hidden from the new frontier. The sentry there was in any case completely disinterested in what was happening. His job was to prevent the Jews who had been set forth into no-man's-land from crossing back over the demarcation line. Whether they starved there or were allowed into Czechoslovakia was no longer his concern, and in any case the rest of the Republic would also be gobbled up within a few weeks. The mousetrap would be snapped shut and Eichmann would then recapture all the Jews whom he had so cavalierly evicted. While the sentry paced his stretch of road and thought of the wonderful days in Vienna when he had gone Jew-hunting with his friends, two strapping men lifted down a large laundry-basket from the cart. The lid was opened and a well-dressed gentleman clambered rather laboriously inside. The lid closed on him and the men carried the basket back to the cart, took out another, and stowed away an elderly man inside. They then placed the two baskets on top of the cart, leaving a small gap between them. A cattle-dealer called Bacher squeezed into the space and leant back against one basket while his feet rested against the other.

The big delivery cart was covered with cross-bars, supposedly to prevent wisps of straw from being scattered by the wind, but actually in order to make it impossible for unwelcome eyes to see inside the vehicle. The gaps were filled with threshed straw, so that there should be enough air for those inside. Stejskal the peasant laid two boards across the basket lids, thus covering the space in which Bacher was sitting from above. A thick hemp rope was thrown over the top and Stejskal pulled the knots through the noose and left the ends of the rope dangling loose behind the cart. His companion pulled the end taut, and the horses began to move. The heavily-laden cart swayed along the roughly-paved lane.

Meanwhile, Erwin Kerner had arrived on his bicycle at the bridge where Hapalek was acting as sentry. They smoked a cigarette together and paid no attention to the cart which was approaching them from the fields. Only when the cart turned from the bridge into the road did Hapalek hail the peasants. A jerk on the reins and the horses stood still. Sergeant-major Hapalek checked the cart, walking round it twice.

"In order, drive on," he said to the peasants.

The horses started to pull and the sergeant-major returned to the bridge. Kerner was sitting on his bicycle, holding on to the iron railings of the bridge with his left hand and waiting to go. Hapalek came up to him.

"Ride a few paces behind the cart, as though you had nothing to do with it."

Kerner gave him his hand. He pushed off from the railings and followed the cart at a short distance.

Bales of straw stood stacked next to the stream before the mill owner even knew that Stejskal had driven into the yard. Bacher took off his leather coat which was covered with straw, shook it out carefully, put it down on top of the basket, and carried the latter together with Stejskal to the delivery van. The two men dashed out of the inn, fetched the second basket from the cart and stowed it away in the van as well. Bacher hastily climbed into the van. The driver started the motor, and his companion took a last look at the inn. They then drove quickly away.

A few yards beyond the crossroads, the van overtook a cyclist. Erwin Kerner rode unhurriedly up to the Reichsstrasse.

Half an hour later, the gate of No. 3, Legionärstrasse closed behind the van. Bacher helped his fellow-sufferer out of the uncomfortable laundry basket. The driver and his mate then filled the baskets with all the sheets and other bed-linen which should have been taken to the Skarolek laundry.

***

The Bohemian border areas had been surrendered. Southern Moravia was occupied. The old Moravian Jewish communities of Nikolsburg, Auspitz, Pohrlitz, Lundensburg and Znaim no longer existed. The Jews had fled from the world-famous spas of Karlsbad, Marienbad and Franzensbad, and the towns of Reichenberg, Gablonz, Aussig and Leimeritz.

Those who had invited refugees from Austria for a meal the day before were now in need of help themselves.

In Brünn, the situation was particularly critical. The eleven thousand Jews there had been joined by families from the villages and dissolved Jewish communities of Southern Moravia. More than two thousand emigrants from Vienna had taken refuge in Brünn immediately after the Anschluss.

Until then, attempts to persuade even a tiny part of the Viennese Jews to leave the town had met with no success. It was not due to unwillingness or lack of means or money on their part, but solely because there were no possibilities of emigrating. Twenty visas had been sent from England and France, but not a single one for Palestine. England had already stated that the White Paper would remain in force, which meant that not one additional visa could be handled. The city police pressed for the departure of the Austrian refugees. The South Moravian Jews were still left in peace. They had the right to choose. The authorities did not trouble about what the Jews were to live on, however. Yesterday, they had still been good citizens, tax-payers and soldiers. Today they were only tolerated, and tomorrow they would be an undesirable element, a foreign body, which had to be eliminated. Until now they had been given asylum. The authorities had hoped that a mass migration would take place, but their hopes were not fulfilled because there was not a single country which was prepared to shelter the multitudes of refugees. Czechoslovakia was hemmed in on all sides by enemy territory.

The representatives of the Zionist groups were well aware of these facts when they met for joint discussions. They were also shattered by the suicide of a young married couple from Vienna. The couple, who had no means of subsistence and were threatened by the police that they would be returned to the new German border, had thrown themselves into the street from the top story of the Jewish community buildings.

Delegates from thirty-one countries took part in the Evian Refugee Conference on Lake Geneva's beautiful south bank. More than twenty overseas countries were represented. These nations possessed enormous areas which were only sparsely populated, and here two young people killed themselves because there was not even a tiny corner on earth for them.

The discussion had already begun when Kerner entered the room. So as not to disturb the proceedings, he crept over to the table on tiptoe and sat down in an empty chair next to Hornik. The secretary of the Jewish community was giving a report on the situation.

There sat this handful of men, their faces lined with worry. What Elbert said hit each one of them hard and bitterly. They heard that after the Anschluss, two hundred refugees, among them many children, had crossed the Swiss border daily, but in July the stream of fugitives had increased so greatly, that the following month, Switzerland had found it necessary to order the return of the refugees to the border. What use was it that the Swiss Children's Immigration Committee had brought some two hundred children to safety, and was ready to accept more? The refugees had to cross the border, and the latter was now closed. Hundreds of children would have to come from the occupied border areas alone. There were thousands of boys and girls from Germany to be saved. More than forty thousand children, the most prized possession, the future of the nation, would have to be transported abroad, but there was no one who would take them in. It was imperative to organize illegal convoys, as the Viennese Jews had done, but the dangers involved were enormous.

Those assembled at the meeting had hoped that the secretary would report to them on rescue work, would give them a tiny spark of hope and faith. He had to tell them, however, how difficult and totally insoluble this problem was, since the pressure of persecution was mounting daily. There was practically no possibility of emigrating. Elbert leafed through his reports, and took off his black, horn-rimmed spectacles. He then introduced Mr. Freibug from Vienna who was sitting next to him.

Everyone looked up in surprise and stared with unconcealed astonishment at the totally unknown blond man who rose with a slight bow.

Freibug had fled from Vienna only a few days earlier. His Aryan appearance had enabled him to discover what the Nazis were planning to do in the near future. As an Austrian artillery officer, he had worked with heavy howitzers at the beginning of World War I. No one had suspected him of being a Jew. Unobtrusively, he frequented circles which were then already closed to Jews. His assured manner, soldierly bearing and blond hair had enabled him until only very recently to move freely about in Vienna, to listen and to observe. What was happening daily there was not reported by the newspapers. Freibug had experienced outbreaks of organized mass fury, had witnessed how women and children were beaten in the streets, how old men were thrown to the ground and trampled in the face. Desecrating graves, despoiling Jewish apartments and arson had become popular sports. The murder of Jewish citizens was no longer punishable by law.

Freibug's voice became more urgent. He begged, he implored his listeners not to wait any longer. They, and above all their children, should flee to safety. They should organize illegal convoys, hire ships or, if there was no other way, even buy them, in order to reach Palestine. He entreated those present not to make the fateful mistake of not believing the emigrants. The Jews of Vienna were now paying dearly for the fact that they had not taken to heart the warnings of Jewish refugees from Germany. What had happened to the Jews there from 1933 onwards was now being repeated in Austria on a much more terrible scale. But what the Austrian Nazis were planning against the Czechoslovakian Jews would be still more beastly and brutal, and the Sudeten German Nazis would make every effort to outdo the Austria mob in sheer violence.

Everyone listened intently. Some shook their heads. Freibug reached for a chairback with his left hand. Drops of sweat appeared on his brow. His voice came in gasps.

"The dregs of the earth, beasts in human form have risen from hell to vent their rage on us. Leave your houses, your fortunes, your social positions. Flee from here while you still can, before this country in which you are living is trampled underfoot. I saw what they did to the civilians in Belgium in 1914 . . ."

His words became unintelligible. A deep groan burst from his lips and his face suddenly became deathly pale. His right hand grabbed at the air. Before Wachsmann could leap to his feet, Freibug had collapsed. Hornik put a glass of water to his bloodless lips. Kerner undid his shirt collar. Selinger sat motionless, his head buried in his hands. He had spent only one night in his home town, the little South Moravian townlet of Auspitz, after the Germans had moved in. In that single night, the synagogue had been burned down, the cemetery desecrated, and the Jewish men beaten. In that first night, his apartment had been devastated, his large leather shop despoiled, and he himself, together with his heavily-pregnant wife, had been chased into no-man's-land.

Freibug had meanwhile recovered sufficiently to leave the room supported by Hornik. Slowly the excitement died down.

There were still a few people who did not wish to believe all the warnings. — Austria, the Sudetenland, that was something else. They were areas inhabited by Germans. But the world would not forsake Czechoslovakia. England, France, Russia — some great power would help the Czechs. A miracle would have to happen. They could not imagine that their factories, houses, businesses, cars, bank accounts and estates, like their fur coats, jewelry and valuable china and art collections might be confiscated. They had worked themselves up to prosperity, indeed to wealth: in the space of three generations, they had not only caught up with their social milieu but far outstripped it. They rationalized that the torrent would be held up by the approaching winter, so that they would still have time to save at least part of their property.

Kerner spoke about the danger and difficulties involved in an illegal journey to Palestine. A few gentlemen only listened with half an ear — they were too deeply concerned with their own worries. — What Kerner was proposing referred primarily to Austrian refugees and now, unfortunately, also to Jews from the Sudetenland. Of course one had to help. Thank goodness one could still do so.

Kerner's voice became more insistent, compelling everyone's attention.

"Those of us who live isolated in the villages are in mortal danger. The Czech police force is powerless and can do nothing against the incitements of the Gymnastic Clubs, the teachers, and Konrad Henlein's other hirelings. The Sudeten German Party is running an inflammatory propaganda campaign and encouraging a boycott and violence. You can read the '*Stürmer*' daily on the windows of my house; you can hear the peasant boys' speaking choruses, and you can see walls plastered with anti-Jewish notices."

So it had already come to this! The poisonous seeds which Konrad Henlein had sown in the fertile ground of Southern Moravia were bearing fruit. There had been hopes that the danger would be averted with the surrender of the border areas, and that the Republic (actually only a residual stump) would be saved. Now each individual suddenly felt that the ground on which he was standing was crumbling beneath him, how his fortune, his possessions, he himself, were standing on the edge of an abyss. The edge itself was already undermined, and would collapse at any moment. There was no foothold, no protection, no hope anywhere. They saw the whirlwind of destruction approaching them without being able to even approximately assess its crushing strength. One had to be either mad or in the depths of despair to find a straw to clutch at in the raging ocean painted by Kerner's last words.

"We must send out ships, because the blockade on Eretz Israel must be broken; not because it is part of any sort of program, but because we have no other possibility of survival."

Kerner sat down amid an excited hum of voices. He seemed unaware of the hubbub and sat, bowed in thought, smoking a cigarette.

Mr. Selinger, who spoke after him, described the desperate situation of the refugees from the occupied areas. A few days earlier, they had still been rich, and had helped the Viennese Jews willingly and generously. Now they were totally destitute and had to be supported by the Jewish community. They had no apartments, no means of existence. Even their citizenship was in doubt. Where could they find the necessary funds for illegal emigration, the three or four thousand crowns which, until then, had been a laughably small sum for them? How could they obtain the necessary clothes and furnishings until such time as they emigrated?

The last speaker was Albert Wachsmann, a tall man with greying hair combed back from his forehead. His voice was hard and clear. For him, illegal emigration was a purely military matter, a campaign which required planning and organization just like an attack on an enemy position which had to be overcome at any price. One wave of immigrants after another, like lines of soldiers in a battle, must reach the shores of Palestine. For him, it was a question of arranging the convoys, organizing an intelligence service, ensuring provisions and health services, supply bases, security and discipline.

Maximum compliance with orders was, for him, a guarantee for the success of every operation.

Wachsmann had finished his speech. He was surrounded by friends offering him their assistance.

It was already nearly midnight when the discussion came to an end. Wachsmann invited Kerner to stay the night with him. For a long time, they sat in the dining-room over black coffee. Wachsmann took a red pen and traced the route which the convoys would take on a rail map. First of all, the railroad from Brünn to Pressburg, then up the Danube to Budapest, Belgrade, Braila, Tulcea and Sulina until the Black Sea. The red line continued beyond Istanbul to Lesbos, Athens, Crete and Cyprus until Haifa.

When they finally went to bed, the first horse-drawn carts laden with vegetables were rattling through the streets. Morning crept, grey and cold, through the windows.

Chapter Six

The free western countries were indebted to Czechoslovakia for having done everything that had been demanded of her. They were well aware of how determined Hitler was to eradicate the Republic from the map, and they were also not unconscious of the situation of the Jews living there, both as citizens and as refugees.

When the Bata combine, which had built an entire city in Zlin after the American pattern, from which it supplied a large part of the world with cheap well-made footwear, transferred its Jewish employees to its overseas branches in order to remove them from the clutches of the Nazis, the Asiatic colonies gave them visas most willingly. Thus, a few Czechoslovakian Jews even landed in Java. It was only to Palestine that they might not travel, to the land of their desire, the only spot on earth where they could have lived as Jews among Jews, the land with which they felt themselves bound in a tradition stretching back for thousands of years and where they would have received help from their brethren. Despite the magnitude of the danger and the extreme pressure, however, there was no change in the number of visas for Palestine. England was not ready to supply even one extra pass.

The Jews began a bitter fight for each visa. They knew, or believed they knew, what to expect from the Nazis, and tried with every means in their power to save as many of their co-religionists as possible. Jewish men who were living legally in Palestine and thus had British visas or passports went to Czechoslovakia, married there, had the newly-wed wife entered on their passports and travelled back to Palestine. Upon arrival in Eretz Israel the couples immediately became divorced. A few remained together. Some forgot to obtain a divorce when they arrived back and only remembered their temporary wives when they came up against the Rabbinate's opposition to their contracting new marriages. These unconsummated marriages saved a number of girls, and the men were undeterred by the fact that they were guilty of bigamy.

54

Again and again, Jews from Palestine travelled to Europe to bring wives and children (at least they were entered as such on the passports) back to Eretz Israel.

***

Within a few days, over six hundred people had registered for the first illegal convoy to Palestine. They had faith in Wachsmann whom the Jewish community, after thorough examination, had entrusted with the organization of illegal emigration. He was free to choose his assistants himself, and to adopt whatever steps he felt correct. He established contact with the heads of the police, and obtained a residence permit for Freibug which was valid until the departure of the first convoy. Freibug had been badly affected by the events in Vienna. His experiences enabled him, however, to organize the security service for the first convoy. Wachsmann had blank passports in the drawer of his writing desk. He filled in the particulars and stuck in the picture of a Viennese Jew. The birthplace in each passport was marked as a small Moravian town, and the nationality could thus be entered as Czechoslovakian. When Wachsmann used up his stock of passports, he went to the police headquarters and returned with a fresh supply.

The convoy management had been established in the offices in the Legionärstrasse. Small groups of young men engaged in lively conversation stood outside the front door until late in the evening. By the entrance to the offices stood a young man in grey riding breeches and brown laced boots which reached almost up to his knees. A wind-cheater and wide leather belt completed his uniform. On the sleeve of his wind-cheater he wore a blue and white armband on which was embroidered a gold Star of David. He asked every caller what he wanted, and then gave him a chit of paper with the name and door number of the worker who was competent to deal with his query. This saved the future member of the convoy a great deal of time and trouble. At the end of the corridor was a small room. A handwritten "No Entrance" sign was affixed to its door with thumbtacks.

At a desk behind the door sat Albert Wachsmann with large quantities of black coffee and even more cigarettes. His jacket, which was cut like a battledress with a high collar, was fully buttoned and gave him the appearance of an officer awaiting a visit from his superior. A map of the Mediterranean countries was attached to the right wall. Opposite the table on a black console stood a bust of Herzl. The room had a second entrance from a large office containing three desks where people were asked various questions and registered for the convoy. In exceptional cases a candidate who had been registered was taken through the narrow concealed door into Wachsmann's room where passports were issued. Most of those who entered the room and were not personally acquainted with Wachsmann thought that he was a police officer. Before someone was entered in the list of candidates for the convoy, he had to answer questions put by Dr. Schwarz, who, together with Hornik, comprised the so-called board of examiners. Erwin Kerner, who almost always arrived at the convoy management offices in the late afternoon to wait for the technical evening classes to begin, found a seat wherever he could, and was always ready to help his friends with the office work. He was sitting next to the anthracite stove one rainy autumn afternoon in order to arrange a meeting with the organizers of the classes when the door was opened gingerly. To Erwin's great astonishment, Karl Träger, who was known all over the town as an idler and loafer, entered the room, his expensive tie hanging somewhat askew out of his jacket. He made a rather disorderly impression, which Erwin attributed to the rain which was pattering ceaselessly against the window panes.

Kerner was only vaguely acquainted with Träger. He knew that the latter came from an extremely rich, very assimilated family, and that Träger's uncle had taken him in ward when his father died, although the young man was already thirty-six years old at the time. The uncle paid Träger a large monthly allowance — some said as much as six thousand crowns. Erwin had also once heard that Träger spent his nights in bars and had a liaison with a caretaker's daughter whom he had supplied with an apartment and a liberal regular allowance.

"What do you want?" Erwin asked Träger rather unsympathetically, without moving from his seat as the latter entered shyly.

"I would like to register for the convoy," replied Träger. Kerner turned to the desk and called to Hornik, "Mr. Träger is here and wants a visa for Palestine."

"That's the best joke in world history," answered Hornik. Everybody laughed. They laughed so loudly that Albert Wachsmann came into the room through the concealed door.

"What's going on here?" he asked severely.

"Mr. Träger is here and wants a visa for Palestine," repeated Hornik.

Albert Wachsmann had noticed the figure in the doorway. His voice softened as he asked paternally, "Do you want to go to Palestine, Mr. Träger? Have you considered what you are going to do there? One has to work in Eretz Israel, you know."

"I shall live on my income," Träger replied.

The girls at the typewriters left their work in the middle, leaped laughing from their chairs, and surrounded the strange animal who wanted to live on his income in Palestine. A blond girl called Ruth giggled.

"Oh Kartshci, it would be such fun if you came with us!"

Träger winked at her. "Wouldn't it just!" he drawled.

Kerner, suddenly interested in the questions which Dr. Schwarz was going to ask, left his warm seat by the stove and sat down at the table next to Hornik.

Dr. Schwarz, to whom all the laughter was totally incomprehensible since, as a stranger to the town, he did not know Träger, took a few forms out of his briefcase.

The usual questions followed: surname, Christian name, age, profession, and address.

"To which organization did you belong?" asked Dr. Schwarz.

"The German Theatrical Society," replied Träger.

"That was once upon a time. Which Jewish organization?" Dr. Schwarz persisted.

"The Jewish community," answered Träger.

"So none," remarked Dr. Schwarz.

Hornik and Kerner sat there tensely, for now Dr. Schwarz was coming to his favorite question.

"What have you done for Judaism, Mr. Träger?" continued Dr. Schwarz.

"I have suffered for Judaism!" said Träger almost tearfully, rubbing his left cheek.

"Where and when?" were Dr. Schwarz's next questions.

"I was thrown out of my girlfriend's apartment in the Hagartenstrasse today and a man whom I've never seen before slapped my face while I was standing at the entrance to the building," Träger said defensively.

"Most probably your Aryan girlfriend's lover," remarked Kerner.

"I would never have expected such meanness from her," said Träger dejectedly. He was about to complain about the amount of gold and valuables he had given the girl, but Kerner interrupted him.

"Imagine you paid a whore. Racial purity is somewhat more expensive."

***

It had been fashionable at one time to be present at every première in the town theater, or to sweat, crushed in among the other dancers, in the marble ballrooms of the "Neues Landhaus" cafe, to the strains of the string orchestra. Now it was very much in vogue, for Jews at least, to attend retraining courses and lectures on agriculture.

Courses in sewing neckties and English cooking enjoyed special popularity, especially among women and girls. The participants in these so-called practical courses contributed towards the expenses of the materials used during the lessons. The lectures on agriculture were organized by Zionist groups, subsidized by the Jewish community and were free for the audience. Margit had signed on for the course in English cooking, and had burnt her finger while cooking some half-raw meat. She mixed ingredients which, according to her mother who was an experienced cook, could not possibly go well together but in this respect, Margit did not heed her mother's opinion.

"You just don't understand," she said. "This is English cooking."

She herself did not enjoy the dishes she prepared and greatly preferred going to a butcher's shop with Erwin when he was free. The food there tasted excellent to her.

Wishing to try out her skill one day, she presented Kerner with a large portion of chestnut pudding which she had prepared according to a recipe from the course. Erwin put the fork to his mouth. The pudding tasted terrible. He looked at Margit's shining eyes. A compliment from him was worth more to her than all the course certificates put together.

"Do you like it?" she asked.

"Hm . . . delicious," answered Erwin, attempting to swallow the bite. "Take a piece for yourself and eat with me," he said cunningly and drew her towards him.

He lifted the fork with a slice of the pudding to her half-open mouth but she immediately spat out her bite.

"How can you eat that stuff? It's quite inedible. Throw it away! Why don't you say something instead of swallowing this snake-fodder?" Margit implored.

She pushed away the plate with the expensive pudding. Both their palates were now urgently in need of some antidote and they ran down the stairs, two happy people. For a moment, their worries were forgotten, and English cooking had been condemned forever as snake-fodder. Naturally Margit gave up the course the very next day. Her friends advised her to join the course in making artificial flowers or sewing neckties. When she told Erwin, he said, "Why Margit? I'm going to work."

"But I won't let myself be supported by you. Life in Palestine is hard," she replied.

***

It was no small matter to organize a convoy of six hundred people, and to equip them with everything they needed. For six hundred people, one had to have as many rucksacks, at least twice as many suitcases, 1,200 blankets and a large number of other things, and for all this one needed money, vast quantities, nothing else. Everything was available in the stores. It was quite another matter, however, to obtain six hundred pairs of brown Canadian boots. These laced up high on the calf and had strong, heavy nailed soles. They had to be made to order and only a first-class shoemaker, a specialist, was competent for this job. Only a skilled artisan, and not some simple cobbler or riding-boots manufacturer could be entrusted with such work, and he had to be sought, and when found, richly rewarded for his labor. The boots had to be fitted at least twice. One had to wait some time for an order, because the bootmaker was extremely busy. At the same time, it was a joy to watch the people who stood around in little groups in the Legionärstrasse. They were young, with confident faces. Their outfits looked suitable for a journey to Africa, and they made a slightly strange impression in the city. One could clearly feel that they were gradually breaking free from their environment. They greeted one another with "Shalom," for in spirit they were already in Eretz Israel.

While they walked around, making purchases and paying last calls on friends and acquaintances, people already started to register for the second convoy. Once again, elderly people and children were kept back since there were grandparents in the town who would willingly keep their grandchildren for a few weeks until the parents had established themselves in Palestine. In the spring, Youth Aliyah would arrange a children's convoy and provide legal visas for them.

As sufficient time still remained until their departure, members of the second convoy were given practical tuition and training in accordance with Wachsmann's program. Most of the young men worked in vegetable gardens, while a few were apprenticed in poultry farms and carpentry workshops. Hornik and Wachsmann seized every opportunity for training members of the convoy.

Three times a week, Mr. Maifeld held Hebrew classes in a small room at the convoy management offices. The room was so full that Mr. Maifeld had only a corner for himself and his much-marvelled-at Hebrew typewriter.

Wachsmann, who was busy almost daily at the police headquarters, worked until late at night, dealt with a large amount of correspondence, and held long telephone conversations with Greek shipping companies. He went to the Ministry of Finance in Prague in order to obtain a license for foreign bills of exchange. Food supplies had to be guaranteed at the intermediate stops; a medical service had to be organized. Transit visas were the greatest worry. Every country closed its borders to the illegal convoy. Difficulties piled up from hour to hour. Refugees from the border areas, who until a few days earlier had still been Czechoslovakian citizens, were suddenly stateless. It had become extremely difficult to obtain passports for these people. Government officials were overrun with applications for citizenship. Czechs from the Sudetenland, the occupied areas of Southern Moravia, stormed the government offices, claiming priority. The officials were tired, cross and uncertain. Who had the time or inclination to deal with the affairs of Jewish emigrants?

Wachsmann worked with seemingly inexhaustible perseverance to prepare the convoy for departure. His closest colleagues pursued the ministries with one telegram after another. When contact had finally been made with the Jewish communities in Budapest, Belgrade, Bucharest and Athens, and a promise of help for the convoy had been received, the news came that the convoy might not make any intermediate stops. Arrangements had to be altered forthwith. It was also very difficult to choose suitable people to direct the convoy. Experience was lacking. No one could know what dangers and difficulties would have to be overcome.

A defense squad was formed, for one could not travel without protection in such troubled times. Since weapons could not be taken with them, rubber hoses and lead bars had to serve as substitutes.

It was even awkward to obtain international postage stamps. As the latter were, however, indispensible for the convoy's intelligence service, Wachsmann had his helpers buy up the stocks in all the smaller post-offices.

Since the occupation of the border areas, life had become harder for the Jews in the Republic. Many relationships with government offices, institutions and friends had been unable to stand the strain. The Jews were left to fend for themselves. During the last evenings before the departure of the convoy, Wachsmann had long conversations with Dr. Mahovsky until the latter commissioned two police officers to accompany the emigrants as far as Rumania.

***

That year, October 28 was very rainy. Leaves fell from the oak trees on the Spielberg. They lay on the wet gravel walks in dirty yellow patches. A flag hung damp and slack from the roof of the old fortress where an artillery regiment was quartered. The sentry took shelter from the rain in the covered gateway. His face was as weary as the Schwarza river, which flowed southwards under the railway bridge with a discontented murmur. The railroad tracks were almost deserted as the city no longer had any connections with the nearby Austrian border areas. The rare passenger trains only had three or four cars to transport the small number of travellers.

Gone were the good old days when on October 28 the population from near and far came to the provincial capital in special trains, in order to be present in the large crowds at the military parade.

The only train was in the shunting-yard. It consisted of ten cars for passengers and another two for luggage. Hornik and Kerner went through the cars together with a railway official. They wrote large numbers in chalk on the doors. Both had turned up the collars of their raincoats against the downpour. After each car had been inspected and marked with a number, it was barred by the railway official. All the windows had already been closed.

That evening, an ancient goods-train locomotive with an asthmatic wheeze towed the train to platform five where it remained until daybreak.

The locomotive then crawled into the smoke-blackened engine room. It had no flag or wreath of flowers on its black rump, as in previous years on October 28.

The city, too, seemed to be dying. The streets which had once been so lively were now empty and silent. Only the rain beat its monotonous drum-roll on the window panes. The wind rose during the night and whistled through the streets until morning. That evening, Kurt Goldreich packed his rucksack. His wife, Grete, put the children to bed as she did every evening, tucked them in and kissed them. She told them about the journey upon which she and their father were embarking, and promised to send them oranges.

"You must be very good and listen to Grandma. In the spring, when it's nice and warm, you'll come and join us together with a lot of other children. In the meantime, we shall build a house and get everything ready for you," Grete promised.

The children were delighted at the prospect of staying with their grandmother. They had no idea where their parents were going. The grandmother, a hale and hearty lady in her fifties, was pleased to have the two children with her for a little while longer in the large, empty apartment. The work which she would have with the three-and-a-half year old girl and the five-year-old boy would be a pleasure and a diversion for her when Grete and Kurt began their journey to Palestine the next morning.

Grete kept her feelings in check as long as the children were awake. She certainly could not show them how deeply it grieved her to leave them for an unlimited period of time.

Kurt Goldreich hid his agitation by packing. Shortly after nine o'clock when the children were already asleep, Margit and Erwin came up the stairs.

"We just wanted to see how you were managing with the children. You really don't have any problems. We had much more difficult cases today, because we had to place children with Czech families," said Erwin, trying to comfort them.

"You don't have any children. You don't know how it hurts me. I am a mother," was Grete's answer.

"We must go now, because I have to be there when you embark at four a.m.," said Erwin, giving Grete his hand.

She sobbed. Margit kissed her cheek.

Kurt accompanied them to the door. They all shook hands. The door closed. Erwin and Margit went downstairs. They walked through the empty, rain-sodden streets to the Legionärstrasse.

***

The hum of voices and the clacking of typewriters could be heard through the concealed door which separated Wachsmann's room from the large office. Kerner hung up his coat on the iron window bar, Albert Wachsmann pushed a few lists across to him for checking. Cigarette smoke lay heavy in the air. Kerner, always thirsty for air, opened the window. The cold night air which streamed in refreshed him. The telephone shrilled on Wachsmann's desk. Albert lifted the receiver and motioned to Kerner to close the window. The conversation was very short.

"Mr. Kerner will be with you at once. Thank you very much." Wachsmann put down the receiver. Erwin was instructed to collect thirty blank passports from Dr. Mahovsky at police headquarters. He wanted to order a taxi but Wachsmann refused.

"You can't call a taxi for this trip. Fritz Rosenberg will drive you there. He has put himself and his car at our disposal tonight. He must be here in one of the rooms," Wachsmann reminded him.

Rosenberg was called. He pushed aside the people standing in the passage. When he reached the door with the sign, "No Entrance," he pulled his jacket straight and combed his hair with his fingers. He did not notice the mark which a strap from his rucksack had left on his face while he slept on it. He knocked and walked in without waiting for an answer.

Erwin had already put on his raincoat.

"Take Kerner quickly to police headquarters and wait for him there," ordered Wachsmann.

They pushed through the crowded passage. Rucksacks and cases lay around in the dimly-lighted entrance hall. A girl in a windcheater and laced boots sat on a medicine chest which had been

63

prepared for the convoy. Her finely-chiselled profile was framed by black hair. Her eyelids were closed, and her chest rose and fell in the regular rhythm of sleep.

"I'd rather drive by night with her than with you," said Rosenberg and stopped beside the girl. Kerner pushed him on. Outside, it was still pouring. They got into the car which was parked in front of the entrance and drove off. Rain flowed down the window panes. The car skidded and came to a stop just in front of the curb.

"This rain!" said Rosenberg, excusing his negligence. He drove on more carefully. The cafés were already closed. The car stopped in front of police headquarters. Two sentries stood outside the gate. Kerner went quickly up to them. After a few minutes he returned. He had hidden the passports in his coat pocket. He walked quickly towards the exit, pulled open the car door, and shook Rosenberg who had fallen asleep from exhaustion. They drove back. In the Basteigasse, they overtook a group of young people going in the direction of the Legionärstrasse. Their clothes and equipment betrayed them as members of the convoy. The car stopped in front of the convoy management offices. The girl in the Canadian boots still had her eyes closed. A few people sat asleep on their luggage in the corridor.

"Did you get all thirty?" asked Wachsmann as the two entered.

"Yes. At five o'clock, I have to hand them over to Dr. Mahovsky at the station," said Kerner.

"Here are the passport photos and lists with the dates of birth. Share the work with Hornik and Rosenberg," Wachsmann said.

"What about the bearers' signatures?" asked Rosenberg.

"Sign them yourselves," answered Wachsmann, and took a few passports for himself.

The first tram went past the window. The rain had stopped. The people sleeping on their rucksacks were shaken awake. They washed their faces hastily and each received a cup of hot black coffee.

They marched to the station in small groups. A narrow bright streak glimmered on the horizon. Relatives and friends stood on the platform. They waved to the people on the train. Small blue and white flags fluttered from the windows of the cars and hosts of hands waved goodbye. Slowly the cars went past. At the end of the platform, where the departing train was already quickening its pace, a little group stood crowded around Dr. Mahovsky who was waving farewell.

Wachsmann, Elberg, Hornik and Kerner called out a last "Shalom" to the convoy.

The train's red tail light cleared the station. Kurt Goldreich looked back from the last platform in the direction of his apartment. His wife, Grete, leaned against the door next to him and wept.

The first convoy had begun its long trek.

Chapter Seven

For a few days, there was little to be done in the offices of the convoy management, although the light in Wachsmann's room still remained burning until midnight. Occasionally, there was a telephone call to ask if there was yet any news of the convoy. Parents who had adult children on the convoy wished to know where the ship was. Wachsmann answered every question with a curt, "No news yet."

Finally a card came from Belgrade. "The ship has passed through the port on the Danube. Everything in perfect order." A few days later, a letter arrived from Istanbul. "The ship took your mail on board today."

"We'll get through. I always told you we would," Harry Waldmann jubilated.

"The ship hasn't yet reached the coast," observed Hornik.

"The difficulties will only begin now," predicted Rosenberg.

"Which won't prevent us from preparing for the next convoy," said Wachsmann who had asked his friends to come to a meeting in his room.

***

Kerner cycled up the Kirschenallee. The trees were bare. A cold wind blew down the street from the Gerichstberg. Kerner bent double over the handlebars so as to lessen the resistance of the wind, and rode to Sulzer's inn. The garden gate was closed. The green wooden board with the black wording, "Sulzer's Inn" had been taken down from the front of the house. Only two rusty hooks on the wall indicated the place where it had hung for over half a century.

Mrs. Sulzer, who had recognized the cyclist when he turned in at the gate, came out and invited him to step inside. Kerner was about to leave his bicycle against the wall, but Mrs. Sulzer stopped him.

66

"It would be better to take it inside. Your tires might be slashed, since people are determined to hurt you and every Jew in general," warned Mrs. Sulzer.

Erwin left a few minutes later and rode to the Hayan estate. He gave his bicycle to the porter and hurried to the steward's office. The door was open. Mr. Kvapil, a portly man in his fifties with red cheeks and a double chin, sat at his desk. In front of him was a row of blue paper bags filled with grain samples. A pair of antlers hung above his head. As a special decoration, they wore Kvapil's grey peaked cap.

Kerner greeted Kvapil briskly and sat down. He patiently endured the thick cigar smoke from which Kvapil's business friends had suffered for years.

"Your father has already told me about your request," the steward began. "So you're finally thinking of training your people for agriculture. About time too! Until now, you've only produced doctors and lawyers."

They went into the castle. In a corner of the slightly musty-smelling vaulted hall stood a suit of armor with its helmet visor down. Severe-looking, slightly mildewed ancestors gazed out of large gold frames at the steward and his companion.

The butler came through a low door panelled in brown wood. His face, which was set in dignified folds, was framed by whiskers such as the late Kaiser Franz Josef had been wont to wear.

"Jan, please inform the countess that Mr. Kerner and I are here," instructed Mr. Kvapil.

The valet examined Erwin, who was intimidated by all the ancestors. His imperial whiskers twitched disapprovingly.

"Have you an appointment?" he asked in sepulchral tones.

"The countess is expecting us," answered the steward, buttoning his jacket over his large stomach with some difficulty. He and Erwin stood in the middle of the room. Jan grasped the doorhandle and opened the door with a deep bow. The countess was together with her daughter. The noble ladies looked very bourgeois. They were simply dressed and behaved very naturally. The butler ceremoniously served tea and biscuits.

"Mr. Kvapil has informed me of your request," said the countess, turning to Erwin. "Please give me a few more details on the subject."

Kerner looked at the glittering diamond cross which hung from a fine gold chain on the lace collar of the countess' blouse. He told her of the persecution of the Jews, of the difficulties encountered by refugees in obtaining residence permits, of people who had been driven out of the surrendered border areas, of the illegal convoys to Palestine and of the necessity for agricultural retraining.

"Are you a Zionist?" asked the countess' daughter.

"Yes, I am a Zionist," said Kerner.

"Is it true that orthodox Jews are waiting and praying for God to take them back to the Holy Land?," asked the countess.

"That is so," Kerner replied.

"Do you personally believe this to be right?" inquired the countess.

"I believe that we must earn God's grace by working hard and building up our country," declared Kerner.

He looked at the sparkling cross on her neck and continued, "In your New Testament it says, 'Pray and work.' It follows that prayer alone is not enough."

"You seem to be well versed in our Bible," remarked the countess.

The steward had told her of Kerner's request to train three people in dairy farming. She gave him her consent.

"We do not agree at all with what is happening outside our estate. We entirely disapprove," said the countess as she rose and shook hands with Erwin and the steward.

Kerner mounted his bicycle, well-satisfied with the result of his mission, and with a sense of accomplishment drove down the road to the Children's Home. The red roofs of the village glowed in the mild late autumn sun. A large lime tree stood behind the Children's Home. Kerner leaned his bicycle against it and walked to a nearby barn which had a ladder leading up to its dormer window. From there, Kerner has a fine view of the picturesquely-situated village.

Suddenly, he had the feeling that something was moving in the dormer window. He saw the ladder come toppling down towards him, and had the presence of mind to jump underneath the lime tree which, he thought, would catch the ladder as it fell. A few branches broke above his head. The crossbar on top of the last rung grazed his left shoulder. He had just enough strength to throw himself onto his bicycle and ride away. His arm hurt as though from a hard blow, and it was difficult for him to hold the handlebars with both hands. When the village was behind him, and he was riding down the Kirschenallee, a rifle bullet whistled past him. The bark of a tree splintered near his head. Erwin immediately took his hands off the brakes and flew along, zigzagging painfully towards his destination. When he reached the Reichsstrasse, he turned in towards the city. The two incidents had convinced him that he was being followed.

The Nazis were becoming more active. Konrad Henlein travelled around, making speeches which all began and ended with "Sieg-Heil" and resembled one another like a row of eggs. Wherever he came, the SDP flags fluttered around the podium. The "Freedom Watch," who accompanied him as bodyguards, stood in rows on either side of him. Hatred of Jews and Czechs gushed out in waves. Scientific works, novels and classics had disappeared from the showcases of the German bookshops, making way for one book.—Hitler's *Mein Kampf* — countless copies of which occupied their former places. The "Stürmer," with its inflammatory caricatures, lay next to "Neuen Tag" and "Grenzboten" in the newspaper stands. A new government was formed with Dr. Emil Hacha as president. The Czechs bore it all with a shrug and listened to the BBC's Czechoslovakian broadcasts. Police raids against Austrian Jews were on the increase. The Slovakians were granted autonomy. Stamps which had hitherto borne the name Czechoslovakia as one word were taken out of circulation and replaced by similar stamps on which the name of the country was hyphenated as Czecho-Slovakia. Business and industry were at a standstill; the country was in agony. The limbless rump lay helpless. Vultures with bloody beaks and sharp claws surrounded it, waiting for their prey.

***

Wachsmann had been given a hint about the forthcoming raids and had quickly informed his friends so that as many emigrants from Vienna — against whom the raids were directed — could be taken away from the city as possible.

Thus Kerner took the Hausner family and Mrs. Glanz, who was no longer safe even in the apartment of her sister, home to join his relatives who had fled to him from South Moravia. Eleven temporary beds had been made up in the four rooms. That evening, Erwin's stepfather called him into his room, and tremulously confided his fears. Erwin only shrugged his shoulders. He kept silent about the attack. In order to change the subject, he talked about the grain samples which he had given his father a few days earlier.

"You shouldn't buy the barley," he said.

It was no use, however. His stepfather examined the barley sample again, and Erwin knew that he had not succeeded in warning him about the danger which everyone could already see was threatening them.

The police raids did not last forever. A few Jews might be caught one day and released a few hours later. It was all only a game of nerves. The Czechs were tired and dispirited. What they had built up for twenty years was crumbling before their eyes.

The first black-uniformed Czech fascists appeared in the streets. The Nazis paid these workmen a daily wage: twenty crowns for each Jew who was beaten up. In order to earn this fee, the thugs strolled through the streets in small groups, looking for solitary old men. They overpowered their victims and thrashed them with their belts.

Squads of white-stockinged Nazis marched through the city. The speaking chorus had been well trained.

"Germany, awake — Judah, drop dead!" It sounded like a record which someone had forgotten to turn off.

Czech fascists covered the walls with the slogan, "Jew, go to Palestine!" The graffiti were large and glaring: they certainly could not be overlooked.

That night the frost thickened. The Obrawa brook was already covered up to its source by a thick layer of ice, and even the much wider Schwarza river only had a narrow ice-free channel along which the water trickled. The windows were covered over with pretty ice-flowers. The snow was piled several feet high in the villages. The hard skids of the peasants sledges smoothed out tracks in the white waste. In the city, a host of workers shovelled the streets clear for traffic. People sat sullenly in their apartments where, in past years, Christmas joy had reigned. The days slipped by, grey and unfriendly. Instead of Christmas carols, and bell chimes, the radio broadcast Nazi marches. Instead of "Hail Mary's" there were shouts of "Sieg-Heil!" Christian brotherly love was ousted by Nazi hate. The solemn Christmas mood had vanished from the city. Only in the more remote Czech villages nestled in hollows between hills covered with dark pine forests did people try, at least for a few hours, to forget their everyday cares. In the little mountain village of Lissitz, peasants found it difficult to make ends meet and worked as woodcutters and cartdrivers during the winter months. They had to work in the snow and frost, unlike the rich peasants in the Brünn district who sat around in warm inns. Once a year, however, on New Year's Eve, when they took leave of the old year and ushered in the new one, they too, drank and danced.

Erwin Kerner received a letter from Jan Horacek, inviting him to the New Year's Eve ball in Lissitz. Erwin loved Lissitz. It lay peacefully and picturesquely among the pine forests. Each time he went he was charmed by the shining houses with their tiny, well-kept gardens. He met Margit at a pre-arranged time and they took the train to Raiz. The cars were almost empty, badly heated and somewhat neglected. The railway officials in the smaller stations scarcely poked their red peaked caps out of their turned-up coat collars. A paralyzing uncertainty crippled everyone and everything. The couple were happy to leave the train at Raiz. Jan Horacek stood in front of the station with a sledge and took some heavy blankets off his horses. When he saw Margit and Erwin, he removed the mitten from his right hand in order to greet them with a vigorous handshake. They climbed into the sledge and Horacek wrapped them up in the blankets which were still warm from the horses' bodies. The horses began to trot. Lumps of snow flew into the sledge from their hooves. The small bells on the harness jingled brightly and gaily. The horses slowed their trot to a walk when the street began to steepen. Horacek called encouragingly, "Kappa, Koketta, home!" and they began to trot again.

"These animals are good, but surely you haven't had them for long?" asked Erwin.

"The army gave them to me as reserve horses after the mobilization and I have to return them when they ask for them. They have too many horses in the army, but if they need them some day, I'll willingly give them back. I'm looking after them well so that they'll stay strong. When our time comes, I'll enlist together with the horses," said Horacek.

The animals pricked up their ears and trotted down the street.

71

They arrived in the village which lay like a toy in a gentle hollow between the wooded hills. The sledge stopped in front of the gateway to Horacek's farm, and they unharnessed the horses, and then went straight to the cows, who knelt, well-groomed and ruminating, on their straw. This was always the procedure when Kerner came to visit: they invariably went through the farmyard before entering the house, because Horacek liked to show off his well-kept livestock. After a few moments, they went into the roomy kitchen.

Margit sat down against the warm tiles of the slow-combustion stove. She wore Mrs. Horacek's lined slippers on her feet. The heavy oak table was covered with a white cloth. A loaf of peasant's bread and a large kitchen knife lay in the middle. Horacek took the loaf, made the sign of the cross on it with the knife, and gave it to Erwin. The latter, who was familiar with the peasant custom, cut off two slices and gave one to Margit at the stove. "God bless this bread," he said, as was customary. "May He bless it," answered the Horaceks. The lady of the house brought tea in large cups. The brew was strong, and well-laced with rum. Mrs. Horacek put a dish of honey and butter in front of the guests. The thick, knotty logs crackled and snapped in the stove. A pleasant warmth and the scent of resinous wood filled the kitchen.

"How's business?" asked Erwin.

"Business?" Horacek grimaced as though he had bitten into a lemon. He was going mad: his entire barley crop was still lying in the granary. No one wanted to buy. He had fattened the pigs before Christmas until they weighed 165 pounds and, as every year, had hoped to receive a good price for them at that weight. There were no customers, however, and now he had to carry on feeding the animals. He was laying out more money every day. Over four hundred pounds of honey was stowed away in the cellar, and there was no one to buy it.

"Business is at a standstill in the city too," said Erwin. "People are hoarding their money because they are afraid of what the future will bring."

There was a knock at the door. Horacek called, "Come in," and Father Adametz entered the room. Everyone rose to greet the priest and Mrs. Horacek brought in an upholstered chair. Father Adametz took off his long, fur-lined coat and sat down at the table.

"How are you, Reverend Father?" asked Kerner.

"As well as can be expected of an old man these days," he sighed. They talked about the intrigues of the Sudeten Germans.

"My venerable fellow-priest, Church Counsellor Stranetzký, has been pastor of your community for thirty-five years," remarked Father Adametz.

"Yes, but that didn't stop his flock from disturbing Divine Service on Corpus Christi Day," replied Erwin.

Father Adametz shook his head nervously. "Is that true? Is it possible?" he asked incredulously.

"It is indeed true, Reverend Father, and that is far from all they have done," Kerner said angrily.

"There is a change taking place," said the priest, "a change straight from Liberalism to Nationalism — and from there the path goes directly down to hell, to bestiality." Father Adametz pointed underneath his chair. There — in that direction, somewhere in the bowels of the earth, lay hell, according to the ideas which had been handed down over the ages. It was from there that bestiality arose.

Silence reigned once again in the room. Father Adametz rose.

"Keep your spirits up," he said to Margit, lifting her chin with his forefinger. "We are all in God's care. May He protect us from all evil."

The band was playing a waltz when they arrived at the Sokol Gymnasium. Horacek ran his fingers energetically through his hair, bowed to Margit and led her onto the floor.

Kerner had no choice but to partner the mayor's wife, who was as corpulent as befitted her dignified position. Horacek winked significantly at him and drank a glass of wine behind his wife's back. The ball went on until midnight when the band sounded a noisy flourish. The lights went out in the hall. Shouts of "A happy new year! A happy new year!" came from all sides. Erwin felt for Margit's hand and kissed her without saying a word. The lights went up again. People threw streamers at one another. Margit and Erwin laughed as they became entangled in a pink streamer.

"It's the New Year. Let's drink a pledge of brotherhood," said Horacek. Kratochvil uncorked a bottle and poured two glasses full. Horacek and Kerner stood opposite one another. Both were the same height, with wide shoulders and hair similarly combed back. They looked into one another's eyes and slowly drained their

***

73

glasses. Then they kissed one another on both cheeks and shook hands heartily.

"Now you are brothers," said Kratochvil jovially. It sounded almost solemn. They sat another half hour together, letting the couples dance past them. Towards one o'clock, Margit and Erwin took their leave of the gathering.

The city was noisy, smoky and littered with dirty heaps of snow. Kerner accompanied Margit to her apartment and then travelled home. He walked down the Bahngasse to the market-place and turned in at the Schlössl. The few people whom he met in the street did not try to disguise their hatred of him. A sickle-moon was just rising as he entered the house. Kerner's sheep-dog leapt happily at him and followed his every step. He took her into the house. At dinner, Kerner told his parents about the pleasant time which he had had in the city. Towards nine o'clock, the elderly couple went to bed. Kerner sat down at his desk in order to work. The dog lay at his feet, her intelligent head resting on her paws. The fire in the stove slowly burned down. Outside, the wind whistled around the corner-house. Suddenly, the dog pricked up her ears. She stood up and ran to the window. Kerner was struck by her unusual behavior. He turned off the table lamp and tip-toed, bent double, into the dining-room. The dog barked, and at the same moment, a shot rang out. The window panes rattled. Kerner stood in a corner of the dining-room and waited. His mother called from the bedroom. Erwin crept soundlessly along the carpeted floor to his parents' room.

"Don't turn on the light and keep calm," he said softly. The dog gradually stopped barking. The danger was past. Erwin's mother wept. All three spent a sleepless night. In the morning, Erwin's stepfather wanted to inform the police, but Erwin objected. The next day, Erwin's travelled to the city by bus and went straight to Wachsmann at the convoy management offices.

"I must leave with the next transport," he said abruptly.

"Out of the question," replied Wachsmann without looking up from the reports which lay on his desk.

"Someone tried to shoot me again yesterday," said Kerner.

"You can't leave now. The difficulties which were predicted for the convoy have begun to take place. The 'Parita' has run aground in Tel Aviv. The Brünn convoy was shelled in the bay of Haifa and had to turn back to Greece," Wachsmann informed him.

After a silence lasting several minutes, Kerner asked, "When do you think you can be ready with the next convoy?"

"As soon as the thaw sets in and the Danube steamer company starts operating again," replied Wachsmann.

"I want to go with this convoy," Kerner announced emphatically.

For days, Kerner did not go back to the village. He worked hard to sell the corner-house by the Schlössl, looked for agents, and even advertised in newspapers. Sometimes a buyer came his way, but no contract was ever signed. The Czechs did not want to buy a house in a Nazi village. The Germans waited for the Jews to run away. The price of houses dropped from day to day.

A thick layer of March fog covered the city. It commingled with the smoke from the factory chimney and people found it difficult to breathe. The opaque air threatened disaster.

The Viennese and Pressburg radio stations broadcast endless propaganda against Jews and Czechs. Radio Pressburg began every transmission with the words, "Na straz." "The Jews are our misfortune, so we must get rid of them. A Jewish child has the devil in his blood. He should not sit next to our children in school." These and similar words of wisdom flew like swarms of ravens through the ether. There was no point in turning off the radio because the loudspeakers bawled the identical propaganda out into the street.

Czech teachers who had worked for years in Slovakia came back to Moravia in order to avoid the Hlinka guard. A few Jewish families still fled to the city. Wachsmann again worked until late at night. The Jewish orphanage was filled to overflowing and extra rooms were necessary. The convoy management looked for another location, and their work was disrupted. Another convoy was planned for March 13. The candidates were already gathered in the city. Jews who came from the Slovakian areas could make no contact with their relatives. A mild wind cracked the ice on the rivers. Finally, the decisive telegram came: "The Danube is clear of ice," it announced.

"We're going," people who had come to the convoy management offices to inquire about the situation called to one another. While the Nazis in the suburbs were already creeping into the city under cover of darkness, and the city's security forces stood passively by while the Nazis' speaking choruses blurted out their vile propaganda at night, the leaders of the departing convoy gathered in Wachsmann's room in order to receive last-minute instructions. The guards for this transport had been considerably reinforced, for the news which had come from Pressburg during the last few hours had aroused fears that there would be untoward incidents.

Elbert, the secretary of the community, and Hornik were present when the convoy departed. The members of the convoy were well-equipped and strictly organized. Elbert saw them climb into the cars in a calm and disciplined fashion, squarely facing the future, happy and determined. What a contrast they made with the few Czechs who were working there at that hour! The latter shivered in the cold morning air. Their faces were pale and exhausted, and they kept their eyes closed as though they were afraid to look at one another. Wachsmann, Rosenberg and Kerner had taken leave of their friends in the offices. They worked feverishly and were nervous and very tired. Just before five o'clock, Hornik telephoned to inform them that the convoy had finally left.

***

German rowdies brawled in the streets. They now wore their swastikas quite openly. The entrances to the government offices were barricaded by the police who had received army reinforcements for the purpose. A large group of German students marched from the "German House" down the Rasingasse across the Freiheitsplatz and thence along Masaryk street to the railway station. Shop windows were smashed in the large Jewish stores, and the mob stole everything they could lay their hands on. The police did not intervene. The voice of the speaking choruses reverberated in the streets:

"We want to go home to the Reich! One nation, one Reich, one Führer! Germany, awake — Judah, drop dead!"

A swastika flag was carried around under the noses of the police. The latter did not interfere. Security men stood, weary and dejected, by the roadblocks. They waited for orders, but no orders came.

Evening fell in the town, and the shops shut at dusk. Most shop windows were unlighted. Cafés were closed. It began to snow. The tram cars were empty. A large, glaringly-illuminated picture of Hitler stood in the window of Brecher's bookshop. In front of the picture was a whole showcase with copies of "Mein Kampf." The few pedestrians who passed the shop spat at the window. Newsvendors sold "Grenzboten" and "Neuen Tag" by the clock in the main square. Shortly before nine o'clock that evening, Kerner and Wachsman entered the convoy management offices. Rosenberg and Hornik were sitting by the stove. There was no one else there.

"Any news?" asked Wachsmann.

"There was a call from Pressburg half an hour ago. The convoy has sailed from the Danube port."

Another 650 people, nearly all of them from Vienna, were out of the clutches of the Nazis.

***

Crowds of people stood around the newspaper kiosks, staring at the headlines in the morning papers. The letters were large and black, as in a death announcement.

"GERMAN TROOPS HAVE OCCUPIED MORAVIAN OSTRAU. GERMAN ARMY MARCHES ON PRAGUE."

The crowd read the news, their lips moving soundlessly. They shivered in the chilly morning air. The world had abandoned this brave, industrious nation, and had prevented them from using arms to defend themselves. They had stood idly by while Hitler, like a voracious beast of prey, had torn the limbs from the living body of the Republic. Now the enemy had invaded the Republic itself. The nation's arch-adversary was marching on Prague, the ancient beloved city of a hundred towers, the heart of Europe.

It was March 15, 1939. The country was covered by an unusually heavy snowfall for the time of year. The rapacious German wolves overran the borders from all sides. Not a single shot was fired. The "Zbrojovka" arms factory in Brünn was famous the world over. Its storerooms were stuffed with weapons. Soldiers filled the barracks. Reservists, the National Guard and Sokol were all prepared and waiting, but no one called them out. The snow fell, the white shroud covered the land.

Czechoslovakia, the sanctuary of Middle European Jewry, was dead.

German students with swastika armbands took up positions at

the cross-roads next to the policemen, who continued to fulfill their duties. Large squads of Nazis with miniature swastika flags marched towards the station.

The gate of the police headquarters was closed. A strong contingent of sentries stood behind the iron gate. Thin columns of smoke rose from the building's ancient chimney. The officials were hastily burning bundles of reports. A gust of wind blew down a small avalanche from the roof. Albert Wachsmann stepped back a pace so that the fine, cold snow should not fall on his face. Kerner had disappeared round the corner.

Wachsmann met Kerner outside the convoy management office. They walked along for a while in silence. When they saw that they were not being followed, Wachsmann said softly, "I burned the passports."

A Nazi flag fluttered from the Obrawa inn. The Müllan family stood at the door. They were hoarse from shouting "Sieg-Heil!" Wehrmacht trucks rolled over the old bridge. At the entrance to the village, in an avenue of cherry trees whose branches were starkly outlined against the sky, the mayor, Franz Scheibl, waited with representatives of the community. He stood beside a large, oval signboard on which was written:

Country - Moravia
Political district - Brünn
Local community - Mödritz
Height above sea level - 670 feet

Underneath the sign-board was a large placard on a wooden post, which proclaimed in yellow Gothic lettering: "THIS VILLAGE IS JUDENREIN."

Heavy Gestapo boots came thundering up the stairs. The doorbell rang at the convoy management offices and before anyone could answer it, the Gestapo were hammering on the door with their fists.

"Open up — Geheime Staatspolizei!"

Albert Wachsmann opened the door. Four Gestapo men entered. "We just want to see what's going on here," said their leader.

Wachsmann took them into the large office and showed them the card-indexes of the convoys which had already left.

"So a group of Jews still left on March 13. Hmm . . . a pity we marched in two days too late. We could have caught a nice lot of fat fish there. Where are the other little Jews who work here?

78

Probably crept underground when we marched in, hey?"

Wachsmann did not reply.

"So, the Jews are emigrating to Palestine. Well, the King of England will be happy. He'll be crowned King of the Jews now!"

The Gestapo men neighed loudly in appreciation of this witticism.

"Work will stop here for the time being until further notice. The Jews who have been registered for the next convoy remain registered."

The man then became official. He shouted so that the window panes rattled.

"Every Jewish emigration office is under the direct control of Stürmbannführer Adolf Eichmann. Mr. Eichmann will decide the number of Jews who may leave the country. Nothing may be done without his express permission. You are responsible to me for everything that goes on here."

The Gestapo man then executed an about turn such as Wachsmann had only seen equalled on the parade ground for perfection. His three companions wheeled too, as though in response to a command, and marched to the door which the last one through closed with a bang.

***

A few Czech policemen were taken away from the police headquarters in a prison truck.

A hearse came for Dr. Mahovsky, who had shot himself through the head when the Gestapo opened the door to his office. The German army marched down Masaryk Street to the Freiheitsplatz. The entire population of the town — which meant, of course, the twenty thousand Germans — greeted it with cheers. The negligible minority of 200,000 Czechs had nothing to say. The eleven thousand Jews from now on no longer counted as people. Streets and squares in the town were immediately renamed. Masaryk Street became Hermann Göring Street and led, as was only natural, to Adolf Hitler square.

The troops marched in on March 15. Two days later, the great Führer himself visited the town. In honor of the occasion, the Czech municipal governors were removed from office and imprisoned in the Spielberg fortress. The Nazis in the German-speaking area of Brünn made a special celebration that day. They set the large synagogue in the Stiftgasse on fire, and burned it down completely. The fire-brigade and the police had to watch passively from the neighboring streets. They were only allowed to prevent the fire from spreading to the large factories nearby. The hot breath of the flames penetrated to the synagogue's organ which stood behind the choir loft, and it gave a long-drawn-out groan. Then the flames began to lick the choir loft.

The Jews prayed, deathly pale, in their houses. They saw the blazing fire leap to the heavens and knew how dearly the Germans would have liked to throw the glowing firebrands into their apartments as well.

***

Kerner fled from the city. It was already dark when he reached Horacek's farm, in a state of complete exhaustion. Mrs. Horacek received him. While he warmed himself by the fireside and drank hot coffee, she sent for her husband. Jan came at once.

"It's a good thing you've run away. Stay with us. They won't look for you here," Jan said encouragingly.

"I want to go to Prague tomorrow," insisted Kerner.

"That's quite ridiculous. All the roads to Prague are closed. What do you want to do in Prague anyway? The Nazis are already sitting there," admonished Jan.

Erwin slept until Mrs. Horacek came in and woke him.

"You must eat something, you know. It's already three o'clock," she said.

Kerner rose and looked around the room. It was sparkling clean and pleasantly warm. A hand-basin with warm water stood next to his bed. After a few moments, he went into the kitchen. Kratochvil and Sybal were sitting by the fire and they greeted him. During the afternoon, warm underwear, shoes, blankets and a straw mattress were brought to the Horacek's farm. The remote little Czech village took pains to offer the Jewish refugee everything he needed. Peasants and farmers came to the Horaceks' daily in order to invite Kerner to visit them. The atmosphere of good-fellowship, helpfulness and friendship aided in alleviating Kerner's depression.

Chapter Eight

During the first days of the occupation, the Nazis' greatest delight was to place a few of their wolf cubs in front of Jewish shops with placards saying: "Don't buy from Jews" in order to chase customers away. These tactics were not lucrative enough, however, to finance the raised living standards of the Aryan master-race. How would an SA man from Brünn have looked in the eyes of his cronies if he could not have paid for so many rounds of beer in the inn? Where was the glamorous SS man in his black uniform to find money for his girlfriends? Life had become expensive, and not every Nazi could get a cushy job in the government. Jewish shops were aryanized according to a well-practiced procedure. An Aryan foreman, often a young shop boy, could receive a naturally flourishing business to manage and would take care that the Jew who had built up the business after years of work or had even founded it, moved into the gun-turrets on the Spielberg. The foreman made sure that all liabilities were paid in cash, with which he then — being after all entitled to the money as an Aryan — lined his deep pockets. He sold the stock at a loss or let it run out in order to help the black market. In the windows of the shop, which were now bare of goods, he placed a picture of Hitler and a board with the inscription: "Under Aryan Management."

German lawyers regarded it as their inalienable and Führer-given right to chase their Jewish colleagues out of the law offices and thus aryanize the latter. Jewish municipal officials were already thrown out on March 15 without being compensated in any way whatsoever. Jewish bank accounts were blocked. The German government rationed food, and issued coupons for bread, sugar, meat and fats. Jews were only apportioned very meager rations, upon which it was impossible to survive. They were not given any textile coupons and were expected, according to the law, to buy their clothing and shoes from the rag-and-bone man. All this, however, was not sufficient harassment in the eyes of the master-race. Czech peasants still offered their products in the fowl and vegetable markets. They sold to everyone and made a decent living. It made no difference to the peasants and dealers whether the buyer was a German, Czech or even a Jew. Why, there were even Czechs who reserved their wares for long-standing Jewish customers. This state of affairs was unworthy of the now politically-aligned provincial Moravian capital. The new German government was industrious, however, and redeemed the honor of the city by an auxiliary law according to which Jews might only do their shopping after eleven o'clock a.m. The markets were, of course, empty at that hour. Only a few half-rotten vegetable leaves moldered in the garbage cans. The market police and the caretakers saw to it that the decree was strictly enforced. Never had the caretakers been so important to the government as now. First of all, their title was standardized. Caretakers received a promotion to a certain extent. What sort of a name was "caretaker" anyway? Was a caretaker on a par with a carpenter, a smith or shoemaker? A member of the Party should not tolerate such a degrading form of address. In consideration of his particular function and his outstanding services to the movement in spying upon the occupants of his building, he was given a rank parallel to that of the gymnasts.

Gymnastic clubs had a squad leader and a cashier. It was only natural that the man who prowled around after closing time at night in a bedraggled dressing-gown and down-at-heel felt slippers and let in residents in exchange for a tip should now receive the title of house-keeper. If he were particularly diligent, he could even become a block-keeper, whose job it was to spy on a whole block of houses, and he thus became an important pillar of the regime. His activities were manifold. He had to keep a close watch on the residents of the house, to sniff out every visitor, and above all to decorate the house copiously with Nazi flags. If, however, by some special good fortune the landlord of the house was Jewish, then the caretaker naturally became the Aryan supervisor, and as such kept the rent for himself. The house-keepers' sons were in the SA and their daughters sat around in cafes and night-clubs. The advent of the Thousand-Year Reich had heralded the golden age of caretakers in the city. The swastika flags fluttered conspicuously. Almost daily, the Führer was cheered. The town rang with shouts of "Sieg-Heil!" and the Nazis drank to the Führer's health until both the Schnaps bottles and their brains were completely drained.

The Jews of the city were now not only miserable and desperate, but in actual need. Businesses had been shut down or aryanized, Jewish employees dismissed without notice, bank accounts were blocked and doctors and lawyers forbidden to practise. The Gestapo ransacked Jewish apartments with the full authority of the government. The SA plundered without any orders and beat up Jews. Czech Fascists who received a daily wage for their labors, attacked defenseless old men in the street. Jews were generously assigned rear seats in the trams. Jews were forbidden to be outside their houses between eight p.m. and six a.m. Stateless Jews were interned in the Spielberg where they joined co-religionists who had been imprisoned for no reason whatsoever.

Czechs were brought before the People's Court for the smallest offenses and the death penalty was imposed in almost every case. A poor Czech who had cut off the leather straps on the window of a railway car was condemned by the People's Court to be hanged. The sentence was announced on every advertisement pillar. The man appealed.

The Czech nation sent a petition to the Protector of the Reich, Baron von Neurath. Twenty-four hours after the sentence had been passed, the man was hanged in the courtyard of the Court of Justice. A haystack was fired in a village. The Czech peasant responsible was sentenced to death by the People's Court for sabotage and hanged. A university professor who had directed the veterinary service of the Czechoslovakian Legion in Russia during World War I was beaten up in the street. The Czech police, were not disbanded but were forbidden to take any action against German citizens. Large signs saying: "No entry to Jews and dogs" hung on the gates of the Au Gardens, which Emperor Joseph II had donated to his people 150 years earlier. A few Czech cafes had separate sections for Jews. The Esplanade cafe, a purely Jewish concern, was naturally strictly out of bounds for all non-Jews. Jewish women whose husbands had been arrested by the Gestapo immediately after the occupation received letters from the management of the Dachau concentration camp. The letters were brief and their contents always the same.

"The urn containing the ashes of your husband will be forwarded to you against payment of fifty marks."

Some women sent the money; others put their heads in the oven.

The Jewish burial society, the "Chevra Kadisha," had its hands full. The spring sun, which usually roused everything to new life, shone on freshly-dug mounds of earth. "Those who lie here are lucky," exclaimed the mourners as they left the Jewish cemetery after the burial of one of their friends.

***

Kerner did not know much about what was going on in the city. He was hidden in a remote village and had no contact with the town. He drove into the woods with Horacek and loaded the cart with logs and firewood, cleaned the cowstall or groomed the horses. In the evening, he sat with the peasants in the kitchen and smoked the cheapest kind of cigarettes. At night, however, alone in the room which Jan had placed at his disposal, he lay for a long time on his bed without being able to fall asleep. The wind which blew from the snow-covered hills made him shiver even under the thick horse-blanket. The room was unheated. Sometimes he seemed to hear his dog howling. When he dozed off, he imagined he heard Margit's voice calling him and he woke up with a start. The room was cold, dark and silent.

Passover approached and the Deutsch family, the only Jews in the village, invited Kerner to the Seder. They sat round the festive table — Deutsch the engineer, his wife, their twelve-year-old son and Erwin Kerner. The Deutsches had fled from Slovakia to Mr. Deutsch's elderly sisters.

"This is the bread of affliction which our fathers ate," said Mr. Deutsch, taking a Matza from the Seder-plate and holding it up to the serious faces around the table. They continued reading the Haggadah and when they came to the words, "We were slaves to Pharaoh in Egypt," the women heaved a sigh. When the meal was over, they sat for a long time and spoke about their own present and most bitter servitude, from which they could see no salvation. When Kerner took leave of them to return to his room at the Horaceks', he looked once again at the festive table with the sad people around it. He felt sorry for them in their helplessness.

"This year we are here, but next year we shall be in Jerusalem, in the land of freedom," he said, and his voice sounded confident.

84

***

Every day, SA divisions marched through the streets. The standard-bearers were followed by orchestras; then came the caretakers' sons in rows of four, the suburban gardeners, and the whole uniformed mob. At the end of each column marched a group of civilians armed with heavy rubber clubs. Every passer-by who saw the standard being carried past had to stand still, raise his arm in the Nazi salute, and shout, "Sieg-Heil!"

The Czechs loathed the daily marches, as they loathed the streets of their own town which were eternally draped in glaring red flags.

Whoever saw a division drumming along in the distance tried to disappear down the nearest side street or to hide in the entrance to an apartment block. No one wanted to pay the required mark of respect. Nazis, however, greeted the columns with raised right arms and frenzied shouts of "Sieg-Heil!"

People who remained in the streets out of the curiosity or carelessness and did not salute the flag were beaten up with the rubber coshes. They were left lying on the sidewalk streaming with blood, their noses broken. An ambulance from the Czech Red Cross had to take them away after the march was over. To add insult to injury, the innocent victims of these beatings were compelled to sign a declaration in the hospital stating that they had been hurt in a street accident.

The gun-turrets on the Spielberg became more crowded daily. If there were too many prisoners, then a group was deported by train. The wives of the internees were given notice on the day before the train left, and were permitted to see their husbands once more, bring them small parcels and even, if the SA sentry was in a good mood, to talk to them for a short while. On many occasions, long lines of women stood waiting on the Spielberg. In the late afternoon, the guard informed them that they would no longer be able to speak to their husbands that day. Parcels could be given to the guard. The women had denied themselves and their children their last bite in order to give it to the unfortunate husband and father. With trembling fingers, they wrote the names on the parcels. They wrote the letters large and clear so that the guard would not have to search too long for the recipient. If the

85

women were lucky enough to see their husbands once more or if a prisoner was released (which occurred rarely), then it became known that they had never received the parcel.

Occasionally, Jewish shop-owners were released. They had to return to their aryanized businesses in order to help the trusty supervisor to collect the debts or to give him professional advice. Once the money had been collected or his professional advice was no longer necessary, the Jew was invariably remanded to the Spielberg again, or, since he would certainly not be needed again, was deported to Germany. There were great differences in the treatment of prisoners. Senior Czech police officers were particularly favored. They were strictly supervised, kept in isolated cells and forbidden to receive visitors or, of course, even small parcels.

Kratochvil went to fetch Margit from the town. They went to the Au Gardens and caught a bus which brought them to Lissitz within an hour. Erwin stood waiting for them at the gate of a peasant's house. He seemed to take no notice of the bus when it stopped. Firstly a few workers alighted, then Kratochvil, who surveyed the street carefully, and lastly Margit, who looked shyly and uncertainly about her. Erwin went up to her and took her to the somewhat isolated room in which Horacek had placed him. The room was poorly furnished but extremely clean. The wide wooden bed was covered with a brown horse-blanket. There was a little table covered with a white cloth, and a wine glass with primroses stood on it. A hard, heavy peasant's chair and a chest covered with a colored cloth completed the meager furnishings. Erwin helped Margit off with her coat and hung it on the window-bar. He put his pillow on the chair and gently helped her into it. Then he pushed up the chest in order to sit next to her. The tension she had held in for so long was released in stammered phrases and tears. Erwin sat silently next to her. Outside it was already completely dark. He closed the shutter and lit the petrol lamp. It mild light illuminated the room dimly. Margit had cried until she could cry no more, and she felt better.

"Why didn't you send us any news about yourself? I was terribly worried about you. Your mother also didn't know where you were. Wachsmann and Hornik asked me about you several times. It would have relieved all of us to know you were here," she said reproachfully.

"I didn't want to endanger you and myself unnecessarily. The letters might have been censored," he explained.

"How is it here? Do you have enough to eat? You don't look well. Your hands are so rough and calloused. I'll leave you some money so that things should be a bit easier for you," she pleaded.

But Erwin shook his head.

***

After lunch, they waited for the news which was supposed to be broadcast from Brünn at one o'clock. A few minutes before one, there was an interval signal. Kerner looked at the clock on the wall. The times did not seem to agree. Horacek broke off what he was saying in the middle and waited with visible excitement for the news to begin. The first bars of the Czech national anthem came across the air.

"This is the Free Czechoslovakian Service," Kerner stood up hastily and went to the door in order to watch the street.

"You can sit down. We've already posted look-outs," Kratochvil informed him.

The news began.

"Jan Masaryk, the Czechoslovakian ambassador in London, will broadcast on the BBC tomorrow evening at nine o'clock Middle European time."

The Nazis have taken over the Brünn tram company and dismissed all Czechoslovakian employees. "We ask all citizens not to use the trams until the men have been reinstated."

What else the news reader said could not be heard. The broadcast was jammed and it was impossible to understand a single word. At one o'clock the Brünn station began to broadcast the news, which was given firstly in German. The renowned exhibition, "The Eternal Jew," which had arrived from Munich, was praised as a special cultural achievement. It had started a four-week long enlightenment campaign against the Jewish "Pestilence." The everyday announcements followed: sentences passed by the People's Court on Czech saboteurs. Jan turned off the radio. He was not interested in what the Brünn service had to say.

***

A narrow crescent moon shone in the sky. Jan Horacek waited in front of the entrance to his farm.

Margit and Erwin walked through the farmyard. They passed the stalls and went down the scrupulously swept passage into the house where Kratochvil was up late mending a wicker basket. The kitchen was dark and empty. Only a very narrow glimmer of light came from the door of Kratochvil's room. The windows were thickly curtained. There was silence in the room. The radio was playing very softly. Everyone attempted to adjust the set, trying one wave length after another. They were on the point of giving up when the interval signal sounded softly but quite clearly:

> Bum bumbum bum
> Bum bumbum bum
> Bum bumbum bum

"Vola Londyn." (London calling.)

Everyone jumped as though electrified, and crowded around the loudspeaker holding their breaths. They sat leaning forward and listened to the words which came to them over the ether. They knew the voice which was speaking to them. It was their own flesh and blood, the voice of the Czechoslovakian nation — the Czech ambassador, the son of the dead president, was speaking to them. Jan Masaryk was calling them. Jan Masaryk was their representative in the free world. While the city echoed from the yells of the torch-light processions which were swaggering through the streets, while the SA prepared its bloody celebration of the anniversary of the Swedish defeat in Brünn, a handful of people sat in a Lissitz farm and listened with heavy hearts and tears in their eyes to the words of Jan Masaryk.

Chapter Nine

Nearly three hundred years earlier, towards the end of the Thirty Years' War, the Swedes under Torstenson had besieged the city of Brünn and the fortress on the Spielberg. They had burned down the neighboring villages and farms, despoiled and beaten the peasants, and turned flourishing Moravia into such a wilderness that packs of wolves roamed through the Schwarza valley. The Swedes could not overcome the city and the Spielberg, however, either by storming them or by starving out the inhabitants. Their stone cannon balls could not wear down the mighty walls of the citadel; they remained stuck fast. The long siege demoralized Torstenson's army, and the general was supposed to have sworn to raise the siege if he was unable to take the citadel by midday on August 15.

The brave defender of the fortress, Radvit de Souche, a Frenchman who was fighting for the Austrians, learned of Torstenson's decision through his spies. As he could not change the calendar date, he ordered the bell ringers in the Jakobsdom to chime midday at eleven o'clock on August 15.

History was not recorded whether the Swedes had clocks and learned of the deception, or whether Torstenson already gave the order to raise the siege at ten o'clock. In any event, the besiegers departed at eleven o'clock and from that day onwards, August 15 became a holiday in Brünn and was celebrated yearly until 1918 with torch-light processions and marches.

When the Czechoslovakian Republic abolished the old Austrian traditions, the local celebration was deemed unnecessary and done away with forthwith.

The celebration was reestablished after the German army marched in and turned into a National Socialist holiday, although Radvit de Souche had been a Frenchman and the citizens and students who had fought on the ramparts were Moravians. Moreover, it had never been recorded whether or not the latter

89

had been pure-blooded Aryans. Doubtless, it was decided to allow the local Nazis to celebrate the holiday in order to show them what deep historical connections there had always been between the Old Reich and the "Bohemian and Moravian Protectorate."

A torch-light procession was organized on the evening of August 14. The "German House" was festively illuminated both within and without. At the head of the procession marched a group of halberd-bearers dressed in leather doublets, ruffs and top-boots. They were supposed to represent the Swedes. Their faces, which were half-concealed by their wide Swedish hats, were lit up by the flickering torches. Behind them marched an SA band, then the Hitler Youth with multi-colored Chinese lanterns, the SA, and finally the people of Brünn. The latter consisted of a handful of weak-kneed old men in Tyrolean breeches and white stockings, and their ancient wives in dirndls and black laced bodices who were thus refreshing their memories of the long bygone celebrations under the Austrian monarchy. The procession marched through the center of the town to the Swedish memorial in the Glacis Gardens where the last battles had been fought three hundred years earlier. There, the mayor gave a stirring address in which he made particular use of the words: courage, life and property. The song, "I had a comrade," was then played in honor of the Moravians who had fallen there during the war. A few yards further on, a group of Moravians who had come out of the Zeman cafe were beaten up to the strains of the song, after which the torch-light procession moved off again, marched through the Glacis Gardens to the "German House" and there, after often-repeated thundering shouts of "Sieg-Heil!" sat down at the beer tables.

The memorial to Radvit de Souche on the Spielberg was not visited. The Frenchman who had defended the fortress so courageously was not worthy of a torch-light procession.

Jewish prisoners in the Spielberg gun-turrets looked longingly out at the memorial. A full moon shone behind the bust of the fortress commander and enveloped him in a halo which was far more beautiful, solemn and sublime than all the smoking torches and singed Chinese lanterns of the Nazi procession.

Processions, speeches and beer were stirring things which made the heart of every Party member beat faster. The grand drinking orgy after the torch-light procession lasted until morning. The SA units stationed in the suburbs and surrounding villages had come to the town in all their uniformed glory. They intended to enhance their reputations by performing some great warlike deed. They had worked off their intoxication in the Jahn gymnasium at the foot of the Spielberg, had eaten an enormous snack in the "Big Tankard" bar, and considerably boosted their fighting spirit by singing nationalist songs. Now they and their SA friends from the city marched in groups to the Esplanade cafe.

They barricaded the Jesuitengasse, stationed themselves in the adjoining Mozartgasse, and closed off the Basteigasse and the entrance to the Glacis Gardens. The cafe was surrounded and besieged on all sides, like the town of Brünn three hundred years earlier on August 15. A few Jews sat on the narrow wooden terrace in front of the cafe. They immediately went inside, closed the windows and barricaded the doors. The Nazi ring tightened. Eleven o'clock struck from the Jakobsdom. The SA men checked their watches in the customary manner of soldiers attacking at a specified hour. The church bells began to strike midday, as befitted the occasion and thus gave the agreed signal for the attack. The cafe's large plate-glass windows were shattered. The splinters covered the parquet floor and the tables. They flew into the coffee cups and the waxen faces of the frightened guests.

Before the SA took the cafe by storm, they bombarded it heavily with stones from a heap of rubble which had been brought there three days earlier, and for which there had appeared to be no use. The barricaded folding doors at the entrance broke under the kicks of heavy Gestapo boots. Drunk with victory, the veteran fighters stormed the cafe.

The head waiter had just succeeded in informing the police of the attack. Although the latter were less than five minutes away from the cafe, it was half an hour before an adequate force of municipal police — unarmed of course — appeared on the scene.

In the meantime, the SA had received reinforcements. The Hitler Youth were given an illustrated lesson in how to deal with Jews and even allowed to take part in the fight or at least to contribute to the SA's victory by shouting "Sieg-Heil!"

SA women had also assembled in front of the Esplanade cafe. They gave a very good imitation of hyenas on a battlefield.

The SA threw deathly-pale Jewish women and girls out into the street, where they were received by the Hitler Youth chanting: "Germany, awake — Judah, drop dead!" and the valkyries fell upon them and tore off their earrings, mutilating their victims' ear-lobes at the same time. The cries of the wounded women mingled with the hysterical war cry of the hyenas and the noise reached such a frightful pitch that it penetrated to the open windows of the Gestapo office in the Mozartgasse. The gentlemen there were extremely busy at that moment trying to persuade a Jewish hotel owner from Vienna, whom they had discovered in the city, to surrender his property to them. They pressed their burning cigarette ends on his forehead and at the same time, broke his lower teeth with the coal scuttle. Two gentlemen, who were thus officially employed, left their work in the middle and slowly made their way in all their uniformed glory to the Esplanade cafe. They arrived just as the SA was attempting to throw the Jews under some passing trams, in which honorable activity they were being hindered by the Czech police.

The Gestapo men drew the Czech police officer's attention to the fact that he might only employ his men to control the traffic. It was not part of the police force's duties to take action against ethnic German citizens of the Protectorate. The SA was roused still further by the appearance of the gentlemen from the Gestapo. They again attempted to throw Jews under a passing tram. Since the police could not begin a hand-to-hand fight with the SA in order to rescue the Jews from their clutches, they stood in tightly-closed ranks along the tram lines in order to catch Jews who were thrown there. Czech officials who were coming out of their offices for their midday break and workers from the textile factories squeezed in among the policemen and formed a living wall in order to frustrate the SA's devilish intentions. Meanwhile, SA heroes searched the ruins of the cafe. They battered the kitchen equipment against the walls, poured out the coffee and refreshed themselves on the spot with the few bottles of alcoholic drinks.

In a hidden corner of the cafe they found the myopic Dr. Dresdner. They pulled him out by his collar. "Hey, folks! We've caught another fat Jew. Look out! He's coming your way," shouted a strapping SA man as he threw his victim down the stairs. Unfortunately, Dr. Dresdner fell so badly that he could not get up immediately. The SA men standing outside fell on him. They trod on his face with their boots. They stamped on him. Before the police could intervene, Dr. Dresdner was dead. A large pool of blood stained the pavement. Blood stuck to the curb. Drops of blood from the women's mangled ear-lobes spattered the street. When ambulances from the Czech Red Cross arrived, the Nazis had already marched off. The wounded who could still walk had disappeared without receiving first aid. Not far from the entrance where Dr. Dresdner lay in a pool of blood, an elderly man was writhing in fearful agony. He was dead before they reached the hospital. A watering cart from the municipal sanitation department drove through the streets. A powerful stream of water washed the blood away. Swastika flags fluttered from the housetops. SA men from the Brünn suburbs had gathered in Hajek's inn on the Kumrowitzer bridge to drink a few pints of beer before they marched home. The mayor's festive address which he was giving in the town hall was broadcast through loudspeakers. August 15, the anniversary of the Swedish defeat, had come to a fitting close.

***

For days, the visit of the exhibition "The Eternal Jew" had been advertised in the newspapers and on posters. Yellow streamers with large crooked letters in a language which read from right to left were hung across the main streets of the city. The crude, shapeless letters were supposed to parody Hebrew writing, and naturally to inflame the masses to vent their outraged feelings in organized riots.

The windows of bookshops also contained nothing but advertisements for this cultural exhibition. The "Stürmer" had taken special pains to place appropriate literature and pictorial material at the public's disposal.

Particularly striking was a large picture reproduced from the "Stürmer" which bore the title: "A Jew at the Fish Market."

The photograph of the Jew with sidelocks and caftan would not in itself have been capable of generating sufficient national fury, and thus the picture bore an additional caption which could not fail to strike every spectator — so large and glaring was it.

"The Jew visits the fish market in order to feast his glittering, bloodthirsty eyes on the killing of the fish." Every normal person who saw the poster was bound to realize that this particular Jew had gone to buy fish. His eyes, as in all newspaper photographs, were quite devoid of any luster; only the Nazis saw them glitter.

Another reproduction from the "Stürmer" showed a Jewish

woman from an old-age home in Karlsbad. The editor of the paper, Julius Streicher, or his worthy colleagues, had added information to the effect that the old-age home had smelt like a rabbit hutch. All these remarks were aimed at poisoning the minds of young non-Jews, at representing the Jews as sub-human objects and at stirring up still more hatred against them so that it could erupt when the Nazis gave the order. Streicher had concentrated his attention on the Bible and the Talmud. He quoted phrases out of context, gave his own interpretation of them, taking care to show thereby that Jews were enemies of the human race. Max Dinter published his trilogy: "The Sin Against the Spirit — The Sin Against the Blood — The Sin Against the Earth." Alfred Rosenberg sold "The Myth of the Twentieth Century." The book was displayed in the shop window like a ravenous wolf. All these publications appealed to the basest instincts of the Nazis who had, in any case, already been fed for years on anti-Jewish propaganda. The books were praised during the exhibition as indispensible research material.

Despite the propaganda machinery which ran uninterruptedly in top gear, the number of visitors to the exhibition left much to be desired. The Germans had to juggle with figures for the sake of publicity and all school-children (naturally according to their class-es) therefore had to visit the exhibition. Even Czech kindergarten children had to look at the new picture book. Their teachers had to explain each picture to them, and the SA guards made sure that they did so thoroughly. The children entered the exhibition hall through a revolving door connected to a device which registered the exact number of visitors. The figures were announced daily on the radio and in the press.

During the exhibition, the Franz-Eher publishing company in-creased its activities. Large posters were stuck on all the walls. The company enjoyed special rights — it was there that the Führer's literary masterpiece, "Mein Kampf," had been published. The latter was ceremoniously given to every bride and bridegroom at their wedding as a gift from the Reich Chancellor. The price of the popular edition was, of course, included in the marriage fees.

One of these posters had a picture of the King of England in the upper right-hand corner. In the bottom left-hand corner, the head of a Jewish soldier with a flat, English steel helmet looked out of

94

an oval frame. A large caption in Gothic lettering enlightened the spectator: "The King of England — The King of the Jews."

Jews who saw the poster did momentarily actually harbor a wish to be subjects of His Majesty, the King of England. They would have been prepared to give up years of their lives for the privilege, and they would also have gladly relinquished the protection of Baron von Neurath, who was pressuring Dr. Emil Hacha to sign the anti-Jewish laws.

The handsome, light-grey gala uniform with the wide carmine lapels in which Mr. von Neurath strutted around the castle in Prague did not, however, impress the poor President of the Bohemian and Moravian Protectorate.

The Jewish inhabitants of these countries, who had possessed Czechoslovakian nationality before the invasion, remained citizens of the Protectorate — which naturally did not indicate that they had any civil rights. As Stürmbannführer Adolf Eichmann did not succeed in striking home with his first blow against the Jews, he started to employ other methods.

The Jews were ordered to give up their apartments in the center of the town and, for the sake of their own security, to concentrate in certain designated streets. The noose began to tighten. The Jews moved. They had no idea that the caretakers were already compiling lists of Jewish residents; the majority were happy to be somewhat separated from the Aryans.

**

When Erwin Kerner finally plucked up the courage to drive to the city in the early morning with a butcher who was bringing slaughtered pigs and calves to the meat market, he found the streets already decked with flags. He got off in the Neugasse in order to walk from there to Park Street. The shortest way to Park Street was through the Au Gardens. Erwin disregarded the metal signboard with the notice, "No entry to Jews and dogs." He walked across the park and arrived at Margit's house just as she was eating breakfast with her parents. He excused himself for coming so early and so unexpectedly, and refused to join them at the table. He felt out of place in his top-boots and laborer's suit in the well-furnished apartment. He gave them two packets of meat wrapped up in linen and prepared to take leave of them. Margit's father found it very hard to come to terms with the fact that Erwin was employed as a farmyard laborer. The white-haired old man had been a Supreme Court Justice until the Germans marched in and had been received several times by the President of the Republic as spokesman for various Jewish delegations.

"Don't you find the work hard?" he asked.

"Not at all. I've already got used to it. While they were threshing, I had to carry heavy sacks of grain to the granary all day long. One just has to have practise," replied Kerner.

It was impossible for the Supreme Court Justice, however, to associate the word "practise" with pigs' carcasses, disembowelled calves and heavy sacks. The very word in that connection gave him palpitations.

Kerner's parents had been forced to leave their house in the village on the day the Germans marched in. They had moved to the Fabrikgasse. Erwin made his way there after he had left Margit's apartment.

His heart thumped violently as he rang the bell. The door was opened a crack and his mother's voice asked, "What do you want, please?"

Kerner's mother had not recognized her son in the dark corridor.

"I would like to step inside," answered Erwin softly. His mother opened the door immediately, as though he were a policeman who wanted to search the house.

It was only when Erwin stepped into the little kitchen and shut the door behind him that she recognized him. Erwin looked around him. He saw the iron bedsteads, the wardrobe, and the table and chairs which his parents had been lent by the Jewish community. There was not a single piece of furniture from his parents' home. The apartment reflected the abject poverty in which they were living.

"Do you need anything? What do you live on?" he asked.

His mother replied with a note of pride in her gentle voice. She took in washing for families who could still afford the luxury, and cleaned apartments for Jews who had been forced to dismiss their Christian maids. Erwin was completely taken aback. None of this had even occurred to him.

Erwin had worked all night long and was tired and sleepy. When he was already in bed, his mother came in. She straightened his pillow, pulled the blanket up to his chin and stroked his hair. He was, after all, still her child who had exhausted himself in order to come and see her.

***

The bus with which Kerner left the city stood at the crossroads near Gurein tightly wedged in a line of lorries. Long columns of German army trucks drove down the street. Uniformed motor-cyclists in steel helmets regulated the traffic, gave orders and drove down the long lines of trucks. Tank units rolled past, followed by howitzers and anti-aircraft guns. Soldiers sat on the gun barrels. SS officers drove down the crowded streets in open cars. After a few hours, the bus began to move again. The tanks had worn deep grooves in the asphalt streets. The bus rattled and jolted along. On the way, it caught up with fresh columns which forced it aside right next to the curb. Singing came out of one of the passing trucks: "Today Germany is ours, and tomorrow the whole world." The bus drove slowly down a long village street which was lined with curious school-children. There were no adults to be seen. The children gazed silently at the soldiers as they passed.

Chapter Ten

On September 1, 1939, Hitler attacked Poland after the British government had refused to allow the country to be chopped up into corridors and motorways. Before war was officially declared, German dive-bombers turned entire towns into smoking heaps of rubble. The Poles resisted the attackers bitterly. The fight for the Eastern Plateau lasted for days. The first allies to come to the aid of the Poles were soldiers from a Czechoslovakian army corps commanded by General Prchala which had fled the country. Before England and France had declared war, the country's fate was sealed. The brave Polish eagle lay writhing the ground with broken wings and the boots of the German army trod it into the mud which the autumn rain had produced in the streets. When the Führer began his great speech in Berlin with the words, "In this historic moment, the German army is marching across the border," Poland was already defeated, but Hitler's plan to engulf it without a fight like Czechoslovakia and Austria had not succeeded. The Poles were the first nation to oppose the heathens with weapons in their hands, and their heroic stand mobilized the whole civilized world against the scourge of humanity. The population fled before the invaders from the bombed towns and villages. Pedestrians and horse-drawn wagons, hand-carts and perambulators blocked the roads. Wheels broke under their burdens. Walking wounded with blood-encrusted, makeshift bandages, children screaming for their mothers, townspeople, peasants and Jews, all tried to reach Warsaw. The dive-bombers roamed the clouds which hung, grey and sad, above the refugees. They swooped down upon the wretched procession and unleashed their bombs. It did not help to leap into the roadside ditches: the aeroplanes' machine guns mowed down the lines of refugees, turned, and flew back, firing their volleys just above the heads of the half-demented fugitives. The Führer plastered the roads with corpses for the sake of his "eastward expansion." The radio proudly announced the

German victories. Loudspeakers bawled in all the streets and squares of the Protectorate. The Czechs went wearily and hopelessly to work. They had hoped that when the Western powers declared war, a joint English and French attack on the Thousand-Year Reich would follow. The German newspapers published the first death notices of soldiers who had fallen in battle. All the notices had the same format: "Our son fell at the Polish front while faithfully fulfilling his duty to our Führer. Proudly and sorrowfully, the parents."

Pride and sorrow, did not, however, prevent the Brünn carpenter, Gerhard Heger, from cursing his Führer, whom he had but yesterday loved so well, when he received the announcement of the heroic death of his only son. Heger's shop was accordingly closed and he himself taken away for educational purposes to the Spielberg.

***

Sturmbannführer Adolf Eichmann's great day came with the commencement of the Polish campaign. While he began centralizing the Jews of Poland into ghettos, he succeeded in spreading the rumor in the other countries governed by the Great German Reich that a Jewish settlement area was being constructed in Poland. Eichmann had selected the little town of Nisko-on-San as the center-point of this area. The Gestapo began to take action against stateless Jews in Moravian Ostrau. Jews were also deported from Prague and Brünn. The gun-turrets on the Spielberg were overflowing, after all, and one had to make room for new prisoners.

A few Viennese Jews who were still living in the city were forced to make the journey to the East in closed cattle trucks; they were a pioneering group responsible for building accommodation in the "settlement area."

Adolf Eichmann travelled through the countries under German control. His tours of inspection took him to Brünn where he honored the Jewish community with a visit, and delivered the following solemn declaration. "We shall win the war and then solve the Jewish question. Should we, however, lose the war, which is of course quite out of the question, then we shall give the Jews a lesson such as they'll never forget."

A few days later, a short notice, which was of the greatest

importance for a few hundred Jews, appeared in the SS newspaper "Das Schwarze Korps." "The emigration center for Jewish overseas emigrants was opened in No. ii Delostrelecka, Prague." War was thus openly declared with the Nazis.

The National Socialist Party began to implement its program of driving out the Jews at all costs. Adolf Eichmann was the Reich delegate in charge of solving the Jewish question.

The convoy management offices in Brünn and Prague began to operate immediately after this announcement appeared. The Jews of Danzig, which was now also incorporated into the German Reich, took the decision to emigrate to Palestine together with their rabbi.

Among thousands, there was an upsurge of fresh hope. They were prepared to leave immediately, but Mr. Eichmann was not in favor of too hasty a departure. He was only interested in having an organization which functioned smoothly and from which he could learn how to organize a convoy — not in order to save people, but in order to freight them in the most expedient way possible as cattle for slaughter.

The desperate Jews obeyed every order given by the Central Office for Jewish Overseas Emigration, thinking that by following the instructions exactly, they could hasten or at least facilitate the departure of the Palestine convoys.

The Thousand-Year Reich's Minister for Jewish Affairs did not, however, particularly wish to organize convoys to Palestine. He was far more interested in lulling the Jews into a false sense of security and showing the subjugated peoples how humanely the master-race was solving the Jewish problem. The emigration center was most proficient in dragging the last dollar out of the plundered Jews and demanding fees from them which, with the best will in the world, they could no longer pay by their own means. Every Jew who wished to be registered for emigration had to travel to Prague, stay there for three days and report to the police station. This naturally involved work on the part of the officials for which one had to pay a fee. The journey to Prague and the three days' stay there were also not free. If the applicant — as was mostly the case — had no more money, then the Jewish community was forced to defray his living expenses. The convoy management offices in Prague and Brünn found it necessary to employ a full-time official to process the applications. The latter

100

also had the arduous task of receiving orders from the Gestapo in the central office and ensuring that they were immediately carried out.

The Jewish community in Prague was instructed to form a security service to keep order in the Delostrecka. The latter were distinguished by yellow "Security Service" armbands, and rewarded by bad language and blows on the part of the Nazis. The Gestapo had set up the emigration center in the Petschek palace in order to demonstrate to the Jews of Prague how subservient they were to their Aryan lords. Petschek was a Jewish industrial magnate and the fact that his home was used for registering the emigrants was nothing but an additional humiliation for the Jews.

Everyone who intended to leave the country first had to pay a "Reich Flight Tax," furnish himself with a certificate to show that he owed no income tax, provide lists of what was contained in his hand luggage and have his clothes valued by a legally confirmed expert (naturally paying the expert for his services). A swarm of parasites grew fat on the misery of the impoverished Jews, sucked their blood and needlessly complicated their lives with constant new orders. At the same time, the declaration of war was followed by shortages in all foodstuffs and consumer goods which resulted in a steep rise in prices. When food was rationed, the Jews hardly received enough ration cards to keep body and soul together. They were therefore forced to pay the high black-market prices for the most necessary staples. The vast majority of Jews no longer earned anything, and since their bank accounts had been frozen, and they were only allowed to remove the most minimal sums from them after receiving permission from the District High Commissioner, their position deteriorated from day to day. The middle-classes were totally ruined and lived on community funds. The rich were exposed even more to underhand trickery. Their fortunes, which they had built up over decades, dissolved before their eyes.

Every night, some fifty people travelled on the express train to Prague. The Prague Jewish community was also obliged to send fifty people daily and at eight a.m., they all had to be assembled in front of the Petschek Palace. People overflowed from the narrow sidewalk onto the roadway. They stood in rows of four with their hats in their hands and their files under their arms. They were not allowed to step on the sidewalk next to the wrought-iron fence of the public gardens. The latter was reserved exclusively for the overlords in their black uniforms who went in and out of the palace. An SS sentry stood at the gate.

The security men from the Jewish community tried their hardest to protect the waiting crowd from being jostled by the SS. They knew from long experience all the latter's cunning tricks which had the sole purpose of harassing the defenseless Jews. As the files containing nine identical copies of the same form had to be given to the officials in immaculate condition, the SS jostled the waiting applicants in an attempt to make them drop the files. If they succeeded in this heroic Teutonic deed, then they stamped on the papers and the latter were consequently damaged so much that they were no longer acceptable. The victim could only pick up the remains of his documents and forms from the dusty street and take them back home. He had paid all the expenses in vain, and had to travel back to Prague when he was summoned. An old man from Prague had already signed a document surrendering all his property to the SS. As he was unable with the best will in the world to obtain the necessary entry visa to emigrate abroad, he had to appear in the Gestapo offices daily, where they snapped at him. Every day he was asked, "What have you done about emigrating?"

The old man would then give a detailed report concerning various consulates he had called upon. Not a single country showed the slightest inclination to give him so much as a transit visa, and the old man had to report every day in the Petschek Palace. Once he was particularly unlucky. He was leaving the building after an interview with the Gestapo and, being still rather dazed, put on his hat before he had reached the SS sentry. The old man, who one could see had once belonged in well-to-do circles, then gave the SS man the summons which had been handed back to him after his session with the Gestapo. The sentry had thought up a particularly ingenious way of letting the summons drop to the ground.

"Well, am I supposed to pick up your papers? Don't you know how to hand over an official document to the SS, you stupid Jew?" barked the sentry.

The old man bent down over the little piece of paper. The SS sentry knocked off his hat with the flat of his hand, and it rolled down the three stone steps to the sidewalk. The old man tried to catch his head-covering. The gallant sentry shouted at him. "Back here, and hand me the summons according to the regulations!" The Jew obeyed. He came up to the sentry, but in his confusion or out of habit, put his hat back on again. The SS sentry knocked it off for the second time. The man trembled in every limb. "When will you learn, you old idiot, that one may only put one's hat on in the street?" roared the sentry, and promised to give the old man a few more genuine Viennese clouts over the ear. The Jew bowed to the young warrior, apologized and departed, leaving his hat lying in the gateway.

***

The Brünn convoy management's representative to the Gestapo in Prague had an extremely difficult job. Every day he had to transmit new instructions and orders to Brünn and then make sure that the latter were immediately executed. One day, every Jew received an additional name to be placed without fail before his own. The convoy management representative hurried to the post office and sent a telegram to Brünn, informing them that all Jewish men were to immediately add "Israel" to their names, and all Jewish women "Sara" to theirs.

The telegram reached the Brünn convoy management office in the evening. Files had already been issued to fifty women and girls who were to travel to Prague that night on the express orders of the Gestapo so that they could report for registration at the emigration center at eight o'clock the next morning.

Thanks to the convoy management's superb organization, the women and girls who had come from small provincial towns the day before were contacted at their relatives' houses in Brünn, and brought back with their files to the convoy management offices. Typewriters clattered until late at night filling out fresh forms, as it was strictly prohibited to make any corrections on the original documents. The District High Commissioner in Brünn even gave the Jews permission to break the eight p.m. curfew for this purpose. After midnight, the exhausted women went straight from the offices to the station. Magda Mandelik-Hirsch was among the group who travelled to Prague. She had not yet had time to get used to her husband's family name, and now she also had to add

"Sara" to her name. The women emerged after a sleepless night. They were worn out from the train journey, and shivered in the chilly morning air. The SS men at the emigration center naturally felt obliged to parade before the women in all their glory and splendor. They forced the women to stand in the street for hours. The slightest whisper was shouted down. A drunk SS man planted himself in front of them. With arms akimbo and a terrible scowl on his face, he shouted, "I've had enough of this jumble-sale! If you don't stop cackling this instant, there'll be real trouble." He eyed the first row of women with loathing. The women stood absolutely silent. The SS hero stretched himself, and strutted up and down the rows like a peacock, clearly trying to create an impression on the women. Magda Mandelik-Hirsch was young and pretty. Her long eyelashes were half-closed from exhaustion. She had fallen asleep on her feet as she waited.

The SS man bawled at her. "Look how you're standing, you slut!"

Magda awoke suddenly but forced herself to remain calm.

At about midday, the first four women were admitted to hand over their files. After a few moments, the door opened and the frightened women hastily left the office. As SS officer demanded to speak to the representative of the Brünn convoy management. The latter came immediately and stood to attention. The SS officer snarled at him.

"Those Jewish blockheads in Brünn don't even know how to spell 'Sara.' Sara has an 'h' on the end. Bring in all the files immediately," and he slammed the door.

The security men from the Prague Jewish community quickly collected all the files. The Brünn representative presented the emigration forms to the SS officer who tore them up, thereby making it impossible for the spelling to be corrected.

"This riffraff from Brünn is to report here with new and correct forms in forty-eight hours. Now scram!" ordered the SS man.

The elegant command "Scram!" was always shouted particularly loudly as it was the latest expression in German, and thus had to be especially emphasized.

Tired and frightened, the women returned to Brünn. Once again, the convoy management worked feverishly to complete the forms. Every Sara received an "h" on the end. Elbert again obtained the travelling expenses from the community fund, and the women once again took the express train to Prague and stood in long lines outside the Petschek Palace. Magda was one of the first four women to hand in their files. The SS officer took her file.

"What name?" he growled.

"What's your name?" seemed to him to be too polite a form of address to a Jew. "What name?" was the latest official phraseology.

Magda stood to attention and answered, "Magda Hirsch nee Mandelik."

The SS officer became red in the face, but he kept himself in check. He opened the file and pointed to the name.

"Read," he ordered brusquely.

"Sarah Magda Hirsch nee Man . . ." read Magda.

The officer interrupted her. He tapped the name again with his finger and looked at the form. His eyes bored into the last letter, the "h" on the end of "Sarah." Then he ripped up the file and threw it at Magda's feet.

"From today onwards, Sarah is no longer to be written with an 'h' " he shouted. "Files with an 'h' are not to be handed in." His voice cracked.

Fifty women travelled back to Brünn. They now had no idea how to write the name correctly. They did know, however, that they would once again have to go to community offices to collect the money for the next trip to Prague.

The blocked bank accounts, aryanized shops and businesses, surrendered valuables and Jews' houses and land became the property of the new masters and confiscated for the benefit of the Third Reich. The more valuables the Nazis swallowed up — legally, according to Hitler's laws — the more voracious their appetites became. On the eve of Yom Kippur, the greatest Jewish festival on which the Jews had fasted and prayed for the past two thousand years, all radio sets had to be handed in to the Jewish community. This decree particularly suited the Nazi rabble from the suburbs, and the cottagers, peasants and caretakers' sons already saw themselves as the owners of handsome and expensive radio sets. Large, valuable wirelesses were trundled through the streets on handcarts. The less enlightened members of the Party with their great protruding eyes had not calculated with the Party's iron discipline, however. They had become used to living out of other people's pockets and it had not yet occurred to them that they were actually only receiving the crumbs, or rather, a few succulent bones to nibble upon. Often, it was true, a piece of meat was still hanging from the bone.

The SS and SA peers, the members of NSKK, all sat much nearer to the honey pot. According to an age-old custom, they fished out the juiciest bites for themselves and left the rest for the serfs. Thus the best radios, most valuable jewels, finest crystal, most beautiful fur coats and precious Meissen figures disappeared directly from the collection point. They were taken in expropriated cars to aryanized apartments. Since the Third Reich had no objection to looting in the annexed or expropriated territories, these methods were simply legalized.

***

One lovely autumn day, two Gestapo men knocked at the door of Elbert's apartment. Mrs. Elbert opened the door a crack. One of the men struck his top-boot in the opening, pushed her back and entered. "House search — Gestapo." he said loudly. Mrs. Elbert suddenly saw two revolvers pointing at her and drew back in alarm. The men immediately went to work. With the air of experienced professionals, they emptied closets of their contents and threw underwear, shoes, clothes, and books into a heap in the middle of the bedroom floor. They found twenty thousand crowns in a little iron chest which they immediately pocketed. They then drew up a short statement and had it signed by Mrs. Elbert. They banged the door of the apartment and disappeared. Elbert, who only came home from the community offices towards evening, found his wife sitting in an armchair, weeping bitterly. She told her husband the whole story. Elbert, who was used to dealing with Nazis, plucked up courage and went to the District High Commissioner.

The latter listened to his complaint and then said, "We gave no orders for your apartment to be searched. You have been deceived by swindlers." Elbert's head swam. The District High Commissioner took down details of the incident.

***

The Slovakian government, which was well aware of the unusual circumstances of its rise to power, began to display its might. It enjoyed wonderful support from the leader of the "Carpatho-

German Party," an engineer named Karmasin who, like his rather better-known colleague from the Party, Konrad Henlein, had lived like a vole during the last years of Czechoslovakia's existence. As the number of Germans living in Slovakia and Carpathian Russia was only very small, Karmasin had been forced to work together with Hlinka Guards, although he hated and despised the Slovakians from the bottom of his Aryan heart.

The Hlinka Guards, the majority of whom possessed nothing apart from their uniform and were lazy to boot, regarded the property of Czechs and Jews with a covetous eye.

The newly-created autonomous Slovakia had to justify its existence in the eyes of the world and Adolf Hitler in particular, and decided to appoint a propaganda minister for this express purpose. This important position, which also involved dealing with cultural affairs, was entrusted to Mr. Sano Mach. The latter was known not so much for his literary activities, which had landed him in prison in Czechoslovakia, as for his alcoholic anti-Semitism. His archenemies — apart from the Jews, of course — were considered by him to be the Czechoslovakian teachers who had continued to function in schools even after Slovakia had declared her independence, as the new state was still short of teachers. As long as these Czechs were active, and through their teaching also influenced the parents of their pupils, Sano Mach feared — and rightly so — for the faithfulness of his Slovakians, who might easily disparage the new government's achievements. Mr. Mach and his ministers had already promised to do a great deal. At that moment, however, they were extremely busy furnishing luxurious apartments for themselves and imposing new taxes upon the country. In order to perform these tasks unhindered, it was desirable for them to get rid of Czech teachers. Mr. Karmasin was naturally in on the plan. The Hlinka Guards received orders to make matters unpleasant for the Czechs. The two sides came to blows and the authorities, deciding that the teachers were a provocative element, expelled them from Slovakia. It was thus that Mrs. Bozena Minarik, her husband and their two-year-old daughter arrived, with scanty baggage and even less money, in Lissitz. Jan Horacek took the family in. As he was Bozena's brother, she was entitled to take refuge in his house.

Erwin moved out of his room. He took shelter with the only Jewish family still living in the village. The latter had run a prosperous grocery business for years, and possessed a house and a few acres of fertile ground. Now the shop was closed and the fields confiscated as Jewish property. According to the detailed estate regulations, Jews could not possess any land in the territory of the Great German Reich.

***

A stormy wind chased the ragged clouds. The forest path was covered with brownish-yellow leaves. Rooks settled inside the farms.

Woodcutters went sullenly to work. It was still dark when they left the village in the morning. The food which they carried wrapped up in red-checked cloths had deteriorated in quality. The so-called bread was a soggy grey dough which stuck to the roof of the mouth. The good grain and golden-yellow wheat from the rich Hann plain went to the Reich. Only inferior barley — animal fodder, in fact — remained for the Czechs. The full-eared brewery barley also went to the Reich, where the consumption of beer proportionate to the enthusiasm for National Socialism, had risen sharply.

Smoked lard and every other type of dripping were now only obtainable at exorbitant prices. Meat was rationed and thus vanished from the market. The sausage which the laborers took to work could have been honorably offered in a vegetarian restaurant. It was only edible if washed down with a large draught of Sliwowitz. Two hours after the woodcutters had left, the cart-drivers followed in order to load the felled trunks onto their long cars and bring them to the railway station in Raiz, where the giant logs began their journey to Hamburg.

The coats of the peasants' horses had become rougher and no longer had the healthy shine of former times. They too were badly fed, and had to work hard in order to transport the logs along the bumpy forest tracks to the railway. The horses had to make a large detour as well, because the Germans were just starting to build a hundred-yard-wide motorway diagonally across the paths and fields. The peasants, whose best fields were being filled with rubble and who received neither land nor compensation in return, did not dare to complain. They avoided the motorway just as workers avoided the builders who sought hired-laborers in the village. The working conditions for Czechs were bad, and certainly could not compare with those of the German foremen. Unfortunately, there was no other work to be had at that time of year.

Erwin walked up the road which led through the forest to Lhotka, in order to take leave of Father Adametz. From time to time, carts passed him, each one loaded with an enormous tree trunk. The path was very steep and the peasants walked beside their horses, holding the reins tightly. They greeted Erwin as they went by. The last cart took the turn rather too quickly, and its left rear wheel skidded into a shallow ditch. The waggoner spurred on his horses with a whip. The latter pulled as hard as they could, but were unable to move the cart. Erwin went up to the horses and let them rest for a moment. Then he seized the rear wheel and while the peasant spurred on the horses, jerked it back onto the side of the road. The peasant offered him his bottle of schnaps. "That was tiring — have a drink. You need a quick one after that." Erwin put the bottle to his lips and took a long drink. He gave the man a cigarette and joined him as he sat by the roadside. The peasant complained that the Germans were cutting down all the forests. They had no business to fell all the trees near Lhotka. They were not at all concerned about how much damage they caused with their motorway. They took away the best fields and built the motorway where it suited them.

The peasant thanked Erwin, rose and returned to his horses. While the heavy cart continued down to the valley with the brakes applied, Erwin climbed on past Heger's house to the village. After making a few inquiries, he found Father Adametz together with his sister, an elderly, wealthy peasant woman. Father Adametz saw him coming and walked a few paces towards him. They sat in a large, airy dining-room. The bells chimed midday from the Lissitz church. Father Adametz's niece, a tall peasant with a snub-nose like a Slav and full, cherry-red lips, laid the table.

"I was particularly anxious to visit you today. I came in order to thank you for the pleasant hours which I was privileged to spend in your company during my stay in Lissitz," said Erwin.

"Do you want to leave us then?" asked Father Adametz.

"Your Reverence knows very well that I want to go to Palestine. I have heard that one can now register for emigration with the Gestapo in Prague," Erwin stated.

Father Adametz interrupted him.

"Be careful. Don't trust this scum from hell. Think it over. We are in the middle of a war. England is the most dangerous adversary of the Third Reich, which calls itself the Thousand-Year Reich. That appellation alone is blasphemous. How can anyone tell whether God has not resolved and decreed that this barbaric and idolatrous state be destroyed tomorrow and blotted from the face of the earth, as Korach was destroyed? Consider whether this Satan will allow you to go to the Holy Land, which is under British sovereignty."

"I must register, otherwise I have no hope of getting away from here," Erwin confided.

The girl came in again with the food. They ate slowly, each one deeply involved in his own thoughts.

As they drank their tea, Father Adametz offered Erwin a cigar.

"You can still come back here after you've registered and wait to see if they will really allow you to emigrate," he said finally.

"The situation has changed. The Germans are building their motorway here. It is too dangerous for me to remain in Lissitz. I can go back to Brünn. There are still nearly ten thousand Jews living there, and it's easier for a single person to disappear than here. I've also heard reports that all the Nazis from my village have been given important jobs in Poland as a reward for their many years of illegal activity. They'll continue their bloodhound activities there," said Erwin with deep resignation.

Father Adametz took his hat and accompanied Erwin back through the garden. They came to the forest path, and looked up at the towering firs and the narrow strips of grey sky above them. Father Adametz stopped. The wind whistled in the trees.

"You will go up to the Holy Land which I, too, was once privileged to visit. You will see Jerusalem, the Holy City, which I too have once seen, but my feet will never again tread upon its holy ground, nor my eyes behold the beauty of Jerusalem. My dear young friend, accept the blessing of an old man. May the Lord our God protect you and guide you upon your journey." Father Adametz shook hands with Erwin, who felt how the priest's hand shook.

Then Father Adametz slowly began the climb back to Lhotka. Erwin watched him until he had disappeared among the pines.

**

Winter came early, and the situation of the impoverished Jews deteriorated still further. There was no work to be had in the Czech villages. The few Jews who had been sheltered by peasants had no means of support. The villagers also feared the ever-increasing pressure of the Nazis and were glad when a Jew found lodgings elsewhere.

In the city, it was unthinkable for a Jew to find work during the winter months. Building had stopped with the onset of the first severe frost, and the Jews who had been employed on a daily basis by Czech contractors were again unemployed.

In former years during the winter months, the poorer classes of the population would sit in the cheapest suburban cinemas, not so much in order to see the ancient films, which tore countless times during the performances, as to obtain shelter from the cold in the well-heated picture-houses. For Jews, however, this too was no longer possible. They were not allowed inside a cinema. The Jewish community helped as much as it could, insofar as the District High Commissioner, who controlled all Jewish property, gave permission for Jews to buy coal. Gone were the days when the cellars of Jewish houses were filled with coal. That winter one was happy to receive a scuttle-full of black dust from the coal merchant.

The dust burned with great difficulty and instead of emitting warmth, produced clouds of irritating smoke which made one's eyes smart. In the Jewish community's warmest room, people sat round a large sawdust stove which it was impossible to regulate once the fuel inside the drum had started burning. Everyone had to leave the room before eight p.m. in any case, and return to their cold apartments.

***

Since Jews had started to register in Prague at the Central Office for Jewish Overseas Emigration, the convoy management offices worked under additional heavy pressure.

Typewriters clacked, forms were filled out, the hot water pipes made the rooms pleasantly warm and the people who went in and out of the offices were more hopeful than anywhere else in the country. Their firm belief in the convoy's departure was the only thing that kept them going.

When Erwin returned to the city, he found a niche for himself in the convoy management offices where he sat unobtrusively during the day. Much had altered there since the last convoy had left two days before the Germans marched in. His old friends with whom he had worked were no longer there. Apart from Albert Wachsmann, all the members of the staff were total strangers to him. For a few days, he watched them, listened to their conversations and tried to build up a picture of their lives and activities in his mind. Gradually, he began to make contact with them and to help them with their work. The gentlemen at the Central Office for Jewish Emigration took good care that there should be plenty of extra work, and the convoy management found it necessary to employ more officials. After receiving permission from the District High Commissioner, Albert Wachsmann took on Erwin as a member of his staff. Erwin was given lists of addresses to process until one day the Gestapo brought the whole office staff to the verge of insanity by their ingenious chicanery. The convoy management was once again ordered to send lists of convoy members to Prague. The lists had to be delivered in fifteen copies, which meant that they had to be typed on stencils, and had to contain the following information:

Serial number, year of birth, place of birth, date of birth, first name, family name, place of residence, nationality, family status, number of children, profession, home address, date of registration at the convoy management offices, registration number at the convoy management, date of registration at the Central Office, and pass number. There were thus sixteen pieces of information to be given concerning each applicant. The lists had scarcely been dispatched to Prague in the required order, however, when a telegram arrived demanding that the column for "Nationality" be placed directly after the serial number. All the lists which had already been sent were therefore declared invalid. When the lists had been altered and taken by messenger on the next express train to Prague, another order arrived demanding a fresh sequence.

After five days, the typists collapsed at their desks. The numbers danced before their exhausted eyes. The night shift dozed off with their fingers on the keys. They no longer knew what they were typing. They made mistakes. Stencils had to be thrown away. Work came to a standstill.

The Gestapo in Prague shouted at the representative of the convoy management and threatened to send him to a concentration camp because he did not give them the correct lists.

"How are you going to organize a convoy if you're not even capable of making a simple register of the members?" the SS officer screamed at the desperate man, who had the onerous task of mediating between the convoy management and the authorities. The SS officers were delighted. In another few days, the Jews would be reduced to begging for a few days' grace in order to deliver the required lists in some sort of acceptable form, or be forced to give up their plans because of their own incompetence. The SS would squeeze the last dollar out of that pack of Jews. The officers would rake in a high ransom if they condescended to accept the lists at all.

Wachsmann was well aware of what was at stake. If he lost this game of nerves which was aimed at driving his staff to distraction, then there would be no question of the convoy's leaving, and over six hundred men, women and children would not depart for Palestine. No one, in fact, would henceforth be able to leave the countries under Germany's control.

***

In mid-December, the thermometer dropped to minus twelve degrees centigrade. An icy wind swept the snow into drifts several feet high. Railway tracks lay buried under the white mass. Snow ploughs, which were used to clear the line, could no longer get through, and long lines of workers had to laboriously shovel the tracks clear. Rivers were covered by a thick layer of ice. The Danube was frozen at Pressburg and totally impassable.

No normal person thought of undertaking a trip in such cold weather. The "Maccabi-Hechalutz" convoy in Prague had sent its members home when the severe frosts began, since a journey up the Danube was out of the question before the beginning of spring. At that precise moment, however, the Gestapo gave orders for the Prague convoy to depart. Those registered for the "Maccabi-Hechalutz" convoy were summoned by express letters and telegrams. They hastened to the capital as quickly as they could, although they felt that it would be impossible to travel in such horrible weather.

At the news of the "Maccabi" convoy's impending departure, the Brünn group also made preparations to start out. The Gestapo, however, had no intention of allowing the Jews to leave. They began a cat and mouse game which gave them their first practical opportunity of organizing a mass convoy.

Over 350 people gathered in Prague in order to set out on their journey. After a few days, they were sent home again in order to wait for better weather. They had scarcely rejoined their families when they were summoned back to Prague. The Gestapo took a sadistic delight in imagining the heartrending farewell scenes, and at the same time relentlessly pursued their aim of forcing the impoverished Jews to spend even more money.

Fritz Heller had already taken leave of his family once. He had been obliged to make the journey to Prague twice and had once again been sent home. On the third occasion, Margit and Erwin accompanied him to the railway station. Heller's parents stayed at home. The three young people had refused to let them accompany them, wishing to spare them the excitement of the leave-taking. They also did not want to give the SA men loitering in the station the pleasure of seeing Mrs. Heller's tears.

The platform was dimly lit by the darkened lamps. The shaded headlights of the incoming express train gave the platform the appearance of a morgue. The locomotive was encrusted in ice. Thick layers of snow covered the roofs of the long railway cars, each of which had three sets of wheels. When the train stopped, some German officers who had come from Vienna got out of a second-class compartment.

The three young people stood in front of an open carriage door. They conversed in low tones and did not look at all agitated. The guard walked down the train with his coat-collar turned up.

"All aboard, please. All aboard!" he shouted.

Fritz and Margit embraced for the last time.

"See that you get out of here as fast as possible," said Fritz.

The guard gave the signal for the train to depart. Margit walked a few paces beside the moving train. Then she and Erwin left the station, each deep in thought. The Gestapo kept its promise and the "Maccabi" convoy actually set out three days later.

After a wait of five days, the first news came from Pressburg. The convoy had come to a standstill, and had to wait for the ice to melt. The "Maccabi" members had actually left the Bohemian and Moravian Protectorate but were stuck fast in Slovakia.

The Gestapo pretended that everything was in perfect order

with the "Maccabi" convoy. It had now departed, and registration for the next convoys could continue.

Once again, fifty people travelled each night from Brünn to Prague with their documents ready in their files. The lists of convoy members were finally accepted by the Gestapo. Whoever received a summons had to appear at the Emigration Center within twenty-four hours. One cold January night, Kerner travelled with a group of applicants. Among the women in the group was Maria Segler, the wife of a doctor who had come to Brünn after the occupation of the Sudetenland in order to take refuge with her father, a German engineer. Dr. Segler had never requested Maria to convert to Judaism. He would have considered, being a person of refined feelings, that such an action amounted to moral coercion, which he would never have imposed on anyone, least of all his Maria. He took advantage of the Czechoslovakian marriage law, remained a Jew and contracted a civil marriage with Maria Kirchner. His Catholic German father-in-law had not taken exception to his actions, and had taken the couple in when Dr. Segler fled to Brünn. Maria was called a few moments after her arrival at the Petschek Palace and requested to come into the office. The SS officer offered her a chair and asked cordially for her file.

Maria, who had already heard a fair amount about the behavior of the Gestapo, was amazed at her punctilious reception. The SS officer leafed through the documents, looking for the certificate of baptism, for he had received information about Maria from Nazi circles in Brünn. When he found the document, he said, "I see from your papers that you are an Aryan and only married to a Jew under civil law."

"I am a Catholic of German descent," answered Maria.

"Under these circumstances, you do not have to register for emigration. We shall be very happy to help you to declare your marriage invalid. I understand that you married a wealthy Jew when you were a penniless girl. Today, however, in the Great German Reich, you are not required to uphold this marriage."

"Excuse me, but your hypothesis is incorrect. I come from a well-to-do family. I married my husband because I loved and respected him," said Maria.

The SS officer remained polite, but grimaced as though racked by terrible pains in his entrails. He tried to make Maria change her mind but she remained firm.

"If you definitely wish to emigrate, then I shall give you an ordinary emigration pass, so as to make things easier for you." He reached for a form, but Mrs. Segler declined to accept his offer.

"I wish to have the same pass as my husband. For me marriage is a sacrament which cannot be violated. As a Catholic, I must remain true to the last words of the marriage ceremony: 'Until death us do part . . . .'"

"If that is what you wish, then I must enter a red 'J' in the passport," grunted the SS officer.

"Please do so," replied Maria.

Thus Mrs. Maria Segler received a red slip — an emigration permit — just like every other applicant, with the formula, "Maria Segler has filed an application . . ."

During the lengthy wait, Erwin had a good opportunity to observe the Gestapo's behavior. They handled the Jews with kid gloves, having most probably received orders to restrain themselves somewhat. They contented themselves for the most part with derisive comments and witty questions. The question which brought the biggest laughs that day was: "Are you also in favor of all the Jews being devoured by sharks?" If the intimidated applicant answered the question loudly and clearly in the affirmative, then bellowing horse-laughs on the part of the supermen ensued for several minutes. During one of these bursts of merriment, Erwin handed over his file, received his red slip and was allowed to leave the room.

With a red pass, one could move around somewhat more freely. If one was caught in the street a few minutes after eight o'clock in the evening and was lucky enough to own one of these documents, then he was released with no more than a reprimand. The German police patrols in the city respected the slips of paper. They apparently set great store on their behavior being regarded as correct by the future emigrants.

***

Once again, groups of fifty applicants had to travel to Prague. Elbert, in his capacity as secretary of the Jewish community, had to appear before the District High Commissioner, in order to receive a permit for the payment of the travelling expenses.

"Why don't these travel-lovers defray their expenses themselves? We can't always take responsibility for the Jews' pleasure trips?" grumbled the District High Commissioner. After lengthy negotiations, he pushed a permit across the table which licensed Elbert to withdraw thirty thousand crowns from blocked Jewish accounts for the purposes of overseeing the emigration. The secretary of the Jewish community, that staunch Zionist Elbert, had moreover to thank the District High Commissioner for permitting him to use this ridiculously small sum, as a dispossessed traveller thanks the highwayman who kindly allows him to depart still retaining the shirt on his back.

***

A rumor sprang up somewhere that the Germans were intending to ship all able-bodied men to labor camps in the Reich. Had this intention been carried out, it would unquestionably have dashed all hopes that the convoys which had been registered would ever leave.

Once again, the community representatives in Prague and Brünn went to their respective District High Commissioners. In Prague, Jacob Edelstein fought with the whole force of his personality — which commanded even the Nazis' respect — for the rights of Jews who already possessed passes. The Prague District High Commissioner and even the Gestapo and the SS looked up to him. Before the war, they had permitted him to travel abroad, not to subsequently allow the Jews to emigrate, but to prove that no country in the world was prepared to accept the Jews. The Nazis had demanded that Jacob Edelstein give them his word of honor that he would return as soon as his mission was ended. He had given it. The Germans were quite convinced that he would not come back, and thus give them an excuse for dealing with the Jews in a quite different manner, but Edelstein returned. He had, unfortunately, been forced to witness how little interest the free world had in saving the Jews, how fruitless the conferences had been and that not a single country had raised even a finger to help his persecuted brethren. He was disbelieved, his reports regarded as exaggerated, in the same way as the letters and statements of Jewish emigrants from Germany had been disregarded. The Germans were still considered to a cultured nation. They lived on

117

the credit that their great poets and thinkers had earned for them. Elbert in Brünn found it somewhat easier to accomplish his demands for Jewish employment. The farms in Moravia were used of old to employing Slovakian workers.

The District High Commissioner's permission for Jews to work on Moravian farms, which Elbert had obtained after a hard struggle, helped Albert Wachsmann to score a double victory. His people could now go on "Hachsharah," earning their living at the same time, and remain together in easily accessible groups until their departure.

Since there was still no question, however, of the convoy's leaving, and the "Maccabi-Hechalutz" convoy in Pressburg was still stuck fast, Wachsmann searched for some means of keeping up the spirits of the convoy members. One day, he called a meeting of all the doctors who were registered for the convoy. Hitherto, convoy members had always been inoculated against cholera and typhus a few days before their departure. The inoculations were, so to speak, the surest sign that the convoy's departure was imminent. If the inoculations could be given, then Wachsmann would have achieved his goal. The doctors were of the opinion that the inoculations were in any case appropriate in wartime, and in fact found it highly desirable to check up at that point on the convoy members' state of health.

Chapter Eleven

The Germans overran Belgium, by-passed the Maginot Line, occupied Holland and Denmark, defeated the British at Dunkirk, forced the King of Norway to flee and marched triumphantly into Paris on June 14. Such unprecedented successes necessitated special celebrations. The victorious world-conquerors in Prague organized a large parade. During the preliminary celebrations both Jews and Czech were bloodily beaten. An unsuspecting group of Jews from Brünn became entangled in the celebrations on their way from the station, and tried to pass through the streets as quickly as possible in order to reach the Prague Jewish community offices. Margit saw the SS's victims. They had been beaten with steel rods and were streaming with blood. She lost the strength to go on. Trembling, her face as white as chalk, she caught the express train to Brünn and travelled back home. That day the Germans in Brünn attempted to attack a group of Jewish and Czech workers who were employed near the city in building a railway.

***

The Thousand-Year Reich now stretched out its claws towards the Jews living in Holland, Belgium, Denmark, France and Norway. These countries, too, had to be made "judenrein." Adolf Eichmann, the Reich delegate for the solution of the Jewish question, sat in Berlin, requested reports on the number of Jews in the newly-subjugated lands, and planned their destruction. His first step was to declare the Danzig, Prague and Brünn convoys full. He had procured the services of a very industrious Jewish merchant, Berthold Storfer by name, who acted as an intermediary between the convoy management and him. One day, after sending a telegram to announce his coming, the commercial adviser arrived in Brünn on the express train from Vienna. He was received by Elbert and the community leaders. Storfer was on his way to Berlin, and broke his journey in Brünn and Prugue.

Stürmbannführer Eichmann was not satisfied with the small ships which had hitherto been used by the convoys. The whole affair dragged far too much for his liking. Storfer was to transport at least four thousand Jews out of the country at a time. This was difficult since it was wartime and sufficient tonnage was difficult to obtain. The main concern, however, was that the British seized every ship which brought illegal immigrants to the coast of Palestine. Under these circumstances, no shipping company was prepared to hire out ships for the convoys, and ships therefore had to be bought. Although Storfer did not spare himself any effort, he was only offered old Greek grain-freighters, and those were at exorbitant prices. Eichmann had even promised to place blocked Jewish accounts at Storfer's disposal in order to finance the purchase of the ships. Complicated negotiations ensued between the commercial adviser and the Greek shipping company, Avegrinos. The question of a flag had to be solved above all, because every ship had to fly the ensign of a neutral country and be entered in a shipping register.

***

The convoy management offices hummed like veritable beehives. Whoever had time came in for a few moments in order to ask whether the date of departure had been set and what Mr. Storfer had said. The entire staff was busy accompanying people to the door in the friendliest possible manner and assuring them that they would be informed concerning the progress of events by circulars.

The telegram which arrived a few days later from Storfer in Athens raised everyone's hopes, although the message was far from cheerful: "Ship's departure delayed due to lack of nails stop Honduras flag unobtainable negotiations continuing Storfer."

The convoy management, after their discussion with Mr. Storfer, was clearly aware of the importance of having a Honduras flag. If it proved unobtainable, then another flag would have to be procured. The concern about the nails, however, was really puzzling. Why did a ship need nails? How could that be a problem. Even Jews could buy a few pounds of nails in any hardware store in the city. In the meantime, the mystery of the nails remained unsolved. People had not yet wound up their daily debates on the subject when another telegram came from the commercial adviser from Vienna.

"Central American consul will issue entry visas at Central Office stop collect foreign currency permits for two dollars per person Storfer."

Albert Wachsmann took the telegram and ran with it to the secretariat of the Jewish community.

***

The departure lists arrived from Prague. There was a sense of embarkation in the air. Felix Neugebauer and Erwin looked through the permits drawn up by the Gestapo for the purchase of medical instruments and ascertained that the majority of instruments and medicines which were designated by the doctors as quite indispensible had been struck off the lists.

The personal baggage allowance of the convoy members was reduced to a ridiculously minuscule amount. Most men had shaving cream, of all things, erased from their lists. Each person was allowed one loaf of bread, five ounces of salami, one box of cheese and forty cigarettes for the journey. The sum of ten marks was also permitted to be exported. As regarded valuables, the Jews might only take their wedding rings. No other jewelry was allowed.

Many people applied to take out several suitcases of underwear and clothing. If they received a permit, then they had to transfer large sums of money from their blocked accounts to the Gestapo, and also have their luggage valued by a legally qualified expert (for whose services they had to pay). Worn-out pieces of clothing were described as "newly purchased" and taxed accordingly, and the lucky owner thus had to pay the full price for his old suit. The "qualified experts" thrived!

***

A Jewish convoy to Palestine started out from the Pressburg Danube port in Slovakia. Slovakia, which had to display its devotion to the Führer for its newly-acquired independence, lost no opportunity to blackmail its Jews. A discarded old paddle-steamer named the "Pentscho" travelled up the river with five hundred young people who had no transit visas and insufficient food supplies. A courage born of despair was responsible for their foolhardy plan to sail for Palestine on such a dilapidated hulk. As the convoy had not been approved by the Gestapo — since Slovakia was officially independent — the "Pentscho" was also not under the protection of Mr. Storfer, the commercial adviser. It was thus purely by chance that the gallant paddle-steamer came to a halt at Sustschuk. Coal, food and money supplies were totally exhausted. The ship was towed into mid-stream by tugs from the harbor and anchored exactly on the borderline between Rumanian and Bulgarian territorial waters.

Bulgarian and Rumanian Jews were only allowed to send sufficient food on board to prevent the passengers from starving to death. A yellow epidemic flag fluttered from the ship's mast. It was naturally strictly forbidden to visit the marooned travellers, and the ship's isolation in any case made a visit impossible.

As no one could see any hope for the "Maccabi" convoy which had been waiting in Pressburg for months for permission to depart, the Jews turned to Storfer, the only person who was considered to be in a position to bring about the convoy's departure.

At the end of July 1940, the Central Emigration Office in Prague informed the Brünn convoy management that only 220 people might leave. The vast majority of the convoy members would have to wait until later.

The uncertainty was nerve-wracking. The convoy members had already been registered for one-and-a-half years. During that time, they had become a disciplined unit which was willing and capable of holding its own even in the most difficult situations. Now they were being divided and torn apart like so many scraps of paper. Some of them favored leaving with the second group. They were afraid of being the first to travel into the unknown. As the Thousand-Year Reich was fully occupied with the subjugation of half of Europe, the Jews in the Bohemian and Moravian Protectorate enjoyed a brief respite. Many believed that the Gestapo would be content with the Jewish segregation laws and that under the worst eventuality, it might only be a question of moving to "Theresienstadt" which was being prepared for the accommodation of Jews.

"Finish dividing up the groups and form a security service.

Elbert has informed me that the 'Maccabi-Hechalutz' convoy in Pressburg is leaving," said Albert Wachsmann when he met his friend Kerner in the morning.

Once again they sat and worked until late at night. They waited for letters from Storfer, for a telephone call from the Gestapo in Prague. Days passed without news. The Gestapo was again playing its deadly game of cat and mouse.

On Saturday, August 31 at 9:30 a.m., the announcement came that the convoy was to take the express train to Vienna at one o'clock on September 2.

The news spread like wildfire. People did not believe it and ran to the convoy management to hear the announcement corroborated at first hand. Both telephones were in constant use. Urgent long-distance calls to the Jewish communities in the provincial towns received no answer because it was Saturday and the community offices were closed.

"Send telegrams to convoy members outside the city," decided Wachsmann. A few boys and girls raced through the streets of the town on their bicycles riding to the most outlying suburbs. Their young faces beamed with happiness. The messages which they brought, which were typed on thin sheets of carbon copy paper, stated:

"Departure on September 2 on the one p.m. express train. Convoy members to assemble at nine a.m. on September 2 in the third class waiting room for baggage inspection."

Albert Wachsmann and Kerner left the office and walked together for a while through the city. They saw the shops with their empty windows, and the glaring notices with "Under Aryan Management" in glaring Gothic lettering beneath the signboards of renowned established Jewish firms. They heard the shouts of "Sieg Heil!" from a group of Hitler Youths on the march. A contemptuous smile came to their lips as they listened to the shrilling of pipes and the drum-rolls. Despite the sunshine, the long rows of houses were grey and dead. The city in which they had lived and worked, the bustling, busy city was no more. The houses bedecked with flags were strange and hostile to them. They were not worth even a moment's thought.

The burden of leave-taking weighed like a nightmare on the relatives who remained behind. Mothers hid their tears from their adult children who came for a last brief visit. The members of the convoy packed their belongings, wrote letters until the small hours and then could not fall asleep. They lay with open eyes and waited for morning. At first light they were already up and out of the house. They pretended that they still had many calls to make, and they avoided the last hours with their relatives. They themselves faced an uncertain future, for they were setting out on a journey whose final destination was unknown. Who could predict whether their voyage would end up in a concentration camp, at the bottom of the sea, or in Palestine?

How many mothers wrung their hands in the depths of despair when their sons and daughters were not there to see it? How many prayers were offered up in those days by fathers who were otherwise quite irreligious?

***

The convoy management office was packed with people. The noisy conversations made work impossible. Any sort of organized activity was unthinkable. Albert Wachsmann quickly gave Felix Neugebauer the necessary instructions for those convoy members who would remain in the city. Then he left the office in order to pack suitcases for himself and his wife and child. For months, he had sacrificed every moment of his life in order to get the convoy under way. He had neglected his family life, eaten up his savings and undermined his health, but he still possessed his upright bearing and unflagging confidence.

It is customary to visit the graves of deceased relatives before the Jewish High Holidays in the fall. Although another five weeks remained until then, many people went to the Jewish cemetery that Sunday morning. Individually and in small groups, they stood by the graves. Long rows of freshly turned-up mounds were surmounted by small wooden boards with the name and date of death of the individual. Too many people had been buried there during the previous year. Magda Hirsch stood with her husband at the fresh grave of her father. A bier was carried out of the mortuary. A young woman who had no more strength to weep, two small children and a few dazed mourners followed the coffin. In an older, somewhat secluded part of the cemetery, between two monuments of black marble, Erwin Kerner stood before his father's grave. The golden inscription on the tombstone was already slightly faded, and the last letters of the name were completely missing. Kerner stood motionless for a few moments in front of the grave of the man who had been his father and whom he had never known. He picked up a few blades of grass, put them on the pedestal, and weighed them down with a pebble. It was his farewell, and last greeting. Then he went slowly down the gravel path towards the exit.

During the morning, there was no room in the convoy management offices. The first members of the convoy from the provincial towns arrived. The members of the "Hachsharah" groups who were registered for the convoy joined them. Some stayed the night at the offices, others lodged with families. Magda and Eliezer Hirsch locked up their apartment and moved into the offices with their luggage. Kerner had invited some relatives to his parents' apartment in order to make the last hours easier for the old people. He only came home late in the evening after having assembled the members of the security service once again in order to give them last-minute instructions about embarkation. He had impressed upon them that they were to stand next to the doors of the railway cars, help load the luggage and be polite and friendly towards the convoy members, but at the same time to keep strict discipline among them.

With a heavy heart, Kerner climbed the stairs to Margit's apartment. The family had postponed their dinner until he came.

He sat next to Margit who was very pale. The Supreme Court Justice handed him a telegram which had arrived that afternoon from Pressburg. Fritz informed them that he would be continuing his journey with the convoy on September 1.

They sat down to supper although most of it was left untouched. Erwin promised to write from every port. The relatives who were remaining behind had agreed with Erwin to write to Mr. Simon Brod, Sultan Hamid Street, Istanbul, who would ensure that the letters were forwarded when he received them in Istanbul. Kerner wrote the address for Margit on a small piece of paper. "What then?" she asked sadly.

So long as Erwin did not write a letter through the Red Cross, she could not contact him. Palestine was enemy territory, and any normal postal connection was therefore out of the question. The only possibility was to write through the Red Cross, and it would take months before such a letter got through.

The Supreme Court Justice went into the kitchen to help his wife clear the table. Margit and Erwin were left alone. The hand of the clock moved forward.

"Please don't come to the station. We have given instructions at the convoy management to leave closest relatives at home. We don't want to make the separation even more difficult. Our oppressors should not have the satisfaction of seeing our tears."

Margit nodded silently. She took a ring from her finger and put it on Erwin's fourth finger. She wept and hid her head in his bosom like a helpless child.

The hall clock gave ten bright chimes. Erwin's time was up. He rose and pulled his jacket straight. Margit called in anguished tones for her mother. Her parents came at once. Her mother had tears in her eyes. Mr. Heller's benevolent face was calm and serious. He was in full control of himself.

"I hope from the bottom of my heart that you will reach your goal and realize all your hopes. I am certain you will do everything humanly possible to help us." He shook Kerner's hand affectionately.

Slowly, Erwin released himself from Margit's arms. Her hands hovered over his face, clung for a second to his arms and then sank weakly to her sides. His lips touched her forehead for the last time. Margit sobbed as he went to the door. Erwin looked sadly at her mother as she shook hands with him and gave him greetings for her son.

The door shut behind him. As he went down the stairs, he pressed his hands against his temples. Then he pulled himself together and strode back with a firm step to his parents' apartment where he would spend his last night.

As he lay awake, he heard his mother crying and the old man, who had taken the place of his father, tossing restlessly on his bed.

He saw the dimly-lighted window in the neighboring house and knew that there, too, a mother was trembling for her child who would leave her forever the next day.

Gradually, dawn approached. A blackbird whistled in the green patch opposite the house. Kerner got up, dressed and began to pack his rucksack. At about seven o'clock, Adolf Hausner and his wife arrived, and shortly afterwards, some friends of his mother and business friends of his father. The little apartment was full of people.

The Hausners took care of Kerner's old father. The latter pulled out his watch nervously and cursed the Nazis who were to blame for his son's emigration. There was a ring at the door. Eliezer and Magda Hirsch entered, both in full travelling-kit. Kerner went from one person to another, bidding them all farewell. He kissed his mother's hand.

Accompanied by his father, he went outside with Magda and Eliezer Hirsch. His brave mother stayed behind with her friends. She had made the leave-taking as easy as she possibly could for her only child.

The nearer they came to the station, the more convoy members they saw dragging their luggage in the same direction. When they reached the city theater, Kerner succeeded in persuading his father to turn back. Albert Wachsmann stood with his wife and small daughter on the steps which led up to the railway station's departure hall. Members of the convoy who crossed Wilson Square and went in to the departure hall stopped for a moment as they passed him.

The hour of departure drew nearer. Customs clearance was over. The German customs official, Alfred Schmatke, waited for the convoy to embark. He still had an important official task to perform. The railway-car doors had to be sealed, as the train would pass through newly-conquered German territory on its way to Vienna.

The bells in the city chimed midday. The luggage — with the exception of the rucksacks which the emigrants were permitted to keep with them — was loaded into the luggage van. Just before the express train arrived from Prague, Elbert came in order to take leave of the convoy in his official capacity as secretary of the Jewish community. He had succeeded in procuring a large barrel of marmalade which, as the luggage van was already sealed, was stored in the first-class car. It was his personal gift to the children in the convoy, whom he did not want to subsist on their scanty portions of dry bread alone. The express train arrived. While the locomotive proceeded to the water faucet, the cars were pushed into place and coupled together, the luggage van being placed between the express train and the four cars containing the members of the convoy.

The railway official in his red cap came out of the station-master's office and walked slowly up the train. The customs inspector, Mr. Schmatke, sealed the fourth car in the presence of the official, then the third and finally the second. The group leaders and two people from the security service stood by the open windows of the sealed doors. Eliezer Hirsch and Erwin stood beside the running board of the first car. The locomotive returned and was coupled to the train. There was a soft crack as the signal arm went up. Elbert shook hands with Hirsch and Kerner, and then with Wachsmann. He obviously found it difficult to speak. Wachsmann and he embraced. The railway official held his watch in his hand. Inspector Schmatke came up to them.

"Have a good journey," he said abruptly.

Wachsmann embarked, followed by Eliezer Hirsch. Kerner leaned forward in order to check for the last time that everything was in order in the cars. The door closed behind him and Inspector Schmatke sealed the first car.

The railway official gave the signal for departure. The locomotive began to move. Its mighty flywheel rotated twice on the spot. The official put his hand to his red cap and saluted. The city disappeared in the smoke of the factory chimneys. It was September 2, 1940. The express train left the station punctually at 1:01 p.m.

Chapter Twelve

The express train was uncoupled when they reached Vienna East. The convoy was left isolated in its four cars. No one noticed that the luggage van with the entire wordly possessions of the impoverished emigrants had been towed away behind the empty express train. A long row of black uniforms lined the platform. The faces above them were scornful.

The master-race had detailed the Gestapo to act as a reception committee. At the extreme end of the line stood an elderly gentleman in civilian clothing, all by himself. His serious rather depressed expression, and the brown document case under his arm made it clear that he did not belong among the gallant heroes assembled on the platform. He was actually only a representative of the Viennese Jewish community who would later have to sign a statement drawn up by the Gestapo declaring how correct the reception at Vienna East had been.

The station-master, accompanied by two Gestapo officers, walked along the four cars and took the seals off the doors. An order came from a loudspeaker.

"Everybody off! Form two lines opposite the cars. First row men, second row women. Leave all hand luggage in the cars."

The security service men leapt down onto the gravel. They helped the women and children off the cars.

"Form up in order of height!" called a Gestapo man.

The men quickly obeyed the order. The women took a little longer. The Gestapo man began to bawl.

"How long is this going to last? I'll make you get a move on. Do you think we've got nothing better to do than to watch you parade?" he shouted, feeling very important. He strode around theatrically. The lines stood still. Although no one was talking, he shouted, "Quiet there! Stand still!"

He stopped three paces in front of a slim SS officer, clicked his heels, saluted and reported for duty. The officer acknowledged his salute, turned to the Gestapo men and began to talk to them. Meanwhile, the entire convoy stood motionless and silent, separated by a railway track from the four cars. Minutes passed. Their nerves were stretched to the breaking point. They were afraid that they would be transported by the Gestapo to a concentration camp. The officer called over the representative of the Viennese Jewish community.

"The Jewish community is responsible for the maintenance of these Protectorate Jews and all costs incurred by them so long as they remain in Vienna. Understood?" growled the SS officer.

The Jewish community representative was obliged to take note of this information. To make any reply, or even to voice a personal opinion, was not permitted. Once again, a Gestapo man walked out to the rows of men and women.

"Count heads!" he commanded.

A second black-uniformed man walked through the rows, staring at each woman in turn and treading on the heels of the men.

The Gestapo counted. They counted a second time, and then again. The numbers did not agree.

"Two people are missing. Who's in charge here?" asked the officer, who was walking up and down the rows during the counting. Albert Wachsmann came forward.

"Mr. Schmatke, the customs official, inspected 226 convoy members at the railway station in Brünn," said Wachsmann.

"How many people are there in the convoy?" was the officer's next question.

Wachsmann took the list which had been signed by the customs official out of the pocket of his jacket.

The officer raised his voice accusatively, "We were told that there would be 228. Where have the extra two disappeared to?"

"A few days before the convoy left, two convoy members received written permission from the Gestapo in Brünn to travel to Vienna. They were crossed off the list by Mr. Schmatke during the customs inspection. In the copy of the statement which I have with me, they are marked down as not having shown up for departure," explained Wachsmann.

"Give me the statement," demanded the officer.

Wachsmann showed him the document.

He explained it and said, "I shall telephone the Brünn Gestapo to inquire about the matter. So long as I receive no answer, no one is to embark. Understood?"

The officer went into the station-master's office followed by two of his men.

The convoy stood in two rows. Gestapo men walked up and down with grim faces, watching to make certain that there was no talking.

An old goods-train locomotive drove in, and was coupled to the four empty cars. While the SS officer telephoned to find the whereabouts of two missing youths, in the middle of a war which had jolted Europe to its very foundation, the Jews waited in terror of their lives. After half an hour which seemed an eternity, the officer reappeared, followed by his two henchmen. He planted himself in front of the rows of convoy members and looked at his watch.

"The convoy is to embark within two minutes," he yelled. The security service men bounded to the doors of the cars to help the women and children climb up. The Gestapo men, who loved such chaotic scenes, laughed loudly as the Jews dashed towards the cars. The representative of the Viennese Jewish community, who was forced to witness this stylish, athletic Gestapo order, lowered his eyes, expecting the watching mob to fall furiously upon the Jews at any moment.

In order to compound the chaos, the officer gave the signal to depart. The goods-train locomotive began to move, puffing stridently. The security men jumped quickly onto the moving train. Someone banged the door of the first car, and a window pane smashed. There was a whistle in the station and the train braked immediately.

A Gestapo man leapt to the car.

"Who broke the window pane?" he demanded.

No one answered.

"The damage must be paid for on the spot," he screamed. The Jewish community representative came hurrying on the scene.

"The Viennese Jewish community will be responsible for the damage," he said quietly.

The Gestapo man called a guard to draw up a statement assessing the damage done to government property, which the Jewish community representative then signed. The sum which was estimated for repairing the damage would have sufficed to replace a plate-glass window in a Ring Street cafe.

Having concluded their official business, the Gestapo man and the guard left the first car in order to grace the next with their presence. The train began to move. The locomotive passed grey rows of houses interspersed with wooden palings covered with posters as it puffed its way to the Danube port. The Jewish community representative travelled with the convoy. He distributed postcards to the passengers, inviting them to write to their relatives, and declaring himself willing to post the cards the same day.

It was already dusk when the train came to a halt some hundreds of yards in front of the Danube Steamer Company's dockside buildings. The lighting was dimmed. The convoy members left the train and went to the luggage van which they believed to be at the end of the train. Not finding it there, they went to the front, but the luggage van was not behind the locomotive either. They became desperate. Their last possessions had disappeared. They had nothing now but what they stood up in, or had packed in their rucksacks or handbags.

Wachsmann did not allow himself to be intimidated. He was prepared to do anything in order to have the luggage back, for without medicines, medical instruments and the scanty belongings of the convoy members, the journey could definitely not be continued. He went to the representative of the Viennese Jewish community, requesting him to intervene. Then he asked the station-master to contact Vienna East in order to inquire whether the car had been uncoupled there. He also asked for help from the Gestapo men who had accompanied the train to the port. The station-master disclaimed any responsibility. The Gestapo men maintained that they had only taken over four cars at Vienna East. Wachsmann realized that he would never get the baggage back in that way. He had learned from Elbert before leaving Brünn that the Danube steamers which were to transport the convoy as far as Tulcea would carry Germans from Rumania, who were returning to Germany in accordance with the "Home to the Reich" campaign, as passengers on the return trip. The Germans were getting rich from the convoy. The Jews paid for the journey to Tulcea and back, as it was only logical that the ships should return to their home port at Vienna. The "Melk," "Schönbrunn," "Uranus," and "Helios" steamers had to bring the Rumanian Germans back up the Danube from Tulcea to Vienna. Wachsmann based his plan on the Nazis' crafty dealing. If the convoy did not embark now, then the Germanic mass-migration would be delayed.

During the following hours, some four thousand Jews would have to embark at the Viennese port. The first group from Brünn had already arrived. Two groups from Prague, a large-sized contingent from Berlin and another from the former Free City of Danzig were already on their way. After lengthy telephone calls, the traffic controller's office in Vienna East admitted that the luggage van had been uncoupled by mistake and would reach the Danube port early on the morning of September 3. The luggage van was there the next morning.

The customs officials and the Gestapo stood behind long tables in the hall in order to ransack the luggage once again. Since the emigrants, who were hindered by the weight of their baggage, only came to the control in small groups, and the Nazis certainly had better things to do, they endeavored to get the business over and done with as quickly as possible. They ordered the first arrivals to open their suitcases, threw the contents on the floor, shook out the rucksacks and rummaged through the handbags. Sometimes, they also demanded to see the travellers' wallets, and checked their contents — which consisted of the generously permitted sum of ten marks — very carefully. Then, after crossing the emigrants' names off a list, they made the latter pass through a wooden barrier. The convoy members thus had to snatch up their belongings at top speed and make their way to the "Melk" with open cases.

Pithy Viennese expressions urging the emigrants to hurry could be heard every so often from the hall. Only the Jews said nothing. They dragged their luggage to the "Melk" as fast as they could, trying to clear the police guard and disappear inside the ship as quickly as possible.

The security service had meanwhile brought all the convoy members into the hall, and helped to bring up the women's baggage. The Gestapo looked at their helpfulness askance. Now the security men themselves stood beside their luggage at the entrance to the hall.

The security service, who were distinguishable by their armbands, were checked particularly thoroughly. Most of their cases landed at the exit after a well-aimed kick. Wachsmann and Kerner were the last to be checked.

"You have a license to export foreign currency for the maintenance of the convoy during the journey. Where is the money?" inquired the customs officer.

"I shall receive it in Rumania from Mr. Storfer, the commercial adviser who has been commissioned by the Gestapo center in Prague," answered Wachsmann.

"What sort of Jewish trick is that? Someone who has an export license for foreign currency must have the money on him," was the livid response of the customs man.

"Please inquire from the Gestapo whether my statement is correct. The money is intended for maintaining the convoy on the ocean steamer," explained Wachsmann.

The customs officer discussed the matter with two Gestapo officials in the hall who were supervising the customs clearance. They called over the SS officer who was in charge of the entire embarkation. He confirmed Wachsmann's statement.

The river Danube which flowed past the "Melk" had washed up many a Jewish corpse onto dry land. Whether the unfortunate person had committed suicide or had been killed during a Jewish purge remained the river's secret.

On the morning of September 3, the Prague contingent arrived. They were, if possible, subjected to even worse abuse during customs clearance than the Brünn group had been the previous evening. They boarded the "Melk" under police escort. A tall man in Canadian boots with a peaked cap surmounting his roughly-chiselled face, carried a knapsack which was packed with military precision and a suitcase. A twelve-year-old boy held the hand of a little girl who looked no older than nine. Both children carried rucksacks which were far too heavy for them. An exceedingly delicate woman, also heavily laden with luggage, followed behind the children. Two sturdy young lads in riding-breeches followed. They too carried knapsacks, and wore peaked caps and wide leather belts. The tall man, who had the sun-burned skin of a colonial officer, turned to Eliezer Hirsch, whose armband distinguished him as a member of the security service.

"I am the leader of the Prague 'Betar' convoy. Please tell the leader of your convoy that I wish to speak to him immediately."

While Eliezer Hirsch carried out this request, the two attendants put down their luggage. The children and the delicate woman sat down on it. The tall man surveyed the men with the blue and white armbands who were ensuring the smooth running of the embarkation. He turned to the two attendants who were standing behind him.

"We have a well-organized group here. It won't be difficult to make contact with them."

After a discussion between the two convoy leaders, the groups were amalgamated. The Prague convoy was well-organized, and consisted for the most part of young people. The Gestapo had allowed them to take some food with them, but forbade them to export medicines. Instead, the group possessed an old typewriter.

Alfred Kronberger, the leader of the Prague convoy, had served for many years in the French Foreign Legion, and had been given the position of supply officer in view of his experience in provisioning. During their discussion, he immediately declared himself ready to cede the leadership of the two groups to Wachsmann, saying that he would be content to be his second-in-command, and deal in the first place with the maintenance of the convoy. He suggested that the two security services be merged. Mr. Gruber, an experienced bank official from Prague, acted as the convoy's secretary.

For three days, the "Melk" lay in port. The food issued by the ship's kitchen was meager and bad. Drinking water had to be rationed immediately. There was a shortage of sleeping quarters, as the "Melk" was an excursion steamer, and only equipped with facilities for some 250 tourists. Now there were over eight hundred people on board, who were joined just before the ship's departure by another fifty or so, whom the Gestapo had brought directly from the Buchenwald concentration camp. They arrived with nothing but the clothes they were wearing, and were so frightened that they avoided all conversation. The Gestapo had permitted the emigration of another two thousand Jews from Germany, Austria and Danzig. These groups had been taken to Pressburg, and kept isolated there in bad hotels with insufficient food in order that they should not make contact with the Jewish community, although the latter had to defray all their expenses. The "Maccabi-Hechalutz" convoy had finally departed from Pressburg, and, like the other convoys, was crammed together on a small Danube steamer.

The ships left Vienna in the early morning of September 6.

They reached Budapest in the late afternoon and anchored side by side on the quay.

The figures of the passers-by on land were clearly visible from the steamer. The elegant women and prosperous burghers did not dream that these four ships, "Melk," "Uranus," "Schönbrunn," and "Helios" were full of Jews whom Mr. Eichmann had so magnanimously allowed to emigrate. After the stop in Budapest, which lasted only one night, the steamers continued their journey up the Danube in the direction of Giurgiu.

Chapter Thirteen

The "Helios" was the first ship to reach the Danube port at Giurgiu at about midday the next day. Rumanian police had already barricaded the port long before the ship arrived. The "Uranus" arrived shortly afterwards, followed during the afternoon by the "Schönbrunn" and the "Melk." The four steamers docked next to each another with the "Melk" last.

The Gestapo motorboat which checked the four ships every day, also landed in Giurgiu. The gentlemen who disembarked from the boat were greeted most cordially and submissively by the Rumanian police. After a discussion — which was more like a transmission of orders — the Rumanian police officers in their extraordinary uniforms accompanied the Gestapo men back to the quay. The motorboat with the swastika mounted in its bows then chugged upstream past the "Melk."

A ship was anchored near the steamers in the middle of the Danube. People on board the "Melk" had not noticed it when they arrived because all eyes were on the other three ships with their passengers — who were as crowded together on deck as on the "Melk." Only now did they see the ship which loomed, grey and gloomy, out of the water. No smoke rose from its chimney and no boat could be seen anywhere in its vicinity. It looked empty and dead. A yellow epidemic flag fluttered from its mast. The last rays of the evening sun lit up the wretched dockyards and the house windows gleamed like molten gold. The ship in mid-stream, however, was not touched by this lustre. Grey and macabre, it hid in the slowly deepening dusk.

The Rumanian port authorities had had the ship towed into mid-stream and anchored exactly on the border between Rumanian and Bulgarian territorial waters. They were now, as far as their government's not over-scrupulous conscience was concerned, no longer responsible for the fate of the ghost ship. Their Bulgarian neighbors for their part had no intention whatsoever of bothering about a steamer which had been towed across from Rumania. They believed that they had done enough by allowing the Jews in their country to gather food supplies for the ship. All that remained to be clarified now was the legally interesting question of whether a permit had to be obtained for transporting the victuals to the ship. Prestige forbade them to make such a request of the Rumanians.

The Rumanian Jews perceived it as their fraternal duty to help their unfortunate brethren, and as they were familiar with the laws of social etiquette in their country, they found ways and means of discreetly conveying a present to the local police commander. In return, they obtained permission to give food supplies to the police, who in turn promised to take care of their delivery to the steamer. The Rumanian authorities were particularly concerned about the health of their Jewish subjects and therefore prohibited them access to the allegedly infected ship. The Giurgiu police, however, definitely had no intention of contracting cholera, typhus, or even the plague on the ship, although no port doctor had been on board to confirm the presence of contagious diseases. It would have been difficult for the latter to do so, in fact, since port doctors only existed in the protocols of the police. Slovakia had naturally not given its Jewish citizens any money for the journey, and the Nazis had no intention of releasing blocked Jewish accounts in Germany or the Protectorate. Mr. Storfer, the commercial adviser, thus had no possibility of looking after the interests of the passengers on board the ship. The Rumanians knew that they would be very favorably regarded by the Germans if they allowed the ship and its entire human freight to perish.

A rowboat approached the "Melk" in the twilight. A young man and woman seemed to be returning from an excursion. A few people looked down at the boat from the deck of the "Melk." The young man rowed almost up to the ship and called out, "Before you lies the 'Pentscho' with five hundred Slovakian Jews on board without food or drinking water."

He repeated his cry and then he and the girl quickly rowed their boat in a wide arc around the dockside and disappeared into the night.

Everyone wanted to help, to give away their last bite of bread, their last cigarette. All the doctors and nurses, as well as the entire security service, received orders to be on the alert that night.

Wachsmann assumed that people from the "Pentscho" would try to reach the ships anchored in the harbor under cover of darkness. A man was sent out to inform the convoy leaders of the "Schönbrunn," "Uranus," and "Helios" what was happening. A long plank, hardly a hand-breadth wide, went from one ship to another. Wachsmann knocked on the cabin door of the captain of the "Melk." The captain — a former officer in the Yugoslavian Marines — had given many signs of his goodwill during the journey, had cared for his passengers so far as it was possible, allowed blankets to be distributed which were not intended for the use of Jewish emigrants, and above all, had kept a strict eye on the kitchen staff. He was obliging, even friendly.

All this had given Wachsmann the courage to confide in the captain. The latter pointed out that they had to be careful since they were in Rumanian territory, and therefore requested Wachsmann not to undertake anything from the "Melk" which might provoke the Rumanian port police. If passengers from the "Pentscho" swam across to the "Melk" during the night, however — which he thought very likely — then he asked that the arrivals be isolated due to the danger of infection. He promised not to hand them over to the port police, and even to intervene on their behalf if they were caught.

Wachsmann left the captain's cabin and walked across the deck to the spot nearest to the "Pentscho." The ship had put on its navigation lights so as not to be rammed by timber freighters during the night. The lights were tiny glimmering dots, The most that petrol-fed stable-lanterns could provide. The watchers tried to pierce the darkness with their eyes. Minutes passed. The ship, which was shrouded in darkness, seemed to be totally deserted. Then a far-away, hardly audible sound rose from the Danube. The men on board the "Melk" held their breaths. A slight, cool breeze carried the cry across to them: "We are hungry!"

Wachsmann shone his torch round in a circle. He heard the sound of a motorboat quickly approaching. A broad beam of light swept the Danube. The side of the "Pentscho" loomed up for a moment in the searchlight and then the latter turned on the "Melk" and the other three steamers.

A Rumanian police boat patrolled the waters between the "Pentscho" and the four ships in the port until morning. On the "Melk" and the other three steamers, the mood was one of deep depression. The "Pentscho" gave them a clear example of what they themselves could expect if they were not allowed to continue their journey. No one knew what the Nazis were plotting with the Rumanian police, nor why they were detained in the port without being brought any provisions. The thought of the ship in midstream gave them no rest. The convoy leaders of the three steamers conferred on the "Uranus" and decided to cut the rations by half for two days in order to be able to provide a little food for the "Pentscho."

During the afternoon, two strong swimmers from the "Pentscho" attempted to reach one of the four ships. They were fished out of the Danube by the police boat which was patrolling the area, and taken to the prison in Giurgiu. The passengers on the deck of the "Melk" saw the totally exhausted swimmers sitting handcuffed in the boat, guarded by two Rumanian policemen. Wachsmann called Kerner over, and told him of a plan he had devised to divert the police with an evening's entertainment on the "Melk." At the same time, Kerner and the security service should transport the food which had been collected from the other three steamers to the "Melk."

The undertaking was fraught with danger. Kerner was to employ his group for the task, and the latter ran the risk of being arrested by the Rumanian police and taken on land. If the "Melk" was then forced to leave the port, what would happen to them? Wachsmann had already spoken to the captain of the "Melk" about what he would do if someone got into difficulties with the police. The captain had promised him not to hand anyone over, and not to leave the port without everyone on board.

"And you trust a captain who commands a ship flying the German flag?" Kerner questioned.

"I believe a Yugoslavian officer, even on board this ship. Besides, I am quite certain that one can do business with the port police," explained Wachsmann.

"What sort of business? Do you have any money, jewelry or goods to offer?" Kerner wanted to know.

Wachsmann replied that if it was absolutely necessary, he would collect a few wedding rings and offer them as a present. Probably a bottle of wine and the smile of a pretty woman would be enough to make the operatic-looking policemen quite docile.

***

The dining-room of the "Melk" looked once again as it had before serving as sleeping accommodation for eighty-five people. The women prepared for the evening in their cabins. Their low-necked blouses matched their boots and riding-breeches to perfection.

Kronberger bought expensive cognac and Tokay wine in the ship's canteen. He paid with vouchers issued by the convoy-management offices. Prices were exorbitant. Wachsmann received countless protests from men and women who refused to agree to a ball in the sight of the starving "Pentscho." It needed all his skill as an orator to convince them of the necessity of the evening's entertainment.

At about six o'clock, the captain of the "Melk" visited his colleagues on the "Uranus," "Helios," and "Schönbrunn" in order to invite them to the ball. Then he went on land in order to transmit the invitation to the port police.

At seven thirty, when the dining-hall was illuminated by every available chandelier, an officer from the port police, arrived, accompanied by the four captains. He was followed by a Rumanian customs inspector and three police sergeants. They exuded a strong odor of perfume. Silver and gold braid glittered on their battledress. The police officer was tall, dressed in an extraordinary uniform; the four ships' captains, on the other hand, were quite simply dressed, apart from the faultless white trousers and dark blue jackets. The orchestra struck up a Danube waltz as befitted the occasion. Wachsmann and Kronberger led the gentlemen to the table, now covered with a white cloth. Glasses clinked festively. While the ball was in full swing in the dining-hall, the security service went into action and began transferring food from the "Schönbrunn." They dragged the heavy sacks across on duck-boards. All of them wore socks in order not to make any noise. Despite all their precautions, Altmann was caught. The heavy hand of the law seized the sack which he was carrying, and a rough voice called out "Halt!"

Two other men who were working nearby let their valuable burdens drop and vanished. The police officers and three sergeants appeared in response to a shrill whistle from the police-men. They were followed by the captain of the "Melk."

141

The unfortunate Altmann stood next to the sack, his arm gripped tightly by the policeman. On the sleeve of his jacket was a blue and white armband, the insignia of his group. His riding-breeches terminated in a pair of white socks.

The officer presented himself to the sergeant. The state of affairs could not be denied, the sack providing weighty evidence against Altmann.

The officer stood in front of Altmann and shouted at him. He wanted to know how he came to be stealing bread and cigarettes. He took the few bottles of water which were also in the sack for alcoholic beverages, and it was a long time before he realized — in disbelief — that they only contained drinking water. How should it have occurred to a Rumanian officer that anyone could be interested in smuggling or stealing drinking water?

Altmann stared straight ahead of him. He did not reply and was taken away to the captain's cabin for interrogation. He walked with his eyes fixed on the ground, a sergeant on either side of him. The policeman who had caught him carried the indispensible piece of evidence — the sack. Wachsmann and Kronberger joined the escort. They did not want to leave Altmann in the hands of the Rumanians under any circumstances.

The entertainment had come to an untimely end due to this incident. People crowded into the narrow passage which led to the captain's cabin. Women voiced their displeasure.

"So irresponsible of him to endanger the whole convoy," said one.

"We've got enough worries of our own. Must we bother about other convoys too?" her friend seconded.

"It seems we must," said a third.

"I'm sorry for the man. I wouldn't like to be in his shoes," declared an elderly gentleman.

They were so excited that they did not notice the signals which were coming from the "Pentscho." The night-breeze blew muffled calls across to the "Melk."

Someone on deck shouted "Quiet!" The hum of voices died down. People stood still, cupped their hands behind their ears in order to hear better and gazed out into the broad river. A lamp was signalling from the "Pentscho" — a tiny dot of light in the darkness. A single voice floated across to them.

S.O.S. S.O.S. S.O.S. and then a chant:

"We are hungry."

S.O.S. S.O.S. S.O.S. and then once again:

"We are hungry."

Women who only a few moments earlier had been laughing at the ball, now shivered. The ghost of grey, hollow-cheeked distress rose before them out of the river and clutched at them with greedy claws. The men stood with bowed heads upon the deck.

The "Melk" did not answer the signals or the calls. Fear and uncertainty had made them dumb.

***

Altmann was taken out of the cabin and left at the kitchen door, watched closely by the Rumanians. The captain continued the discussion in his cabin. Gradually, the police officer's thundering tones quietened somewhat. He could no longer be so clearly heard through the closed door. After an hour, the captain of the "Melk" emerged in order to apologize to his three colleagues from the other steamers whom, in the excitement, he had quite forgotten in the dining-hall. The three captains had preferred, however, to return to their ships after the incident. They did not want to become involved in the affair. Meanwhile, Wachsmann and Kronberger had the opportunity of negotiating alone with the police officer. When the captain of the "Melk" returned to his cabin, he found the three of them engaged in a very friendly conversation. The police officer, who smelled of a hairdressing salon, had decided, after careful consideration, and discussion with the two gentlemen, that the whole affair was only a rash idea on the part of a small group who had undertaken the operation on their own initiative. There was no need, and there had never been any need, to supply the "Pentscho" with food, as this was being done in an exemplary fashion by the Rumanian authorities. As soon as the ship's papers were in order, the convoy could continue its journey. If he did not arrest the guilty party, it was solely because he had great regard for the captain, and because he did not want the ladies and gentlemen who had invited him to the evening's entertainment — which had unfortunately come to an such early conclusion — to suffer for this silly prank. He would very much like to spend a few more hours in their company. The police officer insisted only that the guilty parties be punished on board the ship.

143

The security service was thus relieved of its duties for twenty-four hours.

After long days and nights, the men could finally take off their clothes. They collapsed, dead tired, on the beds in the women's cabins and were asleep the next moment.

Women stood on guard outside the cabins. After two hours, they were relieved by their friends.

At about three o'clock in the morning, the captain accompanied his Rumanian guest back on land. When he returned and walked once again round the ship, he was astonished to meet only women on guard duty.

***

The "Melk" was the first steamer to receive permission to leave Giurgiu. The commander of the port police had a vague feeling on the morning after the ball that the whole celebration on board ship had only been arranged in order to deceive him. In his still somewhat befuddled head, the realization began to dawn that the Yugoslavian captain of the "Melk" was giving his passengers a helping hand and probably knew more about the matter than he admitted. The "Melk" 's papers were in order, and there was no reason to keep the steamer in Giurgiu. It was a matter of perfect indifference to the perfumed officer that the ship's drinking water reserves had to run out and that the captain had requested that the tank be filled.

In order to avoid another incident, he gave the captain to understand that the steamer was to sail past the "Pentscho" without any demonstration of sympathy. In order to emphasize his point, a Rumanian police boat accompanied the "Melk" to the border with Bulgarian territorial waters. The ship steered for the port of Rustschuk. After a few yards, it passed the "Pentscho." The police boat kept close to the steamer. All the passengers crowded onto the side of the deck facing the paddle-steamer. The people on board the "Pentscho" stood closely packed by the railing. They were so near that their faces were recognizable. They called across to the "Melk": "Brothers, don't forget us!"

No one answered. The "Melk" sailed slowly past the greyish-black vessel — a trim river steamer past a ghostly wreck. But the wreck would not give in. Above the yellow epidemic flag rose a blue and white flag with the Star of David and the sound of the "Hatikva" came from the tightly-packed crowd.

***

Altmann was the first to wake after a restful sleep. He found himself in a clean cabin on a comfortable bed, undressed and wrapped in soft blankets. It took him a few moments to remember how he had got there. He dressed, walking on tiptoe so as not to disturb the other sleepers who were snoring in every key imaginable. Outside the cabin, he met a friendly female guard.

"Stay in bed. I'll bring you something to eat at once," she said.

Before he could open his mouth in reply, someone called from the deck, "The steamer launch is coming back."

Altmann looked with astonishment at a harbor which he had never yet seen. The woman smiled.

"While you were all sound asleep, we sailed from Giurgiu to Rustschuk," she explained.

She was interrupted by three short hoots from the ship's siren. People hurried across the deck. They assembled at the gangplank, waving and calling. The captain climbed aboard his ship once again. Men and women formed ranks on either side of the passage to the dining-room.

The captain had hardly stepped on board when he was lifted on the shoulders of some sturdy men and carried through the corridor. Whoever could get near him shook him by the hand. Albert Wachsmann went up to him at the entrance to the dining-hall and thanked him because they had really succeeded, despite all the difficulties involved, in carrying provisions to the "Pentscho."

Chapter Fourteen

The steamer sailed down the Danube, past little Rumanian villages whose clay houses with their thatched roofs bore witness to the poverty of their inhabitants, and finally approached the port of Tulcea. The "Melk" steamed at the head of the flotilla, followed by the "Schönbrunn," "Uranus" and "Helios." The ships stood in the port for hours until the Rumanian customs official was finally brought on board to make yet another customs inspection. He was accompanied by a young police officer and a sergeant who had enough rows of braid on his uniform for a general. The customs official and the sergeant first emptied a bottle of wine in the "Melk" 's dining-hall. The convoy management offered it to the gentlemen in order to put them into a good mood. The young police officer seemed to be quite different from his colleagues. He strolled slowly around the ship, looking sympathetically at the confusion of blankets and sleeping-bags. He talked slightly peculiar German to the children who stared at him curiously and looked without being offensive at the women who still managed, despite the narrow confines of their living quarters and all the other inconveniences to look tolerably well-groomed. After surveying the ship, he asked to speak to the gentlemen from the convoy management, and received lists of the passengers from them. His behavior was extremely correct. The passport control which he carried out was quite different from any of the earlier official procedures. His quiet, refined manner rubbed off slightly on his companion who had made a very thorough job of the bottle of wine and small snack offered to him, and otherwise contented himself with opening a few pieces of luggage in order to search them for dutiable goods. After the passport control, which in spite of everything lasted several hours, the police officer informed the passengers on board the "Melk" that he would give them permission to embark on one of the three ocean steamers which were waiting for them at Tulcea. The ocean steamers, which bore the

146

names "Atlantic," "Pacific," and "Canisbay," were in fact old Greek freighters.

Most of the convoy members would have gladly chosen one of the two larger ships as they promised greater freedom of movement, and the convoy was prepared to accept another group if necessary. Wachsmann, Kronberger and Kerner, however, decided to take the smaller "Canisbay."

The "Melk" crawled past a few barges to the end of the dock where the "Canisbay" was anchored by the flat quay. The Rumanian police boat docked with the "Melk" next to the ocean steamer. The young officer went on board the steamer together with a sergeant. After greeting the captain of the "Melk" briefly, he asked to speak to the leader of the convoy.

"Which ship have you decided to take?" he asked.

"We shall take the 'Canisbay,' " answered Wachsmann.

Kerner, Eliezer Hirsch, Altmann and a mechanic named Jacob Grünthal climbed across to the "Canisbay." A few fat grey rats that were nibbling at some stray ears of corn scurried away. Nails, pieces of wood, a broken handle from a hammer and bits of paper littered the floor. There were wooden bunks everywhere which looked like shelves in a haberdashery store. They were divided into three tiers, the distance between them being just over a yard. The boards were new and had not been planed. Work on the bunks had obviously been finished only a few days earlier. A wooden structure on the upper deck had eight wooden plank-beds. A notice saying "Hospital" hung on the badly-fitting door. On one of the plank-beds lay a blue cardboard bag containing a few stray nails. The label with the firm's name was torn off, and only a small strip was still left hanging there. "Made in Hungary," read Eliezer Hirsch.

"So Mr. Storfer was right when he telegraphed that there were no nails," said Kerner.

They continued walking and came to four narrow wooden doors behind which were the unspeakably primitive WC's. The drains were blocked and there was a frightful stench. Two more lively rats flew past from some corner. Hirsch shuddered in disgust. There were rats on every ship, and they would have to come to terms with that fact.

"What's going to happen when these rats run over our women-folk's feet?" asked Altmann.

147

"The women will scream and frighten the rats and then, since neither side wants to jump into the river, they will quietly share the hold," answered Kerner.

While Grünthal tested screws, pistons, valves, wheels and so forth, the three men went up to the bridge, which made a slightly less dreary impression. They discussed how to divide the living quarters among the separate groups and ascertained at the same time that there were far too few sleeping places. The sound of hammering came from the engine room when Grünthal was examining the fittings.

"He'll smash this pocket-size battleship cum rat-carrier into matchwood if he doesn't watch out," grumbled Eliezer Hirsch.

Grünthal finished his work and came to join them.

"We can sail in it," said Kerner, turning to him. As the ship had come from Greece, one might suppose that the engines worked. They were ancient however, and badly looked after. Grünthal could not check whether the hull was in order, nor could he look at the screws. People began bringing their luggage on board. It was no easy task; they had been cooped up on the "Melk" for too long.

When they arrived on the "Canisbay," however, and saw the dirt, the rough wooden bunks and wretched sanitary arrangements, they began to complain. Many remained on deck and refused to go below.

Albert Wachsmann had to use all his persuasive powers to calm the convoy members down. New groups from the "Melk" pushed their way on board.

The Rumanian sergeant took everyone's passport. He had found a large cardboard box in which he placed the travelling documents. Some passes disappeared into his pocket. The convoy members would in any case have to destroy their papers before reaching the coast of Palestine. The "Canisbay" was the last vessel that they would use. The policeman paid close attention to the passport photographs. He took no interest in the traffic jam on deck. Let the Jews sort themselves out alone. What business was it of his? The complaints became louder.

The ship had no drinking water for the journey, someone said in an undertone. His neighbor heard it and passed on the news. By the time it had been repeated along a whole row of people, the "Canisbay" had received a great deal of its attention. The din was

148

suddenly drowned by a ship's siren. A steamer was advancing upstream, lowing like a cow. Someone from the "Melk" called out: "The 'Pentscho' is coming, the 'Pentscho' is coming."

The people standing on the "Canisbay" hurried to the railing in order to see the approaching ship. The old steamer chugged past them, lying at an angle in the water. Its paddle-wheel ground into the water and whipped it up into a high wall of foam.

In the bright sunshine, the "Pentscho" had a less ghostly appearance. Perhaps it was because its passengers stood waving and singing, tightly packed together on the deck. Their ship was sailing towards the sea, their dearly desired goal, towards freedom, and this filled them with joy, courage and pride. They could not guess that the ship would strike a reef near Rhodes in the dead of night, that they were escaping an attack from the Slovakian Hlinka Guards, that they would have to languish in an Italian prison until Mussolini's downfall.

The rickety steamer had passed the "Canisbay" by a ship's length. The convoy members on the "Canisbay" still waved to the disappearing ship. They were cheerful, excited and more hopeful. The "Canisbay" now seemed less wretched to them. Compared to the "Pentscho" it was a big ship. One could quickly get rid of the dirt.

The bells in Tulcea chimed midday. Kerner pricked up his ears. He had not heard bells chiming during the entire journey. It seemed to him as though he were hearing the bells of his native village. He closed his eyes for a moment, and pictures from the past rose in his mind's eye. His parents' house with the high courtyard walls; the copper dome of the Votthard church; the Obrawa river and the fields; the big novices saying, "German peasant! Don't let a Jewish doctor enter your yard"; the broken window panes and Rudi Scheibl brandishing a wooden club. There was Horacek and he heard the rustling of the trees in Lissitz. There were his old parents and Margit sobbing. Someone pushed a suitcase against Kerner's knee as he went past and jolted him out of his reverie. The echo from the bells died away. He looked around and saw group after group of people coming on board. Men went together with their young wives. Despite all the shortages, they were bright and curious, and boarded the dirty ship with youthful confidence. He, however, was alone, without any loving companion.

149

The security service men were now bringing across the convoy management's luggage — chests with medicines, medical instruments, buckets and large cooking pots. These men in the heavy boots, were Kerner's only family. He belonged to them: he was their father, brother and friend.

Passengers on the "Schönbrunn" and "Helios" began to board the two Avgerinos steamers, the "Atlantic" and the "Pacific." There was an air of lively excitement on the "Canisbay." People hammered and swept. Buckets full of garbage were lifted out of the hull and tipped into the Danube. People stowed away their luggage next to the bunks, thus blocking the gangways. The water tank was empty, and there was no trace of the captain and crew. The boiler had no steam, and the galley was closed.

The convoy members fetched ship's biscuits which Kronberger was distributing outside the hospital by the light of an emergency lamp. Then they crawled into the wooden bunks. They lay closely packed in their blankets and sleeping-bags like large rolls of dark fabric. The sentry's step on the deck, brief flashes from the electric lamps and a tiny oil flame which gave a pale light in the two cabins occupied by the security service were the only signs that the "Canisbay" sheltered human beings.

Kerner threw himself on a plank-bed after inspecting the sentries. He was so tired that he immediately fell into a deep sleep, although he was still fully dressed and wearing his boots. The oil lamp smoked and flickered. The cabin smelt of mold and the floor was damp. Kerner's off-duty workers snored on the hard bedsteads above and beside him. After midnight, someone shook him by the shoulder. Kerner turned his face to the wall in order to continue sleeping. A voice called to him excitedly.

"Let me sleep," he growled angrily.

Still numbed with sleep, he heard someone shouting from the deck, "Water is coming in."

Kerner jumped up and crawled up the narrow spiral staircase. He shivered in the cool night air. People were crowding around the gangplank — a footbridge constructed of two tree trunks — which was dimly lighted by four emergency lamps.

"Women and children first," someone called from amidships.

"Leave the ship in an orderly manner. Do not take any luggage with you."

That was Kronberger calling — Kerner recognized his voice.

He followed the sound of the voice until he bumped into Kronberger next to the hospital emergency lamp. He found a couple of thick ropes on deck by the light of his torch. He dragged them across to the gangplank.

"Where's Wachsmann?" he asked the sentry who was having extreme difficulty in only allowing women and children to pass.

"He's checking the ship's water level," the sentry answered.

The night was pitch black. The broad jetty was soaked by a recent rainfall. The passengers from the "Canisbay" who had been forced to hurry on land stood huddled together. They were ready to drop from exhaustion and did not dare to move even a few yards inland.

Albert Wachsmann checked the entire ship together with Kronberger. In the sleeping quarters in the hold, the water reached to their ankles. The freighter, which was now lighter by the weight of eight hundred people, was no longer sinking.

Gradually the people on the shore made out the shape of a railway embankment in the dark. They went across the muddy shore towards it. Many of them fell asleep there from total exhaustion.

The Danube was covered by impenetrable fog. Only when it became light did the convoy members notice that policemen had taken up positions along the railway line. Two industrious men who knew Rumanian had begun to talk with these representatives of state security. They exchanged goods. Propelling pencils, fountain pens, and highly-polished tin-plate cigarette cases were very popular. In exchange, the policemen offered maize bread and a sausage which no dog would have looked at in normal times.

At about nine o'clock, the friendly police officer appeared. He found Albert Wachsmann, expressed his sympathy over what had happened and promised to see to the repairing of the ship.

It was only a question of a leaking spot in the ship's wall. In the opinion of the Rumanian authorities, the "Canisbay" had been slightly overloaded, and would be seaworthy again within the next few days. The officer recommended that only half the passengers go back on board, and the other half lodge temporarily in a "camp."

Albert Wachsmann and his staff interpreted the word "camp" in a completely different context from that intended by the officer. They left him in no doubt that they would resist any transfer to a camp. The officer, who was most astonished at their refusal, took pains to explain that this was an empty camp, and requested that the leaders look over the accommodation themselves. He admitted that the camp was far from comfortable, but that this was the only available lodging for the other half of the convoy members at that moment.

The convoy members overcame their fear and unease. The ship which was supposed to take them to their destination, had already sprung a leak in the quiet Danube harbor. What would happen to it when it was battered by huge breakers in the open sea? The officer had spoken of dividing the convoy and staying in a camp. They were very distrustful of the words "dividing" and "camp." They suspected a trap on the part of the Rumanian police.

Albert Wachsmann found a crowd of people waiting for him when he returned from the camp. Everyone was staring at him. Everyone wanted to know what the situation was with the camp. It was a long time before he could make himself heard.

"Will this camp be administered and supervised by the police?" asked someone in the crowd.

"Why isn't Mr. Storfer here?" shouted another. A discontented murmur arose.

Several minutes passed before Wachsmann could reply to these questions. The camp consisted of long wooden barracks which normally served as a granary. The floor was built of strong, wide boards. Grains of wheat were stuck in the crevices between them. A cold draught from the Danube penetrated through the holes and gaps in the badly joined wooden walls. There was not a single door in the whole barracks. One entered straight from the muddy yard outside the granary into the makeshift sleeping quarters. During the first night, there was a heavy rainfall which turned the already soaked delta area into a complete morass. Nevertheless, people fell into a deep sleep and even felt refreshed and stronger when they awoke since they had not lain as before, packed together like sardines.

The next morning, when the wind was chasing grey clouds across the sky, a policeman adorned with a great deal of silver braid, appeared in the camp. He began to make a profitable business out of supplying the convoy members with drinking water, for there was no sign of a water pipe or a stream in the vicinity of the granary or in the adjoining timber yard. Drinking water had to be brought from the harbor. Kronberger, who was not at all willing to pay for delivery, wanted to go on board ship in order to ask the convoy management to intervene with the police, but was hindered by the police officials. Only after lengthy negotiations and after he had paid the glamorous policeman in cigarettes for his services, was Kronberger allowed to go on board the ship.

Meanwhile, the appearance of the "Canisbay" freighter had undergone a change. While the Tulcea fire-brigade tried to pump the "Canisbay" dry with their single hose, the steamer changed its name. The word "Canisbay" had disappeared under the dark paint with which the whole ship had been overhauled and slightly beneath it, the name "Milos" was painted in large letters.

A thin dirty stream of water ran out of the "Milos" into the Danube. It was at least a positive sign. The journey would be continued within the next few days. The mood in the camp became more confident. There were also abundant diversions for the convoy members. First of all, latrines had to be dug. The police official raked in a large quantity of cigarettes in exchange for the necessary materials.

Daily life in the camp took on a quite different form from that on board the crowded ship. Men went to work. They repaired the faulty boards, dug latrines, and built a primitive hut over them. They shovelled out the dirt, sat together during breaks and smoked Rumanian cigarettes which bore the name "National" and were of most inferior quality. The police guards received fountain pens, pocketbooks and neckties. They had their hair cut by Karl Schönfeld, who had retrained as a hairdresser. Dr. Rumpler, the dentist, even treated the police sergeant for a cavity. The good doctor could stand no more than ten minutes of this activity, although the sergeant sat patiently on an empty box with his mouth wide open. The patient's nose, which had a reddish tinge due to all the alcohol the sergeant had consumed, twitched every time the dentist trod on the pedal of his drill and grated against the tooth. The smell of bad spirits from the sergeant's mouth hit the dentist full in the face.

For all these services, the policemen brought cigarettes, white bread, salami and cheese. Business flourished. The women were busy washing the clothes which had lain for so long inside the suitcases. They stuck two poles, which still bore the remains of a dove-cote, into the ground, and fastened lines from them to the first windows in the granary. Now pale blue underpants, heavy woolen socks, handkerchiefs and white shirts hung next to pink corsets and red striped bath towels. The women were happy to be able to air out the blankets and sleeping-bags — a most necessary task. The children in the camp led a particularly lively life. They did not realize their situation and did not worry whether the convoy would continue its journey. As far as they were concerned, they might continue living in the camp for weeks. They were quite satisfied, and wanted nothing more. After the confinement and restrictions to which they had been subjected on the boat, they felt very happy.

The children put a board across a tree trunk and used it as a see-saw. They made a ball out of torn socks, and could play with it for hours. If the wonderful ball fell apart and half a sock dangled from it, they were not bothered in the least. They quickly found a piece of string somewhere with which to patch the ball up again. Joseph Kohn, who had just celebrated his seventeenth birthday, sat with a group of children between twelve and fifteen years of age on the sunny wooden fence outside the camp. He was the children's leader. They were repeating the "Ballad of Trumpeldor" in chorus. In a slightly hoarse voice, Joseph declaimed:

"Know ye the ballad of Trumpeldor,
Who lost his arm in Port Arthur at war?"
The boys and girls entered in chorus:
"Trumpeldor was a rising star,
He'd been made a lieutenant by the Czar."
Joseph continued, raising his voice:
"The new lieutenant was really a Jew,
and now in a commanding tone:
"Soldiers attention! Present arms all of you!"
The group of children was most enthusiastic. Their eyes sparkled. Seriously and ceremoniously, they recited each verse of the ballad until the end.

For them, it was not just a poem such as they had been wont to learn in school. They themselves could be called upon to present arms. Joseph Kohn had told them that within the next few days, they would sail past Gallipoli, the historic battlefield where Trumpeldor and the Jewish Legion had fought against the Turks in the First World War. Joseph Kohn was alone on the convoy. His father had been beaten up by the Nazis in Vienna, and he, his mother and his ten-year-old brother had escaped to Czechoslovakia. When they were about to board the train in Prague, the Gestapo kept back the passports which had already been made out for his mother and brother. Joseph had his own passport and had to begin the journey alone. As he had no one to whom he belonged, he devoted himself with all his youthful fervor to this group of children. The boys and girls liked him, and looked up to him. They came to him with all their desires and complaints.

***

Dr. Bieber and his young wife inhabited two square meters of floor space in a corner at the front of the first granary, just beside the entrance. A square post which propped up the roof marked the end of their living-quarters. An ivory-colored visiting card inscribed with the name of Dr. Fritz Bieber was attached to the post with a thumbtack.

Every evening, after supper had been distributed, Dr. Bieber received guests, and each guest received a beaker of tea. It was, of course, assumed that every visitor would bring his own glass and something to sit on.

The first guests were already gathered at Dr. Bieber's. They sat on their rucksacks, leaning against the wooden wall of the granary. They had taken off their shoes and placed them out in the narrow gangway. When Erwin Kerner laughingly knocked on the post as though it were a closed door, Dr. Bieber called out "Enter" in the very correct tones.

"Please don't walk with your shoes on my new Persian carpet," said Dr. Bieber's wife, Ruth, who was squatting in the corner with her knees drawn up underneath her. Blankets had been spread out. They were not large or thick enough to warrant the proud description "Persian carpet," but they were at the moment at least as valuable as the latter.

Kerner took off his shoes, unfolded the blanket he had brought with him and lay down on top of it. His legs reached as far as the blanket of the couple who lived next to Dr. Bieber, who at the moment were visiting another member of the convoy.

"You are now trespassing on someone else's property," said Dr. Rosenfeld who was sitting next to Dr. Bieber, turning to Kerner. Rosenfeld had formerly been an active lawyer in Vienna.

155

"I take it," replied Erwin in mock-serious tones, "that under the circumstances, your client has instructed you to sue me."

Kronberger and Joseph Kone, who arrived late, greeted the company and sat down at the edge of the blankets. Mrs. Bieber asked for their glasses and poured out hot tea for them. They drank it in little sips.

Kronberger passed around cigarettes. He had made a deal with a Rumanian policeman and exchanged his electric immersion-heater for a packet of "National" cigarettes. Kronberger had been cheated in this transaction, the Rumanian having taken full advantage of his desperate situation. Dr. Rosenfeld called it a rotten swindle. Kronberger shrugged his shoulders. Of course Rosenfeld was right, but he was surrounded by trickery, swindling, robbery and lack of consideration for others. The whole manner in which the convoy had been sent on its way was a disgrace. The Nazis had only allowed the "emigrants" to leave after confiscating all their property. The Gestapo in Vienna had tried to steal the convoy's medical equipment. The convoy members were forbidden to go ashore, and were short of provisions. Even drinking water was scarce, and had been rationed immediately after their departure from Vienna. They had been sold a ship that leaked and it was quite unseaworthy. Rumanian customs officials had stolen suitcases from them during the journey, and now Rumanian policemen guarded them in the granary. They had no protection, no help, and no rights. They had paid their last penny in order to obtain entrance visas for Costa Rica, Panama, Honduras and Nicaragua stamped into their passports. The poorest of the poor were being cheated in the most blatant fashion. None of the South American states knew about these entrance permits.

Were the convoy to even attempt to land in one of those countries, it would be chased away. The Panamanian flag fluttered from the "Milos," but it did not afford the passengers any protection. They were outlawed, beyond the pale, so much driftwood in a turbulent sea. Anyone might persecute them, insult them, rob them and beat them. There was no law to protect them, and no court of justice to which they might appeal.

The light from the stable-lanterns began to fade. In the granary, people straightened their blankets for the night. Ten strokes sounded from the church tower in Tulcea.

The company at Dr. Bieber's rose. Everyone put on his shoes, took

156

his empty glass and thanked his host for the enjoyable evening.

***

Kerner was on duty until midnight. Joseph Kohn went with him. The latter, a clever lad, was still searching for someone to whom he could attach himself.

***

They went outside. A few flickering lamps designated out the position of the "Milos." They walked round the camp. The Rumanian police guards were sleeping on the stairs. A police soldier was sitting on a box, snoring. His rifle was leaning against the wall. Joseph reached out for it, but Kerner took him by the arm and pulled him away.

"You're right, of course," he said to his young companion after they had gone a few steps. "A sentry who sleeps on duty should have his weapons confiscated, and be punished into the bargain. But that would be out of place here, and would cause us great difficulties. I shall send one of our people to watch over the man and his rifle while he sleeps. It's unthinkable what might happen if this policeman's rifle were stolen."

They walked on, met their own guards, sent Altmann to guard the sleeping policeman, and went back into the granary towards eleven p.m.

Kerner shown his torch down the long rows of sleepers wrapped in blankets. A boy lay asleep with his head on the bare boards. He had slipped off his rucksack. Joseph bent down, lifted the child's head carefully and pushed the rucksack underneath. A man was writhing sleeplessly on his pallet, groaning softly.

"Is something the matter?" asked Joseph sympathetically.

"Stomach cramps," replied the man in a whisper.

"Have you had them for long?" asked Kerner.

"Since midday," he answered.

"Did you buy sausage from the Rumanians?" Kerner inquired.

The man nodded. Kerner sent him to Dr. Bieber.

Joseph and Kerner walked down the middle row to where Kerner slept as the latter wanted to fetch cigarettes from his luggage. A figure wrapped in a blanket lay in the middle of the gangway.

157

It lay outside the row, and obviously did not belong there since Kerner's luggage, with the rucksack to which his blankets were securely buckled, stood next to the post. Kerner flashed his torch at the figure. Its beam fell on the face of a pretty, blond girl.

"You can't lie here. You're blocking the way," Kerner commanded.

"Please let me stay here. I'm so tired," the girl pleaded.

"Can I see your convoy papers please?" asked Kerner very politely.

The girl gave him a pass made out in the name of Lea Adler. Kerner assigned her his own place in the row.

***

A crowd of gesticulating people stood outside the granary. A lean police sergeant barred the way to the "Milos." His brown, braided tunic was slightly threadbare, and had obviously done duty for a number of years. It was extremely difficult to come to an understanding with the sergeant who did not wish to talk the language of civilians, let alone of foreign Jews. He had clearly received orders from his officer, but it was his own business how he interpreted those orders and carried them out. He was a policeman representing the government, and he was determined to make a profit from the Jews.

The orders which the man gave in Rumanian were not rendered more comprehensible by the way at which he bawled them at the convoy members.

A lady from the convoy was called over to interpret, and it finally became clear that the Jews were forbidden to go outside the camp. Not even Kronberger might go on board the "Milos." The guardian of public order vigorously refused to let a single person pass.

The passengers on board the "Milos" became uneasy. Breakfast had already been distributed long before, but the convoy members from the camp who generally collected the food did not appear. Loaves of bread lay ready in the hampers. The tea began to cool off. Eliezer Hirsch looked at his watch several times, but the people from the camp, although already long overdue, did not arrive. "Something must have happened there," he thought. He decided not to wait any longer, and informed Wachsmann of the situation.

The passengers on board the "Milos" began to get worried.

They had friends and relatives in the camp which was only a few yards away from them and now showed no signs of life. The most absurd rumors circulated: the Iron Guard had occupied the camp; an epidemic had broken out which could endanger the entire convoy. The rumors were born of fear and nourished by the uncertainty which hovered over the ship like a heavy black cloud. The fact that Albert Wachsmann descended the shaky gangplank accompanied by Dr. Segler, who was carrying his doctor's bag, gave still further stimulus to the epidemic rumor.

The policeman who was on duty by the gangplank together with three shabbily dressed soldiers asked the leader of the convoy where he was going, seemed satisfied with the answer: "to the camp," and let the two men pass.

They approached the gate to the square outside the camp, and saw the police sentries on guard. In the crowd of violently gesticulating men and women, they recognized the figure of Kronberger standing opposite the police sergeant, who was protected by the two yawning soldiers. The sergeant was greatly impressed by the appearance of the two men approaching him. Wachsmann was wearing a battledress with brown horn buttons and a blue and white band with two wide golden stripes — the convoy leader's badge of rank — on the sleeve. Dr. Segler, with his black doctor's bag, definitely gave the impression that he had come to inspect the camp.

The sergeant was firmly convinced that the people approaching him with such supreme self-confidence enjoyed the protection of one of his superiors. The situation was quite normal as far as he was concerned. All his life, he had superiors who had, in exchange for money, been willing to do something, or rather to permit something, which they had hitherto forbidden. For as long as he could remember, these big pikes had swallowed up all the juicy bites, whether in the form of money, wine, delicacies or women. An NCO in the police force had to be satisfied with much more meager baksheesh, and an ordinary policeman or soldier was very content if he received even half the scanty pay due to him. Nothing in this traditional state of affairs could be changed. One only had to understand and exploit the situation for oneself. Negotiations were started with the interpreter's help. At first, the sergeant demanded ten Lei in exchange for every permit to go on board, but after a few moments he reduced it to half that sum, and when it was explained to him that the Jews had no money, he began to bargain for cigarettes. The number ten appeared to signify for him the sum that was worth striving for, or perhaps he liked the number because it presented the least strain on his arithmetical powers; at all events, he demanded ten cigarettes for every permit. Kronberger regarded his demands as outrageous and wanted to report the blackmail to the police officer. He would have preferred still more to give the fellow a punch in the jaw. All the same, one would have to throw the puppy a few crumbs. Kronberger and Wachsmann conferred. The interpreter translated. They declared themselves ready, under certain conditions, to pay the sergeant two cigarettes for every person who went on board the "Milos." The members of the convoy management and the security service, the convoy members who fetched the food, kitchen staff, doctors, nurses, and of course patients, who went on board to be treated, would be exempt from this charge. In order to show his good will, Wachsmann offered cigarettes to the sergeant and the two yawning soldiers.

Dr. Segler meanwhile entered the camp unhindered and went to see Dr. Bieber. He found his colleague and Mrs. Bieber warming up half a bottle of tea on a spirit stove. While the doctors sat on suitcases and discussed the health situation in the camp, the negotiations outside continued. The sergeant appeared to have calculated that at least fifty people would go on board the ship daily, thus bringing him in a hundred cigarettes a day. He did not agree to Wachsmann's demand for special dispensations, since he had to give something to his soldiers too, and their rations might not, of course, be given at the cost of his cigarettes which he believed were as good as in his pocket.

The interpreter translated the sergeant's terms, but Wachsmann stuck to his first offer.

The sergeant haggled for every cigarette. Kronberger contained himself with difficulty from telling the parasite what he thought of him. Wachsmann offered the sergeant another cigarette, and clapped him jovially on the shoulder.

The sergeant, who was overwhelmed by so much friendliness, asked very politely if he might be fed from the ship's kitchen while he was on duty. The nights were cold, and as he and his men were looking after the convoy's security so faithfully, a hot tea and a warm bowl of soup would be very welcome.

"We can agree to that," said Wachsmann.

"If we were to ask this rabble for so much as a sip of water without paying for it, we could die of thirst," grumbled Kronberger.

"One has to throw a hungry dog a bone. If we don't give him anything, then he's sure to be sent to an Iron Guard camp," Wachsmann explained. They went inside the granary.

Wachsmann walked up and down the rows of pallets. He had a friendly word and a ready ear for everyone, apart from the confidence which he radiated. He asked Kerner for a report, and received complaints about the water supply. He promised to arrange for some entertainment in the camp the next day.

Their conversation was interrupted by a loud cry of "Breakfast is now being distributed."

Each person was handed a cup of tea, two slices of bread, a pat of margarine, two tomatoes and an onion. Wachsmann walked up and down. He looked at the women who were preparing a spread for the bread from margarine, tomatoes and onions. He was already familiar with the scene from on board the ship. Here, under even more primitive conditions, where the long rows of pallets could be surveyed at a glance, the impression of general need was even greater. People seemed to be more content than on the "Milos," however. They had somewhat more room at their disposal. As there was sufficient tea, bread and tomatoes available, Kerner asked the food distributors to make the rounds once again.

***

The sergeant was bent on earning as many cigarettes as possible, but Kronberger was equally determined to thwart his intentions. He could not stand the lean Rumanian, and used every trick he knew to outwit him. He had thought up a special stratagem in order to send as many people as possible on board the "Milos" without paying for them. There were women with bandaged arms, and limping men who allegedly could not walk due to foot wounds. Others wore wide bandages over their foreheads or eyes.

Thus twenty people went on board the "Milos" every day for whom the sergeant did not receive a single cigarette. And if an NCO anointed with all kinds of perfume could not earn anything, then his subordinates were obviously even worse off.

The sergeant hatched the only thing which men can hatch — a plan of revenge.

For five days Kronberger succeeded in smuggling people through. Five days and no more. The Rumanian had spent nights preparing his counterattack. On the sixth day, which was a Sunday, when he might assume that his superior officer would not be readily accessible, he prepared for action. He allowed the convoy members on board the "Milos" in the morning as usual, and the midday meal also arrived punctually in the camp. At one o'clock, however, he had the way to latrines barricaded by four ragged soldiers. At the same time, he refused to allow drinking water to be brought, and barred all entrances to the camp.

Kronberger called for Mrs. Rotfeld, the interpreter, in order to reach an understanding with his opponent. Mrs. Rotfeld, who was very patient, finally discovered the reason for the measures. She translated the sergeant's lengthy speech into a single sentence: a camp inmate had tried to sell a soldier a watch.

"Let him show me the man," Kronberger demanded.

"The sergeant says that the deal was broken off when he arrived on the scene, and the seller disappeared in the camp."

Kronberger did not believe a word of it. If the fellow had come on the scene, then he would have concluded the deal himself.

"But I can't tell him that," objected Mrs. Rotfeld. At that moment, the young police officer approached the entrance to the camp. He looked imposing in his uniform. His friendly nature and his youthful, dreamy eyes were in complete contrast to the duties which he had to carry out. Kronberger turned to him. He needed no interpreter now for the officer spoke quite acceptable German. The sergeant, when questioned by his superior, naturally stuck to his accusation. He was in the King's service, and wore a uniform. The matter was quite within the bounds of possibility. The young officer, who seemed to come from a good family, had not arrived on that Sunday afternoon in order to inspect the guards: he was only interested in finding a pretty girl in order to have some fun.

"Trading with the guards is forbidden and must be severely punished. If the man who offered the watch voluntarily reports to me within the next half-hour, then I shall see to it that the rule is relaxed for once," he said to Kronberger. One could clearly see how embarrassing the whole affair was for him.

Kronberger, who wanted to gain time in order to find a way out, suggested that the owner of the watch report to Kerner, who would then hand him over to the convoy management. The officer, however, insisted that the man be brought to him, looked at his wristwatch, and promised to wait exactly half an hour. In the meantime, he wished to observe life in the camp. The convoy members were ordered to assemble in the granary. Kronberger requested that the man come forward. Kerner spoke to them harshly, condemning the forbidden trading which was liable to endanger the entire convoy, and announced that there would be a strict search if the culprit did not confess.

Minutes passed and no one came forward. People stood around in groups discussing the incident and giving vent to their annoyance. Dr. Bieber pleaded that the culprit give himself up. He promised to intervene for him. Once again, minutes passed. Dysentery sufferers disappeared behind the rear-wall of the granary. The officer walked along the rows of pallets, and looked ostentatiously at his watch. From time to time, he stared at a young woman. Thus some fifteen minutes went by. Kronberger walked up and down restlessly. The sergeant's triumph galled him. Kerner nervously smoked his last cigarette. Suddenly someone called out from the nethermost corner of the granary: "Freudenfeld has admitted that he did it."

"Let him come out here to me," ordered Kerner.

A path was cleared through the crowd of people standing in the gangways. A tall boy of about twenty-five years of age came forward.

"How dare you trifle with the convoy's fate with your stupid transactions?" Kerner shouted at him.

Kronberger walked round the youth looking at him from all sides.

"You poor fool! Did you have to do business with the police of all people?" added Kronberger.

Freudenfeld looked rueful. He shrugged his shoulders regretfully and kept quiet.

Lea Adler pushed her way through the tightly-closed ring of spectators.

She went up to Kerner.

"Do you want to intervene for him perhaps?" Kerner asked her sourly.

"No, I don't want to intervene. It isn't necessary, since Freudenfeld definitely couldn't have sold his watch. He never had one." she said.

Kronberger said that he, too, had never seen Freudenfeld wearing a watch. The whole affair was most remarkable.

"Did someone give you a watch to sell?" asked Kronberger.

"No. I wanted to sell my own." answered Freudenfeld.

"Lea Adler says you never had one." continued Kronberger.

"I had it in my case, so no one could have ever seen it on my wrist," was the young man's answer.

"What sort of markings did the watch have?" Kronberger asked.

Freudenfeld did not answer immediately.

"He told his friend a few moments ago that he would voluntarily accept responsibility for the affair in order to save the camp from the Rumanian's cunning tricks," said Lea.

The convoy members now wished to come to an amicable understanding with the officer. In order to satisfy all requirements, Freudenfeld stayed behind. He was guarded by two men, and a suitably official atmosphere was thus created. Kronberger had thought up a completely new stratagem.

The officer sauntered back through the entrance to the granary.

"Help us to bargain with him. A smile from you is worth more than all our arguments," said Kronberger to Lea. Lea demurred but Kronberger would not take no for an answer.

Kerner informed the officer that the man had come forward voluntarily and had admitted having tried to trade his watch for food. The officer should take into consideration, however, that the attempt had been unsuccessful, and that no one had therefore come to any harm.

The officer was hardly listening. His eyes were fixed spellbound on Lea's face. She produced an irrefutable argument in Freudenfeld's favor. It consisted of nothing other than opening her eyes with their long lashes very wide. The officer did not have the man arrested. He was satisfied that he would be sent on board the "Milos" to be punished.

Freudenfeld slowly approached with the rueful air of a condemned man. The scene was beautifully acted. Walter Bogner, an opera singer who had formerly sung lead tenor roles in the German theater, was deeply impressed by Freudenfeld's performance. He declared him ripe for the stage.

The officer was no longer interested in Freudenfeld.

"Have him removed. I don't want to see him anymore in the camp," he commanded.

Kerner wrote a report about the incident to Wachsmann and asked him to punish the culprit severely. The two men who escorted Freudenfeld to the "Milos," however, knew what to report.

Freudenfeld was feted as a hero on board the ship.

Lea Adler had made a big conquest. The officer began to devise ways and means of improving her situation.

Life on board the "Milos" was monotonous. The passengers' only diversion was to talk to people from the camp who described the police's attempts to make life more difficult for them. Those on board the ship suffered less from chicanery, but were on the other hand completely isolated, without any contact with the outside world. They had written letters — insofar as they could procure the money for stamps — and given them to the police for forwarding.

Now the waited with longing for replies in the form of food parcels and cigarettes. Only a few postcards arrived, however, and letters which had been opened by the censor. Most of the letters remained unanswered.

The camp was at an advantage in this respect, as post was dispatched far quicker from there. Soldiers on duty were quite willing to post a letter in the town for a suitable remuneration. In fact, the officer on duty, who arrived at the gate every evening in order to speak to Lea Adler for at least half an hour, accepted letters from her for mailing. The young man had fallen in love with pretty, blond Lea in the truest sense of the word, and he brought chocolate, sardines, toilet soap and French perfume from the town as gifts for her.

Lea thanked him, but tried to decline these gifts. She found the whole business embarrassing, and felt directly compromised. Every evening, the officer appeared at the camp gate and told one of the inmates to ask Lea to come. He waited patiently until she arrived — often quite a while later. Kronberger had to encourage her before she was prepared to go to the fence. When she came back shortly afterwards, she often needed help in order to carry her presents back to the camp. She distributed them, keeping only very little for herself.

Since the officer had begun to take an interest in Lea, conditions in the camp had undergone a significant change for the better. Supplies of drinking water arrived without fail. The NCO's petty tricks stopped. Lea's influence in obtaining such a mild punishment for Freudenfeld was clear proof of how she might intervene on behalf of the camp inmates. In addition — and this was very important for the convoy — she brought news and newspapers from outside. Kronberger and Kerner regarded Lea as a valuable member of the group — a comrade who was fighting with the weapons bestowed upon her by nature and thus fulfilling her duty.

In Rumania, anti-Semitic riots had already taken place in several towns. The Iron Guard had organized the mob, which had plundered Jewish shops in Braila, Galaz, Jassy and other places, and had badly beaten the poor, terrified owners. The police had not interfered. Nazi agents agitated for further action. The newspapers did not carry a single report about the incidents. A small group of Jews succeeded in collecting enough money to bribe the police. They were kept under police protection in Tulcea to be brought on board the ship just before its departure.

Lea Adler, who had received this information from her admirer, hurried to tell Kerner that same evening.

In the morning, the camp was surrounded by a large body of policemen. The entire force which was usually on duty, including the sergeant and the police officer, had been relieved. The presence of these new policemen, who were armed to the teeth, did not bode well for the convoy. After breakfast had been distributed, a strapping officer, accompanied by two giant sergeants, appeared in the granary and demanded that the camp be evacuated without delay. Only after lengthy negotiations did he condescend to inform them that the "Milos" had been pronounced seaworthy by the port authorities and that the convoy might thus no longer remain on Rumanian soil. They were all to go on board ship immediately. No one believed the officer's words. They suspected a trap, fearing that they would be taken inland where there would be no possibilities of escaping. The Danube was the only way to freedom: they all realized that to leave it meant moving towards disaster. To refuse to move was out of the question, however. Rumania had brought in its armed police force against a handful of defenseless Jews.

***

A long procession wended its way from the granary to the "Milos." The earth, which had been softened by the autumn rain, stuck to everyone's shoes in heavy lumps. The luggage was a severe burden under such conditions. The nearer they came to the bank of the Danube, the more difficult conditions became. The Tulcea-Constanza railway line, which crossed the area, constituted the only passable stretch in their journey.

The Rumanian police escort forced the convoy members to leave the railroad tracks, however, and so they dragged themselves on through the morass until the head of the procession reached the "Milos"'s landing stage. An empty passenger car stood on the tracks which were only a few yards away from the Danube. The police squeezed through the narrow alley between the train and the bank of the Danube which was crowded with convoy members from the camp, and boarded the ship. Albert Wachsmann came down the "Milos"'s gangplank. He explained to the officer who was in charge of the proceedings that it was quite impossible to take all the people on board, as the ship did not have enough room for them and was not seaworthy. His arguments were refuted on the grounds that the port authorities had confirmed that the leak had been repaired and that the steamer was fit to travel on the high seas.

The passengers who were crowded together on the "Milos" stood waiting in fearful expectation. What would happen if the other half of the convoy was also accommodated on the ship. There was already insufficient room on board. But what would happen if their brothers did not embark? Someone on the "Milos" shouted: "Give us a larger ship! This freighter is a wreck. We shall all perish on it."

The police began to push the camp inmates onto the gangway by force, but they refused to embark. Kronberger went up to the officer who would not take any notice of Wachsmann's protests.

"Don't you realize that it is quite impossible to cram any more people onto this ship? What you are doing is inhuman. We protest against these methods," Kronberger implored.

The officer shrugged his shoulders.

"I have orders that the embarkation is to be carried out under all circumstances," he said.

Wachsmann remained outwardly calm, but began to negotiate with the officer.

"Please come on board and see for yourself the inhuman conditions in which we are crowded together. It is quite impossible to load this ship any further," Wachsmann explained.

"Give us another ship! This steamer can't hold us all," cried someone.

Kerner, who was waiting at the end of the column for stragglers and making sure that no one remained behind, came forward with four security service men when he heard the cries.

The police began to move in. The excited arguments by the gangplank continued. Kronberger invoked human rights, but in vain. Wachsmann demanded that the port captain be called.

The officer sent the sergeant beside him away with a whispered order. Then he turned to Wachsmann and Kronberger.

"I shall inspect the ship thoroughly to ascertain if there is enough room for all the passengers to be accommodated on board." He grimaced maliciously.

The policemen saw that their officer had gone on board the "Milos" and ceased to prod the convoy members. They stood next to the railway car, ready for instant action. The officer, accompanied by Wachsmann and Kronberger, and surrounded by six policemen armed to the teeth, began to inspect the ship. He pushed his way through the thick crowd of passengers who continually told him in agitated tones how impossible it was to cram them together any further. They were supported by Wachsmann. The officer, however, stated in every cabin which he inspected that it was quite possible to accommodate additional passengers there.

Kronberger contradicted him violently.

"It is quite out of the question. One can't even transport a herd of cattle under such conditions."

"You'll see that it will work. What do you want? Am I to place a luxury steamer at your disposal? There are no ships available at the moment. I didn't ask you to start travelling in the middle of a war. The 'Milos' has been pronounced seaworthy by the port authorities. There is enough room on board. No passenger may remain in Rumania," the officer said with a tone of finality.

A howl arose on all sides. A man sprang forward.

"What you are doing is quite barbarous and a crime against humanity!"

"Arrest him!" shouted the officer.

The policemen jumped on the man and held him fast. A second passenger came forward in his place.

"You have no right to arrest anyone here. We are on neutral

territory. The 'Milos' is flying the Panamanian flag."

The officer gave a mocking laugh.

"You can give your views on international law and neutral territory tonight in the prison jail," he said.

He beckoned to his men. The second passenger was arrested and handcuffed like the first.

Those who had witnessed the incident from nearby tried to control their justifiable anger. They clenched their fists, and looked as though they were about to hurl themselves at the police.

Wachsmann immediately recognized the danger which threatened the entire convoy. Eliezer Hirsch wedged members of the security service between the excited passengers and the police, thus preventing any clash. The officer, who was surrounded by his bodyguard with the two prisoners in their midst, left the ship as quickly as possible. Numerous cries of disgust accompanied his departure.

The policemen on shore began to prod the convoy members with the butts of their rifles. Lea Adler ran like a hunted deer to where Kerner was standing.

"Make our people see sense, for goodness' sake! There are machine guns behind the train," she warned.

She hastened back down the line. She pleaded, implored, adjured the excited convoy members to embark. A group of hefty men had pushed through to the jetty. A scuffle with the police seemed imminent.

The noise was drowned by the whistle of a locomotive. At that moment, Kerner caught sight of the young police officer who had visited Lea in the camp. He rushed up to him.

"Give us a few moments please. We are bringing the people on board. Consider that we have women, children and elderly people here. Please help us to avoid any fighting."

The young officer nodded silently, hurried across to the policemen and gave orders. The men assembled next to the landing stage.

Eliezer Hirsch and the security service cleared the gangplank. Slowly the passengers embarked. Lea Adler stood beside her luggage, her rucksack hoisted on her shoulders, and waited until the last group had gone on board.

The locomotive gave another whistle. The train was slowly pushed along the track. Three machine guns and their crews stood on the bank. Eliezer Kirsch and Kerner observed the machine gunners from the pier as they marched away. Some of the policemen followed, but a large contingent remained to guard the approach to the "Milos."

***

Gradually the excitement died down. Eveybody's attention was taken up by the problem of accommodating the newcomers. Every corner, however tiny, was occupied. Most of the new passengers had to camp on the open deck. The gangways were so full that one had to literally step over the people lying there. Kerner found a narrow bunk high up in the security service quarters. There was scarcely three-quarters of a yard between the bunk and the ceiling from which the lamp dangled right next to his head. Some people were still looking for suitable places. They were prepared to spend the night on deck rather than be crowded together on narrow bunks in the airless sleeping quarters. Lea Adler was among those who could not find anywhere to sleep. She wandered up and down on board until Kerner, who was inspecting the ship with Eliezer Hirsch, found her on the deck.

"If it doesn't bother you to share a room with ten men, then I can give you a bunk with us."

He took her rucksack, and Eliezer carried her suitcase. They climbed down the narrow spiral staircase to the security service quarters.

"We've got a new roommate," Kerner announced to the others. "Kindly behave suitably."

"I wouldn't mind giving up half my bed to her on the spot," grunted Altmann. The others laughed.

"She's got a whole bed to herself, and that suits her perfectly," answered Kerner, thus preventing any further remarks.

***

The next morning, the police officer on duty brought a telegram from Storfer which had already lain for two days in the Tulcea post office. Shortly afterwards, a car came driving up to the landing stage, and the commercial adviser alighted, accompanied by a man of medium height.

Wachsmann came to meet him, and took the visitor into the narrow room which served him as bedroom and office.

The news of Storfer's arrival spread like wildfire. People came running from all the gangways and corners, from berths deep down in the ship's hold where the planks were still wet, and from the bridge where they had come up for a breath of fresh air. They all wanted to see the commercial adviser, to speak to him, to present their complaints to him and pour out their hearts, and above all to ask him questions. There was so much to ask. He came from Vienna after all. Perhaps he had brought letters from relatives, some news from the Protectorate. He must know when the ship would set sail, what provisions they would receive in Istanbul, when they could reckon on arriving in Palestine. Despite their haste to speak to the man whom they longed so ardently to see, however, they came a moment too late and only saw the tail of his frock-coat disappearing round the cabin door. The entrance to the cabin was already barred by security service men.

After Wachsmann had welcomed him, Storfer presented his companion. The latter, Captain George, made a very good impression. He was of medium height, his sympathetic face with its lively eyes tanned deeply by the sun. His black, carefully combed hair was slightly greying at the temples; he seemed to be in his early forties.

Mr. Storfer had been informed by the police directly upon his arrival in Tulcea about the incidents on board the "Milos." He had immediately tried to have the two prisoners released. The police did not wish to let this particularly favorable opportunity of making money slip by without taking advantage. Mr. Storfer paid. He also made large inroads into his money supply in order to obtain an improvement in the ship's provisions. Kronberger complained to him about the behavior of the Rumanian police and authorities. He was consoled with the information that the moment the "Rosita" arrived, the "Milos" would set sail.

Mr. Storfer promised to come on board just before the "Milos" sailed and to give the convoy leader the necessary foreign currency to buy provisions during the journey.

***

The next moment, the narrow cabin was crowded with people. "What did he say?" "When are we sailing?" "Who was the man who came with him?" "Did he bring letters from Vienna?" Everyone had a question, wanted to know something. There was a buzz of voices. Kronberger gave a short report which he ended with the

171

words: "When the 'Rosita' comes, we'll be free."

This short sentence was taken up by the convoy members. It filled them with new hope. They had already heard rumors about the "Rosita." Now these had been confirmed by a competent source. The "Rosita" had sailed from Athens; it might arrive any moment. Their ship, the "Milos," already had a captain. The latter had even gone to the port authorities with Storfer in order to sign various documents. The word-of-mouth wireless on board celebrated a triumph. Everyone was in a more optimistic mood. Even the perpetual grumblers found the lunch — which was distributed late — quite palatable. It only consisted of beans and peas which had neither been cooked for long, nor were served with any oil. A drop of confidence, a thin ray of hope, seasoned the meal.

The convoy-members' account of the conversation was far from correct. In their joy, they had invented a new greeting. There were cries everywhere of "When the 'Rosita' comes, we'll be free."

***

Before Bernard Roller had filed an application to emigrate to Palestine in Prague, whither he had fled after the "Anschluss," he had owned a shooting gallery in the Viennese Prater gardens. For the sum of twenty-five Groschen, one could shoot a bull's eye, become a crack shot, and win a prize. The latter was usually a crudely painted vase, which Mr. Roller handed to the marksman with a bow. The Nazis had "aryanized" the gallery immediately after occupying Vienna, and had turned it into a very profitable business, for shooting was not only important as a form of para-military training, but was also one of the most popular national pastimes. The boy who succeeded in hitting the vibrating figure of a hare at six yards distance would certainly very quickly learn how to dispatch a concentration camp inmate with a shot in the nape of the neck. All that was left to Bernard Roller of his business was his wife, a buxom blond, and his wonderfully tatooed chest which sported an Indian chief in full war paint. A blue and red tatooed snake wriggled along Roller's right arm from the wrist upwards, as though aiming to devour the green and yellow parrot on Roller's biceps. Roller's left arm was decorated with a dragon which leered at an eagle or falcon — it was difficult to determine which of the two.

172

When the weather permitted, Bernard Roller liked to promenade naked to the waist in order to show off his tatoos. He enjoyed the admiration of all the children; it was also understandable that his tatoos earned him the nickname, "Bernard, the living picture book." The adults who had invented this rather ironic appellation did not mean it derogatorily, however. Like most Viennese, Roller liked good food, and knew how to prepare genuine Turkish coffee. He sang Viennese songs, particularly the Cab Song which he sang with extreme sentimentality. He was basically what the Viennese call a "merry soul."

His connections with Judaism had always been of a unique nature. On Pesach, he broke matzot into his coffee until the coffee spoon stood upright by itself, and he shut his shooting gallery on the Jewish High Holidays.

When he applied to emigrate, he began to take a greater interest in Judaism. He had already heard of Dr. Herzl. As a Viennese, he felt honored when Zionism was discussed in his presence.

He had risen to the rank of corporal at the end of World War I under the royal and imperial Austro-Hungarian monarchy, and thus felt attracted to anyone in a position of authority. As long as the old Kaiser lived, he had regarded him as his highest commander-in-chief, and had served him faithfully. He had transferred his civic loyalty initially to Kaiser Karl and then to the President of the Austrian Federal Republic. Now, on this rickety freighter, he was attracted principally to the convoy leader, Albert Wachsmann, who gave orders, issued commands, conducted negotiations, and despite his position, still spoke to people in such a friendly way. The head of the convoy was his idol.

Bernard Roller felt highly honored when Albert Wachsmann spoke to him in passing, offered him a cigarette, or even sat down beside him on the narrow bench on the bridge and questioned him about tatooing. Roller could give exact information on how many needles had been stuck into his skin for each picture, and how many hours it had taken for the precious work of art to be tatooed on his chest. Wachsmann was an attentive listener. This Viennese oddity, as he called Roller, interested him. How had the man lived? What had he learned? How would he earn his living in Palestine? What could he do in order to build up the country?

"To be the manager of a shooting gallery is no profession in

Palestine. You'll have to devote yourself to productive work," he said to Roller.

Roller thought that he would be able to find something, although he believed that it would be quite a good thing if the youth in Palestine were taught how to shoot correctly. To take a rifle in one's hand, press the trigger, and take a look afterwards to see where one had made a hole in the good Lord's windows — that was quite pointless. There had been no such nonsense at Roller's shooting gallery. He had taught his customers how to prime a rifle, take correct aim, and then slowly shoot, all the while keeping one's target firmly in sight. Then the shot would pierce home. This was a job which he would do with pleasure.

"Your thoughts are still with your shooting gallery. You must break away from it. We haven't got an army in which you could be an instructor. That profession is in the hands of the British," Wachsmann interrupted him.

"Then I'll have to wait until we Jews have our own army," he replied.

"Everyone's waiting for that, but it will take time until then, and in the meantime, we must live," explained Wachsmann.

Roller said he would find something. He had worked in a laundry in Prague for a while. His wife knew how to iron. When the Nazis had "aryanized" the business, he had taken a job as a waiter until he ran away because he had been cheated.

"How could you have been cheated when you were a waiter?" asked Wachsmann.

Roller threw his cigarette end on the floor, ground it under his heel, and told him that the café owner had paid him his month's wages with a forged thousand-crown note.

"How did you get rid of it?" Wachsmann asked.

"I didn't," replied Roller. "I've still got it on me as the last remnant of my fortune and a souvenir of Europe."

"Keep that note carefully. Don't tell anyone anything about it," said Wachsmann, bringing the conversation to a close. He let Roller descend the iron stairs alone, while he remained on the bridge. He thought over the story. A thousand crowns was a thousand crowns; whether they were genuine or not made no difference in an age of robbery and deceit.

***

On the eve of the Jewish New Year (Rosh Hashanah), severe rioting broke out once again against Jews in Jassy, Braila and Bucharest. The deeds perpetrated by the Iron Guard were so horrible that no one wanted to believe them. Jewish shops had been plundered in Jassy, their owners beaten in the streets, and schoolgirls raped in public. The police had not intervened. In Bucharest, the brutish mob had driven a group of defenseless Jews to the slaughterhouse, slain them, hung their bodies on butcher's hooks and stamped "Kosher" on the various limbs. This gruesome tale was kept secret by the convoy management.

It was the first day of Rosh Hashanah. All the convoy members were assembled on the foredeck around the only Torah scroll. In a mood befitting the solemnity of the festival, they prayed to God, their Lord and King, that He might inscribe them in the Book of Life. In a prayer which they uttered with deep emotion, they enumerated all the ways in which a human being can die: through illness, fire, water, the enemy's sword and wild animals. The author of the prayer had not thought of dismemberment, shooting in the nape of the neck or gassing. At the time when the prayer was incorporated into the liturgy, culture was still far removed from such modern achievements; it had not yet soared to the heights attained during the twentieth century.

The worshippers on deck did not know how near the destroyer had come to them, nor did they have any notion of the dreadful fate of the Rumanian Jews.

The New Year's festival passed peacefully. For security's sake, the gangplank was drawn up during the afternoon so that the "Milos" had no connection with land. A look-out stood on the bridge. He was instructed to report immediately if anyone approached the ship.

175

Chapter Fifteen

Captain George was treated most obligingly by the port authorities in Tulcea. His captain's commission and Greek passport helped him to avoid many difficulties. Matters were not prejudiced by the fact that the captain appeared in a dark blue suit, that the "Milos" was a rusty old grain freighter which still had no crew and that the cargo of the steamer consisted of outlawed, foreign Jews who were on the point of arriving illegally on the coast of Palestine.

The honorable British ambassador, whose task it would have been to protest against the passage of illegal immigrants to Palestine, sat in Bucharest without intervening. The port authorities and the police in Tulcea thus had no reason to cold-shoulder Captain George. Upon his intervention — and after Mr. Storfer had paid a large ransom — the two "Milos" passengers were released from custody.

Captain George wanted to inspect the provisions which were to be supplied for the journey. He regarded it as his duty to test their quality for himself. He had no second officer or kitchen staff; he did not even have a crew as yet. There was thus no one else to whom he could entrust this task. The supplies were not available. The port authorities made all sorts of excuses. They said that there were such shortages due to the war that they would have difficulty in procuring the provisions in the course of the next few days. The captain did not trust the Rumanians at all. He drew their attention to the fact that there were mountains of vegetables and potatoes in Tulcea; butchers' stalls were overflowing with meat and Rumanian peasants were offering innumerable crates and baskets of eggs for sale in the town markets.

Although the police declared that it would be undesirable for the "Milos" to remain any longer in Tulcea, the port authorities nevertheless made every effort to delay the steamer's departure. As far as the officials were concerned, Jewish convoys were a

marvelous source of income. They had made a fortune by supplying the Jews with provisions. Altogether, the Jews were a
godsend for them.

Captain George saw the storm clouds rising over Rumania.
Disaster threatened. Its advance guards — Nazi agents and the
Iron Guard — gave him cause to fear for his convoy's safety.

He made a quick decision, settled his hotel bill after lengthy
haggling, and sent on board the "Milos" the mail which he had been
given for the passengers. Then he travelled back to "Avgerinos" in
Athens in order to find a crew for the "Milos" and to ensure that the
convoy would receive supplies at least in Greece.

Gruber distributed the mail. There were a few letters and
postcards from relatives and friends at hime, and a telegram
addressed to Wachsmann for the "S.S. Milos, Tulcea Port." The
leader of the convoy members who had remained behind in Brünn
stated that he had received the telegram from Tulcea and asked for
further news. There was not a word about his group departing in
the near future. Those who had received letters read them again
and again until they knew the contents almost by heart. They
could count themselves lucky: most of the convoy members had no
news at all and felt depressed and lonely among their crowd of
fellow passengers. Kerner retired to the bridge with his postcards.
His mother wrote that she was glad to have finally received news
from him. She begged him to look after his health and to dress
warmly during the sea journey. Kerner read anxiety for his well-
being in every line of her clear handwriting.

Margit's card, on the other hand, was quite apathetic. Life was
desolate and grey. There was not a syllable about her emigration.
Instead of closing with an optimistic "see you soon," she ended her
letter with "farewell." When travelling on a perilous journey,
people are usually very communicative when they receive mail
from home. Kerner exploited this tendency to the full in order to
discover what news the other passengers had received. People
showed him cards, read letters to him and willingly told him what
they had learned from their mail.

News had come from friends who were all ready to emigrate,
but there was not a hint about their leaving in the near future.

The mood on board ship improved. The passengers had received letters from their dear ones, and no longer felt so alone in
the world. As a consequence of Storfer's intervention, the rations

were a little less scanty, although the food did not improve. A Rumanian tradesman had obtained permission from the police to sell sausage, sweets, cigarettes and toilet articles on board the "Milos." His prices were exorbitant. Business did not go well but the man remained on the ship and a small room was even placed at his disposal at the urging of the police. He was very fluent and polite, and extremely inquisitive.

Kronberger declared that the tradesman was a loathsome creature and waited impatiently for the first opportunity to throw him out. Wachsmann, on the other hand, recommended that they make use of the man's exquisite politeness to negotiate with him and buy up such goods as cigarettes at a reduced price. At the same time, he advised that they keep an eye on the Rumanian.

Since the evacuation of the camp, there had no longer been any opportunity to obtain news of events in Rumania; the only remaining possibility of discovering something lay in Lea Adler. Her "friend" — as he was generally called in spite of her violent protests — came to the "Milos" almost daily, mostly in the late evening in order to speak to her for an hour. Lea always kept him waiting for a long time, refused to go on shore alone and demanded that Kerner place a guard near her.

***

The "Rosita" came into port. Its white-painted hull was visible from afar, and distinguished the steamer from all the other ships anchored in Tulcea.

The ship was given a rapturous welcome by the passengers on the "Milos." The "Rosita," which had already been expected for days, had finally arrived. The convoy members were free and could continue their journey. The "Rosita" was supposed to wait for the second convoy and transport it to the coast of the Promised Land, the destination of all the small refugee steamers, "Lisel," "Tiger-Hill," "Frossula," and "Sakaria," which had departed from there since the notorious "Anschluss" and which were now, after a break of nearly two years (when no one believed any longer in the possibility of convoys), followed by the "Pentscho," "Atlantic," and "Pacific." The "Milos," the last ship in this migratory wave, was ready to sail.

The "Rosita" was deemed the connecting link, the guarantee for

178

further emigration. Those who saw the ship thought that it would still be possible to bring out small convoys from within Hitler's sphere of influence.

How could those Jews, who had already covered more than half their journey, have dreamed that the "Rosita" was only a subterfuge, a low-down ruse on the part of the Nazis to make the world believe that the Jews could escape? The "Rosita"'s arrival caused great rejoicing on board the "Milos." The Rumanian tradesman immediately reported to the police that the Jews were in a cheerful mood.

***

In Greece, Captain George had succeeded, after much labor, in assembling a six-man crew for the "Milos." The Greek authorities' promise not to create any difficulties for the ship encouraged him to sail the "Milos" out of Rumanian territorial waters as quickly as possible. He travelled back to Tulcea with his crew, and collected lifebelts and ship's biscuits in the port depot. Other provisions were still not available.

Towards midday, he went on board with his crew. Shortly afterwards, a police officer appeared in order to search the "Milos" for arms.

Wachsmann endeavored to persuade the officer to waive the inspection on the grounds that it would be difficult to carry out a search on such a crowded ship. He pointed out that the convoy came from Nazi-occupied territory, and had been continually searched by the Gestapo, so that it was beyond the bounds of possibility that anyone should possess arms.

The officer seemed intent not so much on an actual inspection as on blackmailing the convoy. Wachsmann had realized this from the start and had invited the officer to a little snack in his cabin in order to be able to speak to him undisturbed. He already had experiences in dealing with Rumanian policemen, so he plucked up courage and appealed to the officer.

"We don't have a single weapon on board. I would be very interested, however, in buying a revolver for my own personal protection," Wachsmann said.

"Do you have money to buy arms? I might be able to assist you," said the officer.

"I can give it to you just before we leave," replied Wachsmann.

179

Wachsmann was counting on the foreign currency which he was supposed to receive before they continued their journey.

"The 'Milos' has to leave the port within the next few hours," the officer replied.

"But we don't have any provisions on board; there isn't even a sufficient supply of drinking water. We are still waiting for Mr. Storfer to arrive," was Wachsmann's retort.

The officer replied by explaining, "It is in your own interest to leave the port as quickly as you can. We are bringing another fifteen Jews on board whom we are very anxious should emigrate from Rumania."

Wachsmann did not ask the reason for this sudden alacrity. He already knew about the incidents in Jassy, Braila and Bucharest.

"Your captain has already arrived. He knows what to do. Sail early tomorrow morning. We don't know what will happen during the next few days, or if it will still be possible for you to leave. I'll search the ship for arms now," said the officer.

"But I told you that we don't have any arms, and that I am even willing to buy a gun for myself," Wachsmann repeated.

"How much are you prepared to pay?" asked the other.

"I'll give you a thousand crowns for your revolver," Albert offered.

"A thousand crowns?" asked the officer, barely able to conceal his astonishment.

"Yes, a thousand," Wachsmann repeated.

"Hand it over," said the officer quickly and stretched out his hand.

"Could you please wait a few moments? I'll go and fetch the money," promised Wachsmann.

Wachsmann hurried out. "Don't let anyone into the cabin," he called to Altmann who was on duty nearby. They spent a quarter of an hour searching for Bernard Roller and finally found him in the Greek sailors' cabin; he was showing them his work of art.

Wachsmann took Roller's thousand-crown note and ran back to the cabin. The officer took the note, handed over his service revolver to Wachsmann and waited another few moments until the police had brought a group of fifteen Rumanian Jews on board. The two convoy members who had been released from custody came with them.

Late that evening, Lea Adler stood by the landing stage for the last time. The young police officer had asked that she be there.

His words were filled with emotion, and he said, "You have

rejected my offer and I shall have to accept your refusal. I may have appeared insistent to you, but my feeling was deeply emotional. I wanted to help you to leave this convoy, and keep you here in Rumania as my wife. You look very similar to my mother, whom I only knew from pictures."

Lea suddenly felt sorry for the young man who was so devoted to her and whom she had so consistently discouraged.

As if it served as a motive explaining his actions, he confided, "My mother died when I was born. She was a . . . Jewess."

Lea Adler walked up the landing stage which was immediately drawn up behind her.

The officer gazed at her, saluted and vanished into the night.

Dawn broke. The anchor was raised on the end of a rusty chain. The "Milos" began to move. Mr. Storfer, the commercial adviser, could no longer give the convoy management the foreign bills of exchange which had been authorized by the Gestapo. He had already been arrested and was to share the fate of Elbert and Jacob Edelstein. Adolf Eichmann ordered that he should be given "special treatment."

Chapter Sixteen

The sky was grey and overcast. Gulls shrieked hoarsely, and the thundering of the sea became louder. The Gestapo motorboat, which they had not seen during their stay in Tulcea, accompanied them through the George canal. Passengers on the "Milos"'s bridge saw the two big dredgers constantly at work. A fresh breeze wafted the smell of the sea across to them.

The Nazis could not brave the high seas in a motorboat, and were in any case afraid of meeting British ships. The vessel turned and travelled back up the Danube. Wachsmann saw the detested swastika pennant fluttering in the stern of the departing boat. It became smaller and smaller and finally vanished in the haze. He breathed a sigh of relief, and reflected that the most difficult part of the journey was behind them.

Let the sea surge, the white caps of foam on the bluish-green waves rear up like wildly galloping horses, and storms whip the waves up in fury. The sea's primitive might seemed to him less dangerous than the small Nazi boat. The "Milos" sailed down the last few yards of the Danube. The freighter's calm gliding motion suddenly ceased and the ship, caught by the surging of the sea, began to dance gently. The sky stretched like a huge grey dome over the crests of the waves, until it merged somewhere in the vastness with the water.

Captain George had left Tulcea with insufficient supplies of coal. The water tanks were nearly empty, and only emergency rations were left. The rations, which hardly sufficed for two days, were guarded by a member of the security service. It was forbidden to use drinking water freely, and people were given sea water for their own personal use. The briny water was brought up on board in buckets. The Greek sailors worked in the engine room; the stokers were stripped to the waist. Captain George wanted his crew to receive special treatment, and asked that they be given their own kitchen. Wachsmann refused this request. The six men would come under his direct command like all the passengers if he were master of the ship. Wachsmann was only too well aware of the experiences of other convoys. It had once happened that a convoy from Czechoslovakia had been stuck in Greece with out even being able to send out any mail because the captain, whose exorbitant demands for money could not be met, refused to continue the journey and even prevented letters from being dispatched.

Albert Wachsmann was quite determined not to let the leadership of the convoy slip out of his hands. The "Milos" had been bought with Jewish money. Those two courageous representatives of Czechoslovakian Jewry, Jacob Edelstein in Prague and Elbert in Brünn, had succeeded, after a lengthy struggle with the German District High Commissioners, in having blocked Jewish accounts released in order to acquire the ship. Wachsmann found it unthinkable that he should surrender his powers to the captain.

Mr. Storfer had given the man a very good reference, describing him as a sound seaman and friend of the Jews. Wachsmann granted that he was a sound seaman: he had no choice in the matter. Let the captain be responsible for navigation, but let him work as an employee of the convoy management. He, Wachsmann, would not give up his authority over the passengers — his fellow-Jews. He agreed with Kronberger to present the convoy management's point of view in polite but definite terms to the captain. It occurred to him that the captain might refuse to carry out his duties under such conditions, and he conferred with Dr. Rosenfeld. They agreed to only allow the captain to supervise the sailing of the ship, and to refuse all other demands.

Twenty-five minutes after this discussion had taken place, Eliezer Hirsch and twelve men, all armed with black-lacquered wooden truncheons, barred the way to the bridge. Convoy members, who had been drawn by curiosity and collected around the security service men as they marched up, were ordered to keep calm. Wachsmann, Kronberger and Dr. Rosenfeld ascended the iron steps to the bridge, entered the chart room and greeted the captain. Captain George, who was wearing a Greek merchant-navy uniform, rose behind the desk. The men surrounded him.

Dr. Rosenfeld presented the decisions taken by the convoy management. Captain George insisted upon his right to control the passengers and crew, and did not accept any arguments brought to bear in favor of this particular convoy. Wachsmann explained once again to the captain that the ship had been bought by the convoy management, and the captain should thus consider himself as their employee. A fierce argument developed between the captain and the members of the convoy management.

"Why all the talk? Do you agree or not?" Kronberger interrupted.

"Of course not. I insist upon my unrestricted rights as captain and the terms of my contract with the 'Avgerinos' shipping company," the captain muttered.

The captain, whose professional "amour-propre" had been offended, talked of calling his crew and ordering them to keep order on board. He shouted, banged his fist down on the desk, and called the behavior of the convoy management sheer mutiny. The crew had got wind of the argument in the chart room and, as befitted disciplined sailors, wished to come to the captain's help. They were held up on the stairs, and immediately realized that they could make no headway with the sentries who enjoyed the support of the convoy members. The captain recognized the voices of the crew as they shouted angrily at the sentries in an attempt to intimidate them. He became still more obstinate.

Dr. Rosenfeld could not stem the captain's torrent of words.

"Give me the thing," Wachsmann called to Gruber.

Gruber took the revolver out of his pocket and handed it to Wachsmann. The latter pointed it at the captain's chest and took a step forward.

"Submit to the demands of the convoy management! Any resistance is useless," Wachsmann threatened.

Captain George had to give in. He only demanded suitable food for the crew and that the stokers be relieved.

Wachsmann willingly granted this demand, put his revolver away in his pocket and promised the captain that he would be fed by the convoy management and that a young boy would act as his orderly.

The captain made no reply to this offer, feigning not to have heard it.

The men took their leave of the captain and departed. Two sentries remained behind to guard the bridge; the remaining men from the security service were released.

"I like that Greek. He wasn't easily intimidated, but when he had to give in, he didn't ask anything for himself. He has the crew's well-being at heart," remarked Wachsmann to his companions.

Despite the unpleasant episode, Captain George did not bear a grudge against the convoy management. He fed himself on supplies which he had brought with him in a suitcase, and also refused the services of the boy who had been assigned to him as an orderly. He only went to see if everything was all right in the engine room, and seemed to understand that Wachsmann did not wish the convoy to be directed by someone whom he did not know. The captain had heard abundant tales in Greek ports of how the ships' crews of various convoys had behaved towards the wretched refugees.

How could Wachsmann know that he, Captain George, had the greatest sympathy for the Jews, and that he enthusiastically returned to Piraeus from every trip to Haifa full of praise for the achievements of the Jews in Palestine. How could anyone on the convoy dream that he, a Greek, personally knew the representative of the "Joint" in Athens?

The "Milos" sailed on slowly. The sea was calm. Land had disappeared, and there was only endless sea and grey skies for as far as the eye could see. The rolling of the little steamer began to affect the passengers. The lack of drinking water became unpleasantly noticeable. Water seeped in through the badly-repaired leak in the ship's side. It collected in puddles in the sleeping quarters deep down in the hold, and drove out the inmates, forcing them to seek room in the other dormitories which were already overflowing. The most important Jewish festival, Yom Kippur, occurred while the convoy was on its way to Istanbul. For the last meal before the fast, Kronberger had a thin slice of bread, a small piece of sausage and a glass of unsweetened tea distributed to the passengers. The children, who were not obliged to fast, received in addition, a spoonful of marmalade which had been thinned with water to last them through the festival. The passengers gathered for prayers on the foredeck. They suffered from seasickness which was even more uncomfortable because of their empty stomachs.

When the Day of Atonement was over, they broke their fast on a glass of tea, two small salted potatoes and a paper-thin slice of bread. The next day, the transport management distributed half a loaf of bread among eight passengers. This was naturally far too little to even partially appease their rumbling stomachs, but was nevertheless considered a large ration. Kronberger had decided on its distribution because he assumed that the "Milos" would receive sufficient provisions in Istanbul.

Albert Wachsmann, accompanied by Dr. Rosenfeld, went to the captain once again to ask him to anchor in the port in order to take on food and water. Wachsmann did not have any foreign currency with which to finance the purchase of provisions and coal for the ship, but relied upon making contact with the "Joint." He also wished to take on board the mail which had presumably arrived in the meantime. Captain George received the two leaders amicably, prepared coffee for them and offered Greek cigarettes. His anger had vanished, and a friendly helpfulness had taken its place.

The port and town of Istanbul were a wonderful sight. Steamers, yachts and sailing-ships and boats rocked up and down on the waves. The sun smiled down from a blue sky.

The "Milos" approached the harbor. The passengers crowded by the railing. They nursed the hope that they would be able to anchor there for a few hours, eat their fill and recover a little from the journey. Everyone watched tensely as a Turkish police boat approached them. Captain George called through a megaphone that he wished to fill up with water, coal and bread in the port.

"We do not permit you to land. Move on, move on," the Turk called back. The boat turned back towards the harbor, and the "Milos" sailed slowly on. When they reached the Straits of the Dardanelles, a pilot guided the ship through and told the captain of the German invasion of Rumania. The news spread like wildfire on board the ship. For a few moments, the gnawing hunger was forgotten. It had given way to a paralyzing fear.

At sunrise, the "Milos" was off Gallipoli. The convoy members assembled on the deck. Kronberger ordered the entire security service to form up in ranks. A blue and white flag was hoisted. Wachsmann, Lea Adler and Kerner stood beside the captain.

"Over there is Gallipoli," the captain said, pointing to a settlement which loomed out of the haze on the sandy shore. Apart from the ships anchored in the Bosphorus, they had seen no other steamer.

The "Pacific" and the "Atlantic" had left days before them. As there were no radio or telegraph links between the ships (they had no transmitters, of course), the passengers on the "Milos" knew nothing of how the other two steamers were faring on their journey to the coast of Palestine.

The world had other worries than the fate of the three ships. Diplomats and statesmen had to study Chancellor Hitler's speeches down to the last detail. Not one word of his pearls of wisdom might escape them. Where were they to find time to consider the groaning of people who were breathing their last, exhausted by hunger, despair and hoplessness? Both on the "Atlantic" and the "Pacific," death was claiming many victims.

The ships were not far from land, but were not allowed to put in at any harbor. The survivors had been denied bread, water and coal in Istanbul. It was too great a bother for the Turkish authorities to grant a grave to those who had died during the journey. No country or government was prepared to allow the bodies to be brought to land. A large convoy travelling under inhuman conditions in the middle of a war, a ship upon which people died, could cause an epidemic in the port.

It was the second half of October. During the day it was still quite warm. It was incredibly crowded on all three steamers. There was no cool room, as on modern passenger steamers, which might be turned into a morgue. The coast of Palestine was still far away. Those who had died were stateless — and certainly not citizens of the British Mandate in Palestine. They had been on the point of illegally reaching the land of their desire. There was no alternative but to wrap the corpses in sacks, tie a few pieces of iron to the feet, and let them sink to the bottom of the sea. Even the small linen sack with earth from Palestine — which is given to every dead person so that he can rest at least symbolically in the holy earth — was denied to them. Nearly every day, one of the steamers slowed down and stopped briefly in order to consign a body to the waves. On some days, the "Atlantic" even stopped twice in order to unload its sad burdens.

The "Milos" had so far not had to record a single death. The health situation on board was quite satisfactory, thanks to the well-organized medical service. The doctors had operated on an inflammation of the middle ear with excellent results. A second-degree burn was healing well. Only Mr. Nestler, whose heart condition had considerably worsened during the journey, gave the doctors cause for concern. His wife was constantly by his sick bed. She had been allotted a stretcher to sleep on in the wooden hut which passed for a hospital. The doctors hoped to be able to nurse Mr. Nestler, who was gravely ill, until they reached Palestine, but knew that his days were numbered. The hospital was not completely full. There were a few patients among the passengers, but all of them could sleep on their own pallets. It was not necessary to hospitalize them.

The "Milos" sailed towards Greece at a speed varying between four and six knots. Captain George kept the ship fairly near to the coast, as the scanty coal reserves were fast running out. He was worried by the fact that the water was still penetrating through the badly-repaired leak. The pumps worked for hours on end in order to keep the sleeping quarters in the hold dry. It was quite impossible to venture into the open sea under such conditions.

The last provisions had been used up. The only supplies left consisted of rock-hard ship's biscuits which were beginning to go mouldy. The journey had already lasted for nearly six weeks, and during the entire period, the passengers had received neither fresh vegetables nor fruit. They were happy if they could even tolerably satisfy their hunger with beans and bread. Now the bread was also gone. The first signs of malnutrition became apparent. The water tanks were empty. Only the reserve tank on the foredeck still contained some forty liters of water reserved for children and patients. It was guarded by a sentry. The convoy management's cigarette reserves were also almost completely used up. Only the night watch received one cigarette among six men. Before the men began their guard duty, they sat down side by side on the plank beds, and each of them received one puff of the precious delicacy.

***

A storm sprang up off the island of Lesbos. The "Milos" danced like a nut shell on the high waves. The hull groaned. The storm wind blew across the deck, tore up a wooden plank and whirled it into the roaring sea. There were anxious moments while hissing waves of foam flooded the deck. Captain George maneuvered the "Milos," his hand firmly on the rudder and his eyes fixed on the wild, stormy sea. His passengers held on desperately in order not to be flung into the sea by the breakers. To port, the raging of the elements seemed somewhat weaker, and the passengers sought that side of the ship. Whoever had any strength at all came up from the sleeping quarters on deck. Men and women suffering

188

from seasickness lay groaning on the floor in the narrow, airless gangways. As the luggage had, due to the heavy swell, also slid to port, the freighter threatened to capsize. A Greek sailor — the only one who knew something about steering and who therefore relieved the captain sometimes when the latter slept for a short while in the cabin, stood on the bridge, cupped his hands to his mouth and called:

"Alles pipel ondre side, bitte."

His voice was so powerful that it drowned the raging of the sea.

The passengers heard him and saw him gesticulating and pointing to starboard. They understood his jumbled orders and obeyed. The "Milos" righted itself, but the next moment heeled over to starboard. Once again, the Greek called out, pointing in the opposite direction,

"Alles pipel ondre side, bitte."

The passengers went back and forth. In their distress, they looked up to the Greek and followed his orders each time he gave them. Indeed, they even took up his cry so that it should be heard all over the ship.

Captain George battled his way through to the entrance to the bay of Sigris. Although here, too, the waves rose as high as a house, they did not have the same crushing force as in the ocean. Slowly, the "Milos" approached a poor little fishing port, which emerged from behind a bare hill.

Sigris was not equipped to receive ocean steamers. Ships with even the smallest draught could not come as far as the harbor — if one could call this small stone house and two storehouses a harbor. The captain therefore had no choice but to cast anchor in the bay, where he was at least protected from the sea's wildest onslaughts.

A rowboat approached them from Sigris. It rose up upon a mountaineous wave, plunged down into the valley, hovered on a crest of foam and sank back once again. Wave upon wave bore down upon the boat. Up and down like a ball on the waves, it gradually fought its way nearer. For a moment, it seemed to stand high above the "Milos"; the next moment it was far below it. Conversation took place through a megaphone. The boat could not venture any nearer — it would have been dashed to pieces on the steamer's hull.

Captain George shouted that he wanted to wait in the bay of Sigris until the storm died down, asked if he could obtain bread and water when the storm had abated, and also requested that the port authorities in Athens be informed of the ship's arrival. The man in the boat gave him to understand that Sigris had neither bread nor water, as the storm, which had cut all telephone lines, had also made it impossible to deliver supplies. For lack of any alternative, the captain decided to spend the night in the bay. At dawn, if the storm let up, he would continue sailing towards Piraeus.

No food was distributed on board the "Milos." Tea could not be made due to the water shortage. The children were handed five candies each. They sucked them longingly and forgot their hunger.

Dusk fell. Only a few lighted huts were visible in Sigris. The Greek inhabitants of the island sat inside by their wretched petrol lamps. In the twilight, it seemed as though the small houses had huddled close together. The islanders were afraid of the storm, and the next days when it would be decided whether or not the island would become a battlefield.

The "Milos" lay at anchor, protected from the storm by a rock which jutted out into the sea. The wind whistled and howled in every key. Captain George came down from the chart room in order to inspect the engines, and met the convoy leader on the way. Wachsmann wanted to apologize because the captain had not been served any supper.

"We men will survive. So long as I have my cigarettes, it'll be all right. But it's very difficult for the children," said Captain George.

The storm abated somewhat during the night. Although the wind still howled and the "Milos" tore at her anchor, the waves no longer rose as high as the deck.

Hungry and shivering with cold, the convoy members lay down to sleep. Those suffering from seasickness were exhausted but could not sleep. The "Milos" groaned and creaked. A plank which had come loose fell down on the deck with a crash. A dim lamp burned in the chart room. The captain had decided to spend the night there. Altmann had the second watch amidships. He had been told to listen to the sound of the pumps and to report any change instantly. There was a brief pause in the storm. An uncanny silence reigned for a few seconds.

Altmann listened, held his breath, strained his ears. There was no sound from the pumps. Before the next gust of wind swept over the "Milos," Altmann had already hurried down the spiral staircase. He bumped into Kerner at the door to the sleeping quarters.

They woke up Gruber. The latter climbed quickly on deck and disappeared the next moment into the engine room.

"If that had happened to us in the open sea . . ." Altmann said significantly. Kerner was on the point of sending him back to the cabin to lie down and remain alone on deck when the pumps suddenly started up again, stopped, started, stalled, began to work again, irregularly at first, and finally started to pump regularly.

Due to the lack of food on board the ship, the captain decided to attempt to leave the bay. Once he had sailed out, however, he saw with his practised sailor's eye that he would not be able to prevail against the foaming sea in such a dilapidated freighter. He grabbed the rudder, turned the ship despite the enormous pressure from the waves which caught it for a moment broadside on, sailed back into the bay and cast anchor once again.

The brief quarter of an hour which the attempt had lasted brought on a new attack of seasickness for most of the passengers. Eliezer Hirsch took care of Magda who was suffering badly, until he too dashed up on deck and vomited. Lea and Joseph Kohn helped the children, holding them tight by their lifebelts while they leaned over the railings and vomited into the sea so as not to soil the deck.

Nestler, who was critically ill, suffered terribly. The doctors, who were themselves frail and weak, did their best. Mrs. Nestler wrung her hands in despair. Fritz Hartmann lay groaning next to Gruber. Kronberger tottered across the deck. Even Albert Wachsmann, who tried to maintain his composure, lay wanly in his cabin.

Three days had passed since the last meal. People's tongues, irritated by the salty tang of the sea, stuck to their palates. Their lips were cracked due to the raw air. The rolling motion of the ship, combined with the feeling of imminent danger, had forced even the strongest men to their knees.

As they could not count on obtaining food supplies in the small harbor of Sigris, Captain George steered the ship out of the bay as soon as the storm had let up a little. The "Milos" rolled and pitched in the sea which was still very rough. Whoever had any strength left came up on deck for a breath of air. The vapors in the cabins made even those vomit who had so far withstood seasickness. Whenever the ship lay at an angle in the water, the Greek sailor's accustomed cry came from the bridge:

"Alles pipel ondre side, bitte."

After some hours, the "Milos" approached Athens. The harbor entrance to Piraeus was blocked by mines. Captain George hooted with his siren in order to obtain the services of a pilot to guide the ship through the barricade. There was no answer from the port, and no pilot appeared. The wind increased again. The waves grew higher, and the captain cast anchor. It became darker. The storm and the heavy waves grew more violent. The sirens wailed — short, long, short — and repeated the signal without pause. Finally, a tug arrived which towed the "Milos" to the bay of Salamis. They were not permitted to enter Piraeus harbor as the Greeks had already taken every precaution to ensure against a surprise attack by the Italians. The town and the port were already blacked out. It was the fourth night without food and the passengers were forced to eat the last ship's biscuits which they had previously rejected as inedible. The chocolate which the captain had donated to the children was already used up. Everyone's teeth had suffered from the lack of vitamins; they broke through chewing on the hard biscuits.

It was extremely difficult to maintain the watch that night. The men had to be relieved after only two hours. Fortunately, the bad weather cleared towards dawn. The sky was again studded with stars. At the first glimmer of light, the "Milos" sailed, making for the little fishing harbor of Laurion.

Seventeen-year-old Joseph Kohn was put on temporary guard duty by the water tank. He had already been standing there for four hours, and the time had come for him to be relieved. Kerner came up to him to request that he be patient for a little while longer. If there were no one else, then Kerner himself would take over.

"Give me a biscuit," begged the boy.

"I'm sorry but I don't have any more," replied Kerner.

"A cigarette then," Kohn begged.

"The captain shared his last one with me yesterday. We're cleaned out," was Kerner's explanation.

"Well, I'll have to make do without," replied the youth who was not much more than a child, and who remained at his post.

***

The blue sky of Greece was arched like a dome over a calm sea. After the storm, the air was clear and cool. In the morning sun, the "Milos" approached the port of Laurion. The yellow epidemic flag was hoisted on the mast.

The hoisting of the flag was a ruse planned by Captain George to bring the port doctor on board and induce him to help the starving passengers. There had not, in fact, been a single case of infectious illness on board.

Captain George blew the sirens in order to attract the attention of the port authorities. He came out of the chart room and scanned the port with his binoculars until he sighted a boat quickly approaching them. Now the vessel was already visible to the naked eye. Joseph Kohn had noticed it from his perch high up on the mast.

"A boat's coming," he called out joyfully.

The cry put new life into the feeble convoy members. Many rose from their pallets and went to the railing. Albert Wachsmann, who was pale and tired, came slowly up the iron steps to the bridge.

Meanwhile, the motorboat drew up beside the "Milos." Two Greek officers came on board. Captain George went to meet them. They greeted one another like old friends. Albert Wachsmann received permission to go on land in order to telegraph the representative of the "Joint" in Athens.

The prospect of receiving bread and water worked like a charm on the passengers, giving them strength and confidence.

"A launch is coming towards us from Laurion," called Altmann from the roof of the chart room.

Upon closer inspection, the vessel proved to be a tanker. It drew up alongside the "Milos." A rubber hose was handed across, and the tanker's pumps began to work. Every available water container was filled and taken to the passengers. Mothers brought water to their children, allowing them to drink only slowly. Ernst Hartmann drained his water bottle in one gulp. Shortly after one o'clock, a sail-boat brought nine hundred loaves of bread and baskets of grapes. A little rest, bright sunshine, bread, grapes, fresh drinking water and the additional prospect of receiving a large meal produced a quick and remarkable improvement in the passengers' condition. For the first time since the beginning of the journey, people had behaved humanely towards them. Poor Greece, herself on the brink of precarious military entanglements, gave the "Milos" permission to enter the port of Laurion. Water was boiled in the large cooking pots which had not been used since Tulcea. The second ration of bread was divided for distribution.

Ernst Hartmann came with his mother. The latter lifted the lid of'one of the pots as though she were in the kitchen of her Viennese hotel. A delicious aroma of roasted onions and cooking meat floated over the deck, tickling the nostrils of the sniffing passengers who were waiting in almost devout expectation for their meal.

Chapter Seventeen

The Greeks behaved very humanely towards the refugees. Mr. Levy, the representative of the "Joint," ensured that large supplies of food would be available. Only coal could not be obtained from the Greeks. They themselves had only scanty reserves and these could not be given away when they were mobilizing for war. The "Milos" therefore sailed on very slowly, and was forced to use its scanty and inferior supplies of coal very sparingly.

In the afternoon, as they approached the island of Crete, a thin column of smoke appeared on the horizon. A ship came into view, steering the same course as the "Milos," and seemed, like the latter, to be making only slow progress. People had assembled on the deck of the ship. Light grey smoke rose from the chimney of the approaching freighter. They had met up with the "Atlantic," whose coal supplies were already used up and which was breaking up the wooden bunks on board in order to reach Crete. The port of Candia permitted both ships to anchor as dusk fell.

Mr. Levy had already given instructions from Athens to supply both freighters with food and water. During the loading, which took place in the darkness, the sound of march tunes could be heard from the town. Flickering lights illuminated the walls of the houses. A torch-light procession was moving through the streets of Candia. It was the last march by the worthy Greeks for years to come.

From the moment Albert Wachsmann had learnt of the ultimatum presented by Mussolini to Greece, he had been uneasy, pressing the captain to continue the journey, and not granting the convoy members the break which they so badly needed after the privations they had suffered. He was in a hurry to reach British territorial waters, although he was well aware of what an illegal convoy might expect from the British. Until then, they had met only a few ships and had not yet caught a glimpse of the British flag, ensign of the world's greatest naval power.

Dawn had hardly broken when the "Milos" sailed out into the

open sea. The "Atlantic" followed, but was soon lost to sight due to the snail's pace at which it progressed. At a speed of six knots an hour — more could not be squeezed out of the engines — the "Milos" steamed away.

The stokers at the boilers worked until thick, black drops of sweat covered their naked torsos. They were relieved by volunteers from among the convoy members. Wachsmann roused everyone to even greater efforts. The ship fled from the appalling fate which was likely to engulf Greece at any moment.

***

Nestler's condition had deteriorated greatly in Laurion, despite all the doctors' efforts. After the ship's departure from Candia, the final struggle began. The entrance to the hospital was blocked in order to prevent any noise penetrating to the dying man. Mrs. Nestler was quite helpless. She lay under Lea's supervision in an armchair which had been brought with them from the "Melk," in the cabin which was reserved for doctors on night duty.

The murmur of prayers from religious Jews came from behind the wooden partition where the dying man lay. Every time Mr. Nestler breathed, they repeated the confession of faith, with which Jews have breathed their last through the ages and which a person on his deathbed repeats so long as he is conscious. Towards eleven o'clock, the prayers suddenly stopped. The wooden door was opened. Nestler was dead. The death certificate was drawn up by the doctors and signed by Wachsmann and the captain.

A stretcher amidships, bearing the body of the dead man shrouded in a sack, iron weights at the feet — the entire length covered by a black cloth. Four members of the security service in grey wind-cheaters, with blue and white armbands on the sleeves, formed the guard of honor. The "Milos" slowed down. The deck filled with people. They formed up in groups, like a military funeral cortege. Eliezer Hirsch put his own blue and white armband on the bier. Mrs. Nestler tottered out of the hospital, supported by Kronberger and Gruber. A prayer leader from a small, remote Polish community intoned the prayer for the dead. The engines stopped and the "Milos" stood still.

The corpse was tipped into the sea from the stretcher. For a brief moment, the blue and white armband floated on the waves.

Then the iron weights pulled the corpse quickly under.

The engines started up again. The ship continued to steer towards Cyprus. The deck emptied.

Wachsmann remained looking at the sea for along time, as though he wished to imprint the spot on his memory.

***

Although Wachsmann wanted to reach the British crown colony of Cyprus as quickly as possible so as not to be the target of a possible attack at sea, the captain did not comply with his request. Cyprus could no longer be reached before nightfall. The captain had no wish to stumble upon the minefields anchored before every port, which were hardly visible even by day, and in the darkness meant certain destruction. He preferred to cruise near the island during the night, and to enter Limasol only in the morning.

The approaching meeting with the English formed the chief topic of conversation that evening. Many of the passengers considered it a mistake to dock in Cyprus and, so to speak, run straight into the lion's jaws. They felt that it would be better to avoid the British, make for the coast of Palestine, and disembark somewhere in the dark. They cited the example of the "Parita" whose passengers had succeeded in wading onto the beach at Tel Aviv. The electricity network had been cut by saboteurs, and the whole town was in darkness. They laughed at the Palestine Police who had then occupied an empty freighter, wishing to force it to turn back to Greece. The captain, crew and passengers had, however, vanished without trace. Only the "Parita" remained floating there, month after month, half-submerged — a dangerous wreck which nearly caused the death of many a careless swimmer.

They told the story of another ship carrying a Viennese convoy, which had landed in Netanya and whose illegal passengers had hidden in kibbutzim and settlements until the police had given up the search for them. Kronberger, who greatly regretted the fact that the equipment which they had brought with them would be lost through such a landing, organized groups to break up the ship which, in his opinion, could only put the convoy members ashore in some very out-of-the-way spot. Although the plans were romantic, aggressive and ingenious, they had only one drawback which made them impractical: the "Parita"'s tactics of 1938 were no longer feasible in 1940. Now Great Britain was at war — the most important war in her history. Palestine was under a British Mandate, and its coast consequently well guarded. Kronberger's friends, who were prepared for everything, forgot yet another factor: the "Milos"'s coal supplies would no longer suffice for it to reach the coast of Palestine, for it, too, had already begun to burn wood for fuel. On the morning of October 27, a British patrol boat opened the mine barrier in front of Limasol, and the "Milos" passed through. The barrier closed behind it. Slowly the ship pushed on towards the jetty and was made fast with flimsy ropes. It had used up the last of its strength to reach this destination.

***

When Wachsmann saw a British naval officer coming on board, he could observe simply from the way the man walked that they would not be received with the same friendliness as in Laurion. Captain George found the man who had stepped onto the bridge very unsympathetic. The latter returned his greeting very perfunctorily, and made no move to shake hands with him. Upon being questioned, the captain stated that he wished to sail the ship through the Suez Canal to the Indian Ocean, but had been forced to change his route and dock in Limasol due to lack of coal.

The officer looked suspiciously at the captain, but did not enter into particulars about the ship's destination. He refused to give the captain a permit to go ashore onto the island which was predominantly inhabited by Greeks, but promised him that he would transmit his request for coal to the port captain in Limasol. He left without sparing a glance for the passengers who were gazing at him curiously.

A British warship lay in the harbor like a threatening steel colossus. An Egyptian vessel unloaded bales of cotton. The "Milos" lay completely isolated from the other ships. It was guarded by sentries. It was a warm, clear day, the sea was calm, the sky a friendly blue. Two youths undressed, climbed down the gangway and plunged into the water near the ship. They snatched at a turquoise jelly-fish, and invited their friends to join them in a refreshing bath. Before people could prepare to follow their example however, the British forbade bathing on the grounds that sharks had been sighted near the harbor.

A reporter from the "Cyprus Post," who had come on board together with the naval officer, collected letters for mailing on shore. At the same time, the Cypriot police headquarters radioed a message to the Palestine Police. The British police commander in Cyprus informed the British police commander in Palestine of the arrival of an illegal convoy. Mr. Levy's powers reached as far as Cyprus and the convoy was furnished with all essential commodities. Only coal — the most import commodity of all — could not be supplied by Mr. Levy.

A reporter is a useful person even when a suspicious officer is breathing down his neck and he is consequently unable to practise his profession in peace. If he possesses a sensitive heart, he becomes an indispensible aide, even when working for a government newspaper.

The reporter hunted Wachsmann up in order to ask him about the convoy's experiences during the journey. The "Cyprus Post" took a special interest in the "Milos" convoy.

The "Milos," which reached Limasol on October 27, was the last of the three refugee ships to arrive from Greece.

On October 27, the Italians declared war on Greece and on the same day, Italian and German aeroplanes bombed Athens. When Wachsmann learned from the reporter that Italy had already been at war with Greece for some hours, a cold shudder passed through him. He realized that with a delay of only twenty-four hours, the entire convoy would have been in the operational range of Italian and German bombers, and he could easily imagine what a terrible end that could have meant for them all.

The reporter could not obtain much information from Wachsmann who was extremely worried. He and his entire convoy — who had just escaped certain destruction — were on a freighter without any coal in a British port which might well be the target of air raids.

The British officer had not moved from the reporter's side, and paid close attention to the conversation between him and the leader of the convoy. When Wachsmann began to speak about the lack of coal, the officer remarked that he had transmitted the request for coal to the port commander and received the reply that the coal could be delivered immediately against payment in sterling or dollars.

Albert Wachsmann did not possess these currencies. From

199

where could he have obtained them? Mr. Storfer, the commercial adviser, who should have handed over foreign currency to him, had not appeared when the "Milos" sailed from Tulcea; indeed, nothing more had been heard from him. Wachsmann was thus forced to refuse the offer.

"We are prepared to accept gold in payment for the coal. We shall reckon it at the full exchange value," the officer said dispassionately.

"We have neither money nor gold. We are refugees. It would be an act of simple kindness to enable us to continue our journey," Wachsmann said in an effort to move the officer.

The Englishman was, however, in the first place a tradesman.

"If you pay, you can take the coal on board immediately," replied the officer. No one had noticed that the reporter had taken down this conversation as well.

The reporter surveyed the ship together with the officer, spoke to the children, and noted down with horror the reports of the former internees in Buchenwald concentration camp who showed him the numbers tatooed on their forearms. Before reaching Cyprus, the men had not breathed a word about their experiences in Buchenwald. Now, however, on British territory, they felt secure. The arm of the Gestapo did not reach to Cyprus.

The news of Italy's declaration of war on Greece spread quickly on board the "Milos." One convoy member shouted it to another. Everyone was aware of the peril they had escaped, and were prepared, one and all, to sacrifice the last of their possessions in order to continue their journey and leave Cyprus which lay so close to Greece.

Wachsmann, who cherished the same desire, exploited the mood of the passengers in order to procure the wherewithal to buy coal.

Before supper was distributed, he went through the ship, requesting that wedding rings be given to the convoy management.

After supper, there was silence on board. The harbor buildings and anchored ships lay in darkness. Two searchlights scoured the skies. The bright streaks approached one another, crossed and glided apart again.

The delivery of the valuables which constituted the last remnant of the convoy-members' property and which also possessed great sentimental value for everyone, progressed in perfect calm and order. Not half the convoy members had yet given up their rings when the English officer appeared unexpectedly on board and asked to speak to the convoy leader.

"Your coal was paid for at the port authorities over an hour ago. You may collect it if you wish," the officer stated.

To Wachsmann's astonished question concerning their benefactor's identity, the officer replied that he could give no information.

Quite some time elapsed before the "Milos" arrived at the coal dumps. The captain was very satisfied. The "Milos" was loaded with English bituminous coal, and returned to its former anchorage.

It took far longer to give back the wedding rings than it had taken to collect them. People seemed to be in no hurry at all to retrieve their possessions.

In the afternoon, the water tank was filled. The reporter from the "Cyprus Post" came on board for a few moments. He reported that a Jewish shopkeeper from Limasol had paid for the coal on learning of the refugees' plight.

"Give us the donor's name so that we can thank him," Wachsmann said.

"The gentleman wishes to remain anonymous. He told me that it was his duty to help Jews who wanted to go to Palestine," was all the information that the reporter would supply.

The reporter paused and then he added, "You will still have difficulties, but the worst is definitely behind you. I wish you a good journey."

He said goodbye to Wachsmann and left the ship.

The "Milos" remained in port for another two days. It still had no permit to sail.

Some said that the security situation looked very threatening. Others were of the opinion that the convoy's reception by the Palestine Police had not yet been sufficiently well prepared.

There was no longer any lack of food on board. There were plentiful supplies of drinking water, and the weather was very favorable. The convoy members began to recover and to even feel a sense of optimism.

Chapter Eighteen

Sky and water appeared on the horizon for as far as the eye could see. The sea was calm. Not a single column of smoke was visible to indicate the presence of another steamer in the vicinity. The "Atlantic" and "Pacific" had not been seen any more. It was assumed that they were already far ahead of the "Milos," perhaps had already even reached the port of Haifa. The superior English coal which it had received in Cyprus enabled the "Milos" to travel at a speed of eight knots. The leak had been repaired in a makeshift manner and hardly any water penetrated when the sea was calm. Nevertheless, the sleeping quarters deep down in the hold were still constantly wet.

The look-out posted on the roof kept watch. He searched the horizon in the direction which the captain had indicated. At any moment, he expected the coast of Palestine to emerge from the sea.

Kronberger secretly cherished the hope that it would be possible to land the "Milos" unnoticed on the coast and disappear with the passengers.

"Boat in sight — heading towards us," Eliezer reported. Nothing had yet been seen of the English fleet. The boat came nearer and could now be seen clearly with the naked eye. The passengers assembled on the deck observed it carefully. They thought it was a fishing boat. The sound of a motor could be heard. The vessel held the same course as the "Milos," and overshot it by a ship's length. A shot was fired from a rocket, and a curt command rang out through a megaphone. The "Milos" stopped and the boat came alongside.

An officer and six Englishmen came aboard. Kronberger, Gruber and Dr. Rosenfeld hurried up the steps to the bridge. The British officer followed them with two of his men.

Captain George waited for the Englishman together with the three convoy members.

202

The naval officer came up to the captain. He did not greet him. "Make for Haifa," he commanded.

The passengers looked at one another. No one spoke. Wachsmann looked out to sea through the porthole. He still seemed to be waiting for the British fleet. The motorboat separated from the "Milos" after the boarding party had embarked on the "Milos." A machine gun appeared which had so far been hidden from sight. It was aimed at the freighter. A narrow strip of coast emerged from the sea. The mountains only gradually became recognizable. The ship was near Ras el Nakura (today Rosh Hanikra). The British had captured the boat immediately upon its arrival in the territorial waters of the Holy Land.

The officer turned to the members of the convoy management, calmly lit a cigarette, and asked in faultless German:

"Gentlemen, which of you is Albert Wachsmann?"

"I am," answered Albert, taking a step forward.

"You are the leader of this convoy, You have eight hundred illegal emigrants from Bohemia and Moravia on board," proclaimed the officer.

"We have 883 Jews who have escaped from Hitler. I am, as you have correctly remarked, leader of this convoy. But kindly tell us how you know."

"We already expected you the day before yesterday. We were informed about you before you began your journey. Our Secret Service would be in a sorry state if we didn't know about such a trifle in good time," the officer replied offhandedly.

***

At one p.m. on November 3, twenty-four hours after the twenty-third anniversary of the Balfour Declaration, the "Milos" passed through the mine barricade into the port of Haifa. Oil tankers, freighters, fishing boats, destroyers, and troop carriers were anchored in the harbor. Barges and motorboats, ferries and customs cutters enlivened the picturesque bay. In the middle of the wet dock, at some distance form the other ships, lay the "Pacific." Its passengers were crowded together by the railing. They waved and called to the "Milos" as it slowly passed. A blue and white flag was hoisted on a pole on the "Pacific"'s bridge. Answering cries came from the deck of the "Milos." A blue and white flag fluttered on the roof of the chart room. A thunderous rendering of the "Hatikva" rose from both ships to the heavens. The British forbade the singing of the anthem and ordered the flag on the "Milos" to be taken down.

At one thirty p.m. on November 3, the anchor chain rattled into place. The "Milos" lay isolated in the middle of the harbor. A motorboat drew up alongside. Policemen relieved the boarding party who sped away in a boat towards the city.

Men embraced. Mothers hoisted their little ones on their shoulders.

"Eretz Israel, our country!" they shouted.

Groups of young people, religious men, women, the doctors in their white gowns, Kronberger, the entire security service, the nurses, even Wachsmann, who only held himnself upright with difficulty, joined hands in a long chain. They moved along the deck, their feet stamping out the rhythmical beat of the hora.

They sang the song of King David.

"David meleh Yisrael hai ve-kayam."

Faster and faster they sang, faster and faster the feet stamped on the deck.

Captain George, in a beautifully-cut Greek merchant-navy uniform, came up on deck. The children encircled him, dancing joyfully.

"David meleh Yisrael hai ve-kayam."

A girl of scarcely twelve, who moved with elfin grace and had seemingly been born to dance, seized the captain by the hand. A boy made room for him in the line.

Captain George danced with them, singing the Hebrew song with a somewhat peculiar intonation.

The Greek sailors came up on deck from the engine room. They had put on their best clothes. The hard labor of shovelling coal was finished. They had reached port. They joined the dancers.

An old man, led by a boy who might have been his grandchild, stood at the bottom of the staircase leading up to the bridge. Tears of joy and emotion stood in his eyes.

"This is Eretz Israel, promised to us as an eternal possession. We have come home, my child, we have come home!" he intoned.

The door to the security service's sleeping quarters stood wide open. The black-lacquered wooden truncheons hung in a row, knocking gently against one another. The room was overflowing with people. They sat on the upper bunks with their legs dangling,

204

rocking from side to side to the song of a mouth organ. The whole ship was gripped by an intoxicating joy. The convoy was in port, only a few hundred yards from the coast of the land which was so dear to them. The misery and privations which they had suffered, the dangers they had escaped, were forgotten. The faces of the convoy members were radiant. Was it a reflection of the sun which shone down on them out of a friendly blue sky and gilded the ship's small, dirty portholes? Was it a reflection of the longing of the people who had received this narrow strip of coast from its God as an eternal possession, or was it only the sigh of relief of victims of persecution, outlaws, who had finally reached the light after languishing in a darkness which had threatened to engulf them?

What did it matter if an English boarding party had seized the ship, and boats from the Palestine Police controlled the bay? Palestine, Eretz Israel was no longer a Utopian dream, a pious legend. It actually lay before them. It was close, tangible, no fairy tale. The bay, the coast, the town, the Carmel lit up by God's sun, this was the fulfillment of a thousand-year-old wish, the answer to a prayer.

"Rebuild Your city Jerusalem speedily in our days." This was the Holy Land, liberty, their homeland, salvation and redemption.

Groups of people stood on the deck. Many had placed their luggage next to them, waiting for permission to land. The "Milos" had already lain at anchor for more than four hours. A police boat circled both ships in a wide arc. There was no trace of a landing permit.

The policemen on board the "Milos" had stated that there was no question of landing yet. Albert Wachsmann decided that it would be correct to inform the convoy members of the difficulties still facing them.

On November 3, 1940, exactly twenty-three years and one day after the publication of the Balfour Declaration which gave the Jews the right to return to the land of their fathers, the very same government which had issued the Declaration forced the Jews to wait outside the gates, keeping them and their wives and children crowded together on a ship under conditions which made a mockery out of any form of civilization. Despite the devoted labor of the doctors and nurses, the number of cases of sickness among the children increased rapidly. Crammed into a tiny area like a herd of cattle, without any sort of sanitary installations, deprived for weeks on end of the possibility of leading an existence befitting human beings, they now stood at the gates of their homeland. The country was closed to them, however, due to the White Paper, which prohibited immigration in such large numbers. The refugees from Hitler's bestiality thus had no alternative but to succumb or to break the barricade. The groups on deck stood undecided for a long time, debating and giving vent to their emotions.

A few religious people had gathered round Aron Tennenbaum, prepared to be the first to land. Tennenbaum, who held a Torah Scroll gently pressed against his heart, ran the fingers of his left hand caressingly over the red velvet cover of the scroll which was the only thing he had brought with him from Europe. His wife, his children, the entire community which he had led in prayer had been murdered by the Germans when they marched into Poland. He alone had succeeded in escaping from the burning prayer-house which collapsed behind him in flames and dense smoke. The sun set in the sea behind dark clouds. The edge of the bank of clouds glowed with gold and purple tints. The Holy Land greeted its returning children with the splendor of the sunset.

The solemn mood was disturbed by the chug of engines from the police boat which circled the "Milos" and "Pacific" without pause.

A man who had been interned in Buchenwald concentration camp, one of the group who had been escorted onto the "Melk" by the Gestapo in Vienna, asked, "Will we be sent back to Europe?"

"But that's quite impossible!" someone called out.

"Why don't they allow us to land? Haven't we suffered enough already?" another refugee intoned.

The town, the harbor and all the ships anchored in it were unlighted. The enemy had come considerably closer through his attack on Greece. The harbor, and particularly the oil refinery, might be targets for air raids. Just before the two ships had arrived, an enemy squadron of bombers had destroyed an oil tank. A blackout had been decreed for the whole country. The half moon rose over the "Milos" like a slice of ripe melon. Dr. Bieber went into the makeshift wooden hospital. Four children had just been admitted with aching necks. An exact diagnosis had not yet been made. He went into the room which was reserved for doctors on night duty. The nurse had been instructed to report to him immediately if any of the young patients showed signs of difficulty in breathing. A motorboat circled the two ships. Searchlights scoured the sky.

The arrival of the refugee ships threw the whole of Palestine into a tumult. The Jews pressed the British to respect the Balfour Declaration, the twenty-third anniversary of which had been celebrated on November 2. The Arabs, incited by the expelled Mufti of Jerusalem, celebrated November 2 as a day of mourning, as they did every year. The English felt that their peace had been disturbed by the arrival of the ships. As civilized people, they opposed Hitler's actions against the Jews. That Jews who had been persecuted by the Nazis dared, however, to come to Palestine, was an anathema to them. How could these Jews, at a moment when England was engaged in a life-and-death struggle with the Nazis, when London was being attacked by flying bombs, demand that one should give priority to their problems? The situation in Palestine itself was very precarious.

The Arabs, not only those living in Palestine, were flirting with the Nazis. They were waiting for Hitler to liberate them, that they might overwhelm Jewish settlements and towns, rob and plunder, beat men and rape women. The Jewish self-defense squads, which were rapidly gaining in strength, were more of an impediment to them than Britain which, as the leading Great Power, was responsible for maintaining calm and order in the territory under its mandate. The British had permitted the Jews to set up a settlement police which, although under British command, might nevertheless be employed to defend the Jewish population. This alone was cause enough for the Mufti's followers to hate England. They forgot completely that they, too, possessed a defense force in the Arab Legion which had been created to serve in East Jordan. Naturally the Arab Legion, too, was commanded by British officers. Abdullah, the Prince of the Hashemites and a good friend of the British, had been given fairly wide-reaching autonomous powers over the newly-created Emirate of Transjordan in East Jordan, and had received a British adviser as well as abundant financial help. The British High Commissioner in Jerusalem was the supreme authority for both Palestine and the Emirate of Transjordan.

England was in the process of erecting enormous military bases in the area so that she could repulse a possible Axis attack against the routes to her colonies. The bases could only be built along this strip of coastline — on this narrow piece of land joining Europe, Asia and Africa — for the other bordering countries proved themselves less reliable. Moreover, Palestine had the great advantage in that her civil population might be employed in this endeavor. There were sufficient Jewish skilled workers available to set up military workshops. It was simple to build up a bureaucracy staffed by Jews under the supervision of the British. The country's road network was good, the ports and oil refineries were active, and a rich supply of cheap auxiliary workers from among the poor Arab masses was available for the asking. The country was moving towards prosperity, and the British Mandate was of the opinion that everyone might benefit from it.

For more than a year, no illegal convoy had reached the coast of Palestine. Against the Jews' urging for larger immigration quotas, the British had replied that the country had only limited powers of economic absorption, and had quoted the reports, conclusions and opinions, which had been published in the White Paper, of English commissioners who had spent a few weeks in Palestine and had come to the exact conclusions which appeared appropriate for the British Mandate. The Jews had always fought the White Paper policy, since it deprived them of the possibility of developing the country by prohibiting the immigration of European Jews threatened with destruction by Hitler.

The Arabs, too, attacked the White Paper because, in their opinion, it made too many concessions to the Jews.

There was another, very small but powerful minority which was carrying on a furious propaganda campaign among the Arabs, inciting them against the Jews and the British, and which, although its presence was well-known to the government, was nevertheless permitted free and unrestricted movement in the country.

These were Germans who had already lived for decades in the "Walddorf" and "Wilhelma-Sarona" settlements founded by the German Order of the Knights Templar, and in German colonies in Haifa and Jerusalem. They had become prosperous, even rich. The nearer the war came, the louder Hitler shouted on the radio, the more these Germans tried to undermine law and order. They had abundant resources at their disposal for spreading Nazi propaganda. The German settlers waited faithfully in accordance with the Nazi slogan: "the Day is Nigh"; the Arabs waited for easy booty, and the Jews prepared to sell their lives as dearly as possible. The arrival of the ships in Haifa had given them hope that it might still be possible for small, daring groups to escape the

Nazis. They were determined to stop at nothing in their fight for the rights of the illegal immigrants. The British High Commissioner was inundated with demands from the Jewish authorities to allow the passengers to land. Spokesmen from Zionist organizations, rabbis, men of science, the entire Jewish press, highly-esteemed personalities, and the Jewish National Council intervened. Telegrams were sent to London, America and Canada and all parts of the world where Jews were living, asking for help, intervention and protests.

The High Commissioner did not issue a landing permit. The "Milos" and "Pacific" lay in the harbor, circled continuously by police boats. The arrival of the "Atlantic" had already been announced by the Cypriot police, and the ship was expected to dock shortly.

For two days, the Jews hoped that the High Commissioner would give them a positive answer. They assumed that he possessed a sensitive heart and would take pity on the desperate plight of men, women and children who had escaped death. Nevertheless he refused permission to land. The Jewish Agency intervened in London. England declined to allow Jewish refugees onto Palestinian soil.

The ships lay in port. The passengers knew nothing of what was happening on land. They were isolated and without news. A final decision as to what would happen to the convoy had not yet been made. The High Commissioner would have preferred to send the intruders back to their countries of origin. It was quite immaterial to him what would happen to them there. England was prepared to take the refugees to one of her colonies, and to grant them asylum there for the duration of the war. They would, of course, be interned in a detention camp, for there might well be German agents among them — a Fifth Column which might infiltrate into the British Empire. That the German colonists in Palestine already constituted an active and powerful Fifth Column completely escaped Britain's notice.

The Jews declined all these friendly offers. They could not comprehend the difficulties faced by the British, and only saw the new arrivals' distress and the death struggle of the Jews who had remained under Hitler's domination. The refugees must be able to land in Palestine. It was their human and historic right. The gates of the country must be opened for every Jew who might succeed in reaching Palestine.

The High Commissioner received instructions from the British government to make all the necessary preparations to deport the illegal immigrants. At the same time, an order went out to the British governor of the remote island of Mauritius to prepare the detention camp for the reception of four thousand Jews. The waves of protest which arose throughout all the Jewish settlements in Palestine were suppressed by the police.

The Jewish underground army was now compelled to act. The struggle had begun.

A boat brought provisions to the "Pacific." It was, of course, guarded by the police. Nevertheless, a laborer who was carrying crates onto the ship succeeded in making contact with the convoy management. The laborer was a member of the "Haganah," and had friends on board who also belonged to the "Haganah"'s underground army. The boat unloaded its freight and steered back towards port. The Englishman who had accompanied it had nothing to report. It had not occurred to him for one moment to set foot upon the dirty ship.

A small piece of paper was found in the mailbox of an engineer in Trumpeldor Street in Haifa. The man had emigrated from Vienna a few years earlier. The engineer's wife wracked her brains trying to deduce who might have written the note and how the slip of paper, which had no address on it, had arrived in her mailbox. The handwriting was quite unfamiliar to her. The message was very short.

"Am on the 'Milos.'" Underneath was the signature, "Erwin."

The woman remembered having heard the name mentioned once in a conversation between Leo and Fritz Hausner, two brothers who were living in her apartment as sub-tenants. She gave the note to Leo Hausner when he came home from work that evening. Leo immediately recognized the handwriting of his cousin from whom he had received no news since the outbreak of the war. He requested the woman to inform his brother that he would return home later that evening, and quickly left the apartment. He had already heard about the arrival of the ships. He had no time to consider how the note had reached him. As he also had arrived in the country as an illegal immigrant, he knew what conditions were like on board such ships. He also knew that he would not be able to speak to his cousin so long as the latter was on board the "Milos." The authorities' refusal to grant the boats permission to land was the topic of the day: everyone knew about it and condemned it indignantly.

Leo Hausner hurried to the office of the Jewish Agency. It was only there, at the immigration authorities, that he could hope to be able to do something for Erwin — perhaps to send him cigarettes and chocolate. There was feverish activity in the office. He had difficulty in making his way through the crowd of people standing in the corridor to the door of the immigration office. He began to argue with a man who refused to allow him inside.

"How can you know who's on the ship?" he was asked.

"My cousin is on the 'Milos.' I want to do something for him," said Leo excitedly.

"Until now, we've had no possibility of even making contact with the ships. The 'Milos' is strictly guarded, and is isolated in the middle of the harbor," the man explained to Leo.

The official was at least as excited as Leo. Leo played his trump card. He showed the official the slip of paper. "Here is my cousin's handwriting — he is on the 'Milos.'"

"Please come with me," said the official. "Just tell us your cousin's name and what you know about him. We shall do everything we can to contact him. We are very interested in knowing the number of people on board and their identity." He steered Leo through the door into the office.

Despite the efforts made by the Jewish Agency to obtain permission to send its immigration officers on board the ships or at least to be allowed to take over the provisioning of the convoys, the British authorities firmly refused, strengthened the guard on the harbor still further and themselves continued to supply the ships with food and drinking water. In order to deliver the food, however, the police had to make use of Arab and Jewish workers, as it would have been quite unthinkable to expect an Englishman to compete with the dock workers. They were the masters in the country — which in their eyes was no more than just another small colony in their world-wide empire — and their role was thus to command and to supervise. To have lifted a finger themselves would have meant a loss in prestige: lowering themselves to the level of the 'natives.' Under these circumstances, it was not too difficult for a Jewish worker to unobtrusively press a slip of paper for Kerner into Eliezer Hirsch's hand — the latter being easily distinguishable by his blue and white armband — while unloading sacks of bread onto the "Milos."

The message informed Kerner of the British decision to transfer the passengers on the illegal ships to the "Patria" in order to deport them. He was instructed to send a good swimmer under cover of darkness to inform them of the number of people on board the "Milos." Moreover, as soon as he would be transferred to the "Patria," he was to see if it would be possible to get inside the engine-room.

Kerner felt it advisable to immediately contact Albert Wachsmann. Albert, who was physically very run down, wanted to inform Kronberger, as he himself was temporarily in no position to be of any help.

The two men sat in the security service's sleeping quarters, reading the carefully-worded message through once again, and noted down the names of swimmers who might be suitable for transferring the required information. They called in candidates for the task one by one, inquired about their athletic achievements and then, in an apparently off-hand manner, if the young man would dare to swim ashore during the night. They finally chose a young sportsman who had won a number of prizes in the Bar Kochba swimming club in his native country, and recommended that he carefully imprint the picture of the harbor in his memory while it was still daylight so that he would be sure in which direction to swim when dusk fell.

Although the youth was known to be extremely reliable, Kronberger felt it important that he should now not come into contact with the other passengers, but should eat and then remain in Kerner's company until he started out.

The foredeck was empty during the distribution of the evening meal which took place somewhat earlier than usual. Dusk began to fall. A cable was made fast to the railing. Kronberger and Kerner stood blocking the swimmer with their backs to the deck in order to prevent curious eyes from seeing him as he quickly undressed. The youth let himself down the rope and plunged into the water. He was immediately swallowed up by the twilight. The cable was taken in. Kronberger and Kerner walked across the deck smoking. Eliezer Hirsch called to the passengers in the stern to collect their food.

Far out, almost at the end of the concrete jetty protected by huge boulders, lay the "Patria." A large motorboat, such as was used for round trips in the harbor, travelled back and forth between the "Pacific" and the "Patria." For three days, people on the "Milos" watched the transfer of the "Pacific"'s passengers onto the "Patria." On the third day, a police officer came on board the "Milos" in order to prepare for the transfer of its passengers.

"Where are you going to take us?" asked Kronberger.

"We did not reckon on such a large number of people arriving," answered the officer. "Our quarantine building is not equipped to house such large numbers. As you have come from a war zone, so to speak, it is imperative that you be kept in quarantine for a few days. We have fitted out a modern, spacious passenger steamer called the 'Patria' as a temporary quarantine station. Your convoy members will be examined and inoculated there. Besides, the landing formalities also have to be gone through. I would estimate that you'll be free within a fortnight."

Kronberger accepted the explanation calmly. He had learned the art of self-control from Wachsmann.

The Englishman walked past Kerner who had been standing nearby, seemingly quite by chance during the conversation, and disembarked.

"Did you hear that?" asked Kronberger, turning to Erwin. "The man apparently had orders to tell us that cock-and-bull tale."

Kronberger's self-control vanished. What a scoundrel the man was to tell him such blatant lies!

***

At seven o'clock the next morning, the first group left. Apart from the captain of the motorboat, the passengers were escorted by two policemen and a civilian who also had the unmistakable look of an official. Shortly before eight o'clock, the boat docked alongside the "Milos" again in order to fetch the next group. When the boat returned for the third time, Erwin was already expecting to receive first reports, but no one had come back apart from the English escort. Kronberger advised that the members of the security service remove their armbands. Until then, all the passengers had taken all their luggage with them. In order to have a pretext for returning to the "Milos," Altmann went with only his hand luggage on him; he left his rucksack behind, pretending to have forgotten it. He succeeded in being brought back to the "Milos" in

213

order to fetch his rucksack, and the few moments which were allowed him to take his piece of luggage on board the boat sufficed in order to transmit information to Kerner. The latter thus learned that the "Patria" was strictly guarded by the police. A thorough baggage inspection by the policemen had already been begun during the convoy-members' transfer to the "Patria." The British escort demanded that cigarette cases and pocket knives be handed over.

Dr. Segler disembarked with the patients. Albert Wachsmann was among their number. Captain George would not be deterred from accompanying him as far as the boat. The "Milos" began to empty. Those passengers who still remained on board felt lonely: the sudden abundance of space oppressed them. In the evening, they huddled closer together in their sleeping-bags. The kitchen staff were already on the "Patria." The passengers ate together with the Greek crew, from whom kitchen utensils had been left behind. The Greeks were anxious about their future, and looked to the captain for support. They had no work to do, and were immersed in gloomy thoughts. The last twenty convoy members were ready to be transferred. A few sat next to their luggage, awaiting the arrival of the boat which would take them to the "Patria."

Kronberger and Kerner walked through the ship for the last time. If something had been left behind, then they could take it with them and notify the loser. The unplaned wooden shelves which had served as bunks for the passengers were empty and neglected. A broom leant forgotten in a corner. Fragments of a broken mirror lay next to a celluloid doll which had lost its legs. Rats flitted into their holes as the men walked along. Water was dripping through the leak which had never been properly repaired. They went past a dormitory in the hold which had until then sheltered Kronberger and his family. Kronberger stopped. Sadly, he surveyed the bare room. It seemed to grieve him that he must leave the place forever.

They went back on deck and climbed up the iron staircase to the bridge in order to take leave of the captain.

In the weeks they had travelled together, through all the difficulties and dangers they had faced, they had learned to revere the captain as a man with a dedicated sense of duty. His tact, his friendliness, and above all the love which he showed the children had earned him universal esteem and respect. Everyone was sorry to have to leave him behind on the "Milos" without any possibility of looking after him. The captain was well aware of the difficulties awaiting him. He had to reckon on being punished by the British for having transported an illegal convoy, and being expelled from the country after having served his sentence. He would, as he said, have returned to his homeland with the knowledge that he had helped unjustly persecuted refugees, but he had not imagined that his country, too, might be entangled in the war.

He had left his wife and children behind in Athens. He did not dare to think what the Germans might do to the family of a Greek captain who had conveyed Jews to Palestine.

A high-pitched wail from a siren announced the arrival of the boat. "Give Mr. Wachsmann my regards," said Captain George as the two men shook hands with him.

They climbed down into the boat which had already taken on some of the group. The members of the crew who remained behind on the "Milos" waved. The boat began to move.

Chapter Nineteen

The reception which the Palestine Police had prepared for the last group of passengers from the "Milos" left nothing to the imagination. They rummaged through the baggage at the control, and shouted at the passengers. Families were ruthlessly torn apart, as the policemen felt that men should not share the same rooms as their wives.

The "Patria" had already taken on all the passengers from the "Pacific" and "Milos." There was a huge throng of people in the gangways looking for somewhere to sleep. The police did not bother to organize matters, and had also completely forgotten to punctually provide a midday meal for the convoys. The passengers from the "Pacific" had been brought on board the "Patria," which was already under steam, two days earlier.

The "Pacific" convoy consisted of 1,500 people from the Old Reich, including a large, well-organized "Hechalutz" group. They had left Berlin on August 14, and had been taken to Pressburg in sealed railway cars and kept in strict isolation until September 3, when they had embarked. Six hundred Viennese Jews, who had been waiting in Pressburg for the convoy's departure since December 1939, were added to the group.

Contact was quickly established with passengers from the "Pacific." They had already encountered unpleasant experiences with the British during the few days they had been on board. They told of the bad provisions — a quarter of a loaf of bread, an orange, a piece of halavah and a cup of coffee daily. They also described the arrogance of the Palestine Police stationed on board. The latter had reserved first-class cabins for themselves, while women and children, invalids and old people were crowded together in the gangways and overflowing sleeping quarters.

Despite all the underhand dealing to which they had been exposed during the journey and now also on board the "Patria," however, the "Pacific" convoy members had not lost their vigor and their confidence. They bore up under their trials, and remained disciplined despite the oppressive uncertainty.

All approaches to the engine room were guarded by heavily-armed policemen. Although the British had proved incapable of organizing an orderly assignment of sleeping quarters, and totally refused to cooperate with the Jews, they asserted that they would take care of accommodating the children. They had taken on an elderly Englishwoman as nurse-cum-social-worker who was in charge of a cabin filled to bursting with blankets. The woman, dressed in a white nurse's coat, gave orders and advice and hurried busily to and fro, but she did not distribute the new blankets which were so lovely and soft. She meticulously supervised the British property with which she had been entrusted.

The sleeping quarters overflowed during the night, and were badly ventilated. Showers were available, but these only worked on sea water. The showers for the British personnel, which were especially labelled, were not accessible to the general public. They were supplied with fresh water, which was not available to the Jews.

Repeatedly, the Jewish authorities tried to have the deportation decision cancelled. One wave of protest after another swept through the entire Jewish population. The hunger strike on the "Patria" was unsuccessful. England was quite determined to carry through the deportation, and was only waiting for the arrival of the "Atlantic" to complete this action.

The second-class dining-room served as a makeshift office and assembly hall. The screwed-down tables prevented the room from being used as a dormitory.

Two very friendly gentlemen in civilian clothing, who spoke perfect German, sat at two of the dining-room tables. They had appeared one morning with briefcases and had asked a number of people to come into the dining-room. Two unusually charming policemen were on duty. The officials said that they had a few questions to ask each passenger. There was a large empty space between the tables where these men had made themselves comfortable and the line of those waiting to be questioned, so that the latter could not clearly hear the soft questions and the ensuing replies. Whoever had answered the questions was obliged to leave the dining-room immediately.

Kerner had put himself in the foremost row of those waiting in line in order to catch a few snatches of the conversation at the table. The questions which were asked had absolutely no connection with illegal immigration. They asked the passengers' names, ages, last place of residence, and requested information on sites of military importance. The interrogators seemed to attach particular importance to the last question. Kerner was not kept waiting for long.

"Your name and address please."

Kerner gave them.

"What was your last place of residence?"

"Brünn."

"Could you name military objectives or industrial plants which might be of importance for our war strategy?"

At this question, all the hatred which Kerner felt for the Aryan master-race surged up inside him. Now he had the opportunity to pay them back. In his imagination, he already saw British bomber squadrons flying over the city, and attacking the targets which he would mention.

"If I had a map of the city, I could mark in the most important targets for you. The uniform depot in Prager Street with the barracks opposite and the barracks in Serben Street, and above all the 'Zbrojovka' arms factory." Absorbed in his hate, Erwin did not notice that the official had turned over the sheet of paper and given it to him to sign, which he did without hesitation.

Through his signature, he had unknowingly declared himself willing to be deported to Mauritius. He no more dreamt of it than all the others who were questioned before and after him.

The extremely amiable questioners finished their work at two p.m. as befitted punctual colonial officials. They promised to return the next day, but were never seen again.

The third ship, the "Atlantic," reached the harbor and anchored a few hundred yards from the "Patria." The distance was, however, too great to enable contact to be established. Kerner stood leaning on the railing, and looked across to where he knew Fritz Heller was. How glad he would have been to have him there, to tell him that a last, desperate attempt was about to take place, which, if successful, would enable the passengers of the three gallant ships, the "Milos," "Pacific," and "Atlantic," to land. He wanted to have Fritz Heller by his side during this last, bitter struggle. Perhaps at least one of them would be lucky enough to break through and remain in the country. The convoy management had kept the news of the impending deportation secret, and was careful not to allow it to come to the knowledge of the convoy members as a whole. Even Albert Wachsmann did not know of it. He had now lain for days in his cabin, nursed devotedly by Lea Adler. Dr. Segler had diagnosed scarlet fever. Responsibility weighed heavily on the members of the convoy management. Kerner could not obtain the advice of his experienced friend; indeed, he could not even inform him that their deportation was imminent. The situation required the utmost exertion of all his faculties. He had to feign confidence to his fellow-travellers, encourage them and keep them confident that they would arrive on land within a few days. He had to ensure that the members of the security service patrolled the ship continuously, watching for people who had weakened to the point of collapse by the hunger strike. He stood by the railing, turned his eyes away from the "Atlantic" and looked across to the town which was so near that he could see the buses in the streets. He saw the Technion building, which he recognized from photographs, and the golden dome of the Bahai temple, whose splendor he knew from hearsay. He took leave in spirit of the beloved town which he had never entered, and which he did not know if he would ever see again in his lifetime. The sound of a sob behind him jolted him out of his reverie. He turned around and saw a woman who, with tears in her eyes, was also looking across at the city. Kerner had not noticed her arrival.

"Why are you crying, Mrs. Siebel?"

The woman crumpled up her handkerchief in her hand.

"My daughter, my only child, lives in Haifa. I shall never see her again because they're going to deport us," she said.

Tears ran down her cheeks.

Kerner pulled himself together. His voice was stern.

"Don't make a fuss. Go to your cabin. I know nothing about any deportation."

Mrs. Siebel looked at him. Not a muscle moved in Kerner's face. His eyes met hers unflinchingly.

"Then it isn't true what people on the ship are saying about being deported to Mauritius?" she asked. A tiny glimmer of hope flickered in her eyes.

"We were told by a British officer that the 'Patria' is only a quarantine station. We shall very shortly be on land," Kerner said encouragingly.

Mrs. Siebel pressed his hand and left the deck comforted. Only then did Erwin realize how much the conversation had exhausted him. He paced up and down the deck in order to regain his composure.

Ernst Hartmann, the Viennese hotel owner whose lower jaw had been broken by the Gestapo in Brünn and who was now suffering from a permanent speech defect, came up on deck to look for Kerner. The two had become friendly during the journey.

"Have you got a cigarette?" he asked.

"Not at the moment, but I'm counting on getting one soon from the nurse. We must be careful when we smoke. It is strictly forbidden on board the ship. If we're caught, we'll be put in the ship's prison, and you know that I can't afford that now. Albert Wachsmann is sick with scarlet fever and lying isolated in his cabin. Two of our group leaders are in hospital with a high fever," Kerner told him.

The two men were silent. They heard the chugging of a motor from one of the police boats which were circling the "Patria" incessantly. A young boy ran nimbly across the deck. He stopped when he saw Kerner and handed him a folded note.

Erwin read it through carefully, and then crumpled it up into a tiny ball and flicked it with his finger over the railing into the sea.

"I'm coming immediately," he informed the boy.

The convoy leaders sat in a cramped cabin. They were utterly exhausted and slightly unkempt. The lack of food and soap was clearly visible. The sun sank slowly into the sea. Like a smouldering firebrand, its blood-red rays lit up the narrow room through the porthole. The situation was clear to the convoy leaders. If the British succeeded in deporting them, it would mean the end of emigration from Europe, and the Jews living there would be lost. No country would allow steamers to sail through their stretch of the Danube. Even the Jews in Rumania, Bulgaria and Greece would not escape the destruction which was threatening them. There would no longer be any possibility of rescue. The convoy leaders had received the latest news from land during the night. A Jewish policewoman in the Palestine Police, who had been sent on board the "Patria" to supervise and take care of the women and children, had made contact with them. The last message robbed the convoy leaders of all hope, for the negotiations between representatives of the Jewish Agency and the Mandate authorities had been unsuccessful. The High Commissioner had even had the impudence to refuse the president of the "Va'ad Leumi" (Jewish National Council) — the universally esteemed leader of the delegation, Yitzchak Ben-Zvi — permission to take the part of the illegal immigrants.

Interventions in London were countered with the deportation order. The Jewish community in Palestine was kept down by force. A curfew was imposed on Haifa during the evening and night, the guard at the entrance to the port reinforced by soldiers, the "Patria" encircled continuously by motorboats of the Palestine Police, and the desperate immigrants guarded by a large body of policemen stationed on board the ship.

In this impossible situation, only sabotage of the ship itself could stop the "Patria" from sailing. It was clear to the convoy leaders that every conceivable precaution had to be taken in order to reduce the danger to human life to a minimum. Despite their increased agitation, the men in the cabin spoke very softly. The members of the security service who were on guard in the immediate vicinity of the cabin (in order to give warning of the arrival of the Palestine Police by knocking on the door) did not hear a word of the discussions inside the cabin.

The sun had set in the sea. A blood-red sheen still tinted the waters of the bay.

That day, as every day during the entire journey, the convoy management's order of the day was drawn up and typed out on the only typewriter. Kronberger signed the document in place of Wachsmann, who lay groaning in a feverish daze.

At seven p.m., Kerner went into the "Patria"'s dining-room. The passengers were sitting at the tables, swallowing the thin soup which had been distributed by the ship's kitchen. Many ate chocolate which had been brought on board as a present from the Jewish authorities.

It was Eliezer Hirsch's turn to supervise the security service that evening. He waited at the entrance to the dining-hall in order to inspect all the dormitories together with Kerner before people went to sleep at nine o'clock. The convoy members in the dining-room conversed in whispers. Eliezer Hirsch walked into the middle of the hall with Kerner.

"Quiet, please, while the order of the day is read out," he called.

The conversations in the hall died down. Everyone stood up, came nearer and stood round the two men. Kerner waited until the noise made by the people around him had stopped. His eyes had dark rings under them and were sunk deep into their sockets; his face looked even paler by electric light than by day. His jacket hung loosely at the shoulders and his grey riding-breeches were stuck into a pair of Canadian boots which had lost their lustre. His blue and white armband with the golden border had been freshly washed and was still slightly damp. He looked around him, his glance lingering for a second on the faces near him. He unfolded the sheet of paper and raised it shoulder high so as to catch the light from the ceiling. Silence reigned in the hall.

He read slowly and clearly:

"Order of the day issued by the convoy management.

"1. In the name of all the groups on the 'Patria,' the convoy management protests against the British Mandate's announcement on the radio and in the press that the British navy overcame three illegal ships in Palestinian territorial waters after a violent struggle, and took the passengers prisoner. We know nothing of any struggle and saw not a single British warship except for a Palestine Police boat manned by six policemen which approached us off Ras el Nakura. The crew boarded our ship without any opposition on our part, and gave the captain instructions to dock in the port of Haifa.

"We protest against our imprisonment on the 'Patria' and the description 'prisoners.' We are refugees who have escaped from countries occupied by Hitler in order to settle in our homeland, on the basis of our historic right to do so as well as the Balfour Declaration which was solemnly given by the British government on November 2, 1917.

"We solemnly declare our solidarity with our brethren living in Eretz Israel, the land of our fathers, who are fighting for us and with us to open the gates of this country to all Jews threatened by Hitler.

"2. Tomorrow, November 25, the ship will be given a thorough cleaning. All convoy members are therefore to leave their cabins and dormitories by eight a.m. at the latest, and without exception to come up on deck. Luggage is to remain below. No room is to be entered after eight o'clock until permission has been granted by the convoy management. This order is to be obeyed without fail.

222

"3. It is strictly forbidden to talk to the ship's crew or to members of the Palestine Police on board.

"4. Any case of illness among the convoy members is to immediately be reported to the convoy doctor on duty.

"Issued on November 24,1940, the eighty-fourth day of our Aliyah, on board the 'Patria' in the port of Haifa."

***

The convoy members had listened quietly. Now they crowded around the two men. They had questions to ask. Uncertainty weighed heavily on them. Kerner avoided their questions, and only reiterated the importance of the discipline demanded in the order of the day. He made his way through the throng of people surrounding them. Eliezer Hirsch followed at his heels. They went into every dormitory and every cabin, on the 17,000-ton ship. They proceeded down below where a grey-haired Frenchman from the ship's bakery was distributing rolls to the children on the convoy, and where a Siamese stoker, who happened to be off duty, was giving the same children sweets. They went past the entrance to the engine room, which was guarded by two police sentries, climbed the stairs, and read out the order of the day on deck and next to the ship's prison where swimmers were interned who had been caught by the Palestine Police while attempting to reach land.

At nine p.m., the lights went out. Only the few emergency lamps gave a glow. Whispering still continued in the dormitories. Men from the security service stood by the doors and ordered people to be quiet. Kerner and Eliezer Hirsch fetched their raincoats in order to protect themselves from the cold night air. They stood by the railing and looked across at the dimly-lit houses and streets of the town. Hartmann joined them. He had procured a single cigarette. The three of them shared it, covering the glowing end with the hollow of their hands. A rifle bullet shipped across the waves. Two searchlights scoured the bay. A police boat came quickly over to the patch of light, hove to, and then steered towards the "Patria."

For a few seconds, the searchlight lit up the police force's rifle barrels on the narrow jetty to which the ship had been made fast with ropes. Behing the narrow concrete escarpment protected by gigantic boulders surged the sea. There was not a star in the sky. Somewhere far away in the darkness lay Europe.

Cranes loomed up next to the dimly-lit ships out of the darkness of the port. They were guarded by the police. The "Patria"'s loading crane lifted crates and barrels which quickly disappeared into the ship's hull.

A coal carrier came up alongside the ship's mighty hull. Drops of sweat dripped from the laborers' sooty faces despite the cool night breeze. They were clearly visible in the beam of the searchlights which lit up the carrier at regular intervals. Three pairs of eyes followed the proceedings from the deck.

Hartmann grumbled softly: "To deport refugees, tortured human beings — for that there's tonnage in the middle of a war against Hitler."

Eliezer Hirsch nudged him.

"Quiet! We mustn't be discovered here," her warned.

The three shadows ducked noiselessly in order to avoid the searchlight from the motorboat which circled the "Patria" once again.

The wind rose. Sheet-lightning flickered far out to sea. The night air became damp and cooler. The rumble of thunder became louder and the lightning flashes sharper and more frequent. Large drops clattered onto the deck, singly at first, then faster, until a heavy downpour engulfed the "Patria." After a few moments, the rain let up. The storm moved away across the bay. In the irregular flashes of lightning, the silhouette of the "Milos" emerged for a moment, as it pulled at its anchor chain in the middle of the port, far from the jetty.

***

The upper deck filled with people. The members of the security service went through the ship, ordering lingerers to leave their cabins.

At eight thirty, Kronberger called his closest colleagues to a meeting in the convoy management's cabin. They sat round a small table and waited for Kronberger's report on the situation. Kerner looked nervously at his watch.

"It is 8:45," he said.

Kronberger looked at him before he began to speak.

He had the unpleasant duty to inform them that all legal

224

attempts by the Jewish authorities in Palestine to prevent the deportation to Mauritius had failed.

Kerner looked at his watch again.

"It is now 8:54," he said.

Gruber turned on him.

"What do you keep announcing the time for? It's 8:45, it is 8:54. What's that supposed to mean?"

"Because at nine o'clock something is going to happen," said Kronberger.

Everyone looked at him.

As though in accordance with a premeditated plan, a number of people from the German convoy jumped overboard at nine a.m. The police fired over their heads in order to prevent them from swimming away. They gave chase in their motorboats. At the same moment, men jumped over the railing on the other side of the deck. The British began to fire again.

A muffled explosion shook the ship. The alarm clock fell down from the wall of the cabin onto the table. From the next room came the wailing of an Arab policewoman who was on duty that day and, finding herself without work, had lain down for a short nap.

An English policeman hurried through the empty dining-room to the corridor which led to the cabins.

"Put on lifebelts, put on lifebelts," he called. The "Patria" slowly keeled over to one side. Kronberger tottered out of the door. His briefcase fell to the floor. Gruber took him by the hand and helped him up the steps to the deck.

People clung to the railing in order not to slip over the side as the ship continued to keel over.

A few boys who were in the hold climbed up the banisters as a throng of people was hanging onto the stairs trying to get up. Due to the angle at which the ship was lying, and the weight of the bodies hanging onto them, the stairs became top heavy and collapsed onto the lower deck.

A British naval officer fought to get to the boiler room through the crowd of people shoving to reach the deck. His daring plan to open the vents so as to let the steam out saved the ship from an explosion which would have blown everything to pieces. He paid for his courage with his young life.

A few men still remained in one of the lower-lying dormitories which had been occupied by a group of former Jewish soldiers in the Czechoslovakian army. One of their number stood on guard. At the moment when the explosion took place, he opened the door and helped the men out. A flying piece of iron struck against his head. The door closed. The exit shifted due to the "Patria"'s ever-increasing list, and could no longer be reached from the inside. Bedsteads fell on the heads of those who had been locked in. The water rose quickly, and people and objects were thrown around in confusion. Those who were hit fell down and could no longer get up again. From among the casualties only three men escaped. They had succeeded in keeping themselves afloat by swimming until the "Patria" struck ground broadside on and stopped sinking. The incoming water left them a breathing space of barely half a yard. They held out for hours, banging with pieces of wood which drifted past them against the side of the ship until hours later, the rescue team finally heard the knocking and melted the armor-plates with oxyacetylene torches.

People jumped into the sea from the deck of the "Patria" and swam to the nearby shore. With strength born of despair and mortal terror, they strove to escape from within range of the sinking ship. The side of the deck facing the sea rose ever higher while the side opposite the port sank simultaneously into the sea.

An ominous rumbling came from the upper deck where mattresses and boards had been stored which were to serve as beds for the "Libertad" convoy interred in Atlit, whom the British had also intended to deport in the "Patria." The stacks of boards began to move, tore through a piece of railing and crashed into the sea with a dull thud. Swimmers who were hit by them sank under the waves. The boards covered the sea for yards around like a clean-swept wooden floor. The people who were fighting for their lives underneath them were irretrievably lost. The heavy mattresses also descended. They flew through the air as though flung by a mighty hand, and landed on the unfortunate people who were still trying to cast off a lifeboat from the "Patria."

A police motorboat came rushing over from the harbor. Oil steamers and freighters put out their lifeboats. The crew of an Arab fishingboat rowed with all its might towards the scene of the disaster.

No boat dared to approach the side where boards and mattresses had flung people into the depths. The "Patria" might founder any moment and swallow up the rescuers together with the survivors. All the vessels gathered around the railing which towered high above them in order to catch people who jumped from it. A small police boat rocked up and down on the waves. It ventured near the sinking steamer. A young woman was helped down into the boat on a rope held by two policemen. She had just recently given birth to a baby girl. The new-born baby was tied up into a bundle and thrown down by a policeman. His colleague in the boat caught it and laid it in the arms of the trembling mother.

A man swung over the railing and jumped into the sea. The boat moved a few yards towards him and picked him up, then sailed quickly away in order to take the mother and baby to the hospital. The dripping wet father was allowed to land with them.

Erwin Kerner had been flung against the landing stage, which was already under water. He had had the presence of mind to throw his body to one side and thereby avoid an iron post. There was a small iron platform above his head which was just large enough to protect him from the avalanche of boards and mattresses. He ducked instinctively in order not to be hit. The thundering wave of boards passed over him. He climbed over the railing which was under nearly eighteen inches of water, and tried to scale the side of the steamer. A trembling and rattling shook the ship's mighty body and it threatened to keel over him into the sea. A hard object pushed his head under water for a moment. He let go of the ship with his left hand and thought he was lost. His wristwatch flashed underwater. With renewed strength, he raised his arm again. He lifted his head. The salty tang of the sea burned his lips. His left hand caught hold of the side of a boat which had pushed his head under a moment earlier. He pulled himself up and dropped into the boat. The latter was a lifeboat from the "Patria" which had not been unfastened and was almost half full of water. The huge ship had touched bottom, and had righted itself somewhat. Waves had splashed into the boat, which now hung in the air a few inches above the surface of the water. The "Patria" was no longer sinking, but bales and barrels still flew from the deck into the sea. Kerner sat up to his hips in water and stared at the sea, trying to think of a way to save himself. Magda Hirsch was swimming not far from him. He knew her and wanted to call out to her. There was a humming sound, a dull thud, and a little jet of water spurted up. Where the young woman had been just before,

227

a red-striped barrel now turned in the waves. Kerner stared at the barrel. He covered his eyes with his hand. Someone called his name. Above the rushing of the waves breaking against the ship, the rattling, rumbling and creaking, above the wailing of sirens from ships still calling for help for the "Patria," a human voice penetrated to him.

A man in dripping clothes held onto the railing. His feet sought a foothold on the gently-rocking boards. Slowly, very slowly, the figure approached. Kerner extended out his right hand in order to pull the tottering, totally exhausted man into the boat. The latter finally put a leg over the side of the boat. With his last remaining strength, Kerner dragged him over and let him sink down upon the seat. The exhausted man's breath came in gasps.

"Let's call for help. Someone will surely hear us," he said.

"No boat will come here. No one thinks that anybody is still here. We must decide how we can help ourselves. The ship is now lying quietly. It is no longer sinking. We must rest a moment, Mr. Gruber, and then climb along the side of the ship. Perhaps we can reach the ropes by which the ship is made fast to the jetty."

The waves gently rocked the two men sitting in the boat. Kerner tried to calculate the distance to the place where he supposed the ropes to be.

They stood up and began to climb along the side of the ship, clinging tightly. The slightest projection, an iron ring, sometimes only a slightly larger rivet, afforded them a tiny foothold and eased the heavy burden on their hands. Quite exhausted, they reached the place where the ship's screw projected from the water. Finally, they saw three thin ropes in front of them with which the "Patria" had been made fast. There was only a short space remaining to be covered. With their last reserves strength, they inched their way forwards. Their hands were flayed and bloody. Sweat ran down their chalk-white faces. Their breath came in gasps. Someone called to them to throw off their jackets which were dripping with sea water and hindering their progress. They could not do so, however, for fear of losing their balance. Another half-yard still separated them from the ropes. A hand reached out towards them and seized Gruber's arm. He put his foot on the supporting cable and groped with his right hand for the second line which came up to the height of his chest. He moved his foot slowly forwards and joined the long row of men and women from the upper deck who were tottering towards the jetty on the rope. The third rope stretched just above their heads. Many held onto it with one hand and balanced themelves with the careful, groping step of a tight-rope walker. Although the rope was crowded with people who had come from the ship and were creeping with excruciating slowness along this single shaky line of communication with the shore, there was no panic. Finally, Erwin too put his foot on the rope. Some-one on deck had broken the human chain for a moment with a loud shout of "Stop!" and had thus made a few inches of rope free for him so that he could edge his way into the line. His jacket hindered him, and he shrugged it off into the sea. A rowboat patrolled near the ropes, picking people up who had no more strength to hold on, and carried them to the boulders which protected the narrow cement escarpment of the jetty from the surging of the waves. It then returned to look for more people whose strength was giving out. When Erwin slid off the rope onto dry land, his little remaining strength forsook him completely and he collapsed next to an enormous boulder. People on board the "Patria" crowded together on the upper deck which towered high above the water. Many did not dare to jump off, fearing that they would fall onto the armor-plates. The rescue teams which came hurrying from the port had not yet gone on board. They called to the survivors to jump into the water so that they could be picked up.

A Siamese — one of the stokers who had been employed on the ship — broke through the dense crowd, yelling unintelligibly. He had a small girl under his left arm. He climbed over the railing, still clinging to it with his right hand. He hung for a moment over the waves, then dropped, sank with his burden, rose to the surface again, swam towards a nearby police boat and handed over the child before being taken on board himself.

Aron Tennenbaum had smuggled his community's only Torah scroll through all the Nazis' baggage controls. He did not forget it during the terrible moments of the shipwreck. He raised the scroll with its velvet cover high above the heads of the people who, in their mortal terror, blocked his way to the railing. He turned his eyes towards the blue sky which was reflected in the waves. With the age-old cry of "Shema Yisrael," uttered by every Jew when his life is drawing to a close, he pushed his way through and jumped into the leaping waves. He swam to the shore, and laid the scroll down on the boulder against which Kerner had collapsed.

He leant over him to try and help him.

"Are you hurt?" he asked.

"A bit bruised and exhausted," Kerner answered, rising labor-iously from the boulder.

"We have been saved from great danger. We must say a prayer of thanksgiving," said Tennenbaum.

The believer turned eastwards. He prayed in an undertone, his voice choked with tears. Then the two survivors threw themselves down next to the scroll which was dripping with sea water. The free-thinking Zionist lay next to the orthodox prayer leader of a small, remote community. They kissed the damp sand which had collected around the boulder three times.

While the people on the ropes walked step by step towards the shore and salvation, while clusters of bodies hung on the upper railing and planks, beams, mattresses and barrels killed the swimmers, the most ghastly life-and-death-struggle was taking place in the "Patria"'s closed dining-room. A few days earlier, the British had unscrewed the tables from the parquet floor in order to make room for the deportation of the three hundred members of the "Libertad" convoy who had already been interned in the Atlit camp for two months. The hull's sudden list caused the tables and chairs to slide around. The electric light went out. Water shot into the dining-room through the portholes. People were thrown down by the moving tables. The door to the dining-room suddenly appeared above the heads of the people who were fighting desperately for their lives. The roar of the water as it rushed in, the loud crashes as tables were flung against the walls, and the noise which penetrated from the outside drowned the death cries of people who were trying with all their might to climb onto the tables. When the ship had touched bottom, a man attempted to reach the door high above him by climbing on a pile of chairs and tables. He pulled his wife towards him out of the water. The young woman removed her dripping clothes and tried to climb up on her husband. He was much above the average in height and could reach the door when he stretched his hand upwards. His wife climbed up onto him. She stood for a moment on his shoulders. As she was light and supple, she succeeded in reaching the opening. The man called to her to use his head as a stepping-stone. Her feet, wet with sea water, slipped off his head. She made several more attempts until she finally managed to push herself off from her husband's head and pull herself up through the opening. She cried shrilly for help. Another woman's head emerged from the water in the dining-room. Hands groped at the heap of furniture on which the man was standing. A delicate woman climbed up and tried to catch hold of the man's leg. He did not notice her and pulled himself up through the opening. Two British policemen clutched him by the arms and dragged him up on deck.

They had notice the woman clinging to the pile of tables and called to her to hold fast. She held on, panting. Her clothes were dripping. A lifebelt hung around her narrow shoulders. Someone threw her a rope. She tried to catch it, but it was beyond her reach. It dangled above the water and the jumble of tables and chairs. Finally, she gripped the end of the rope and tried to climb it hand over hand. Helping hands reached out to her through the door opening. Only a few inches remained for her to cover.

Her head drooped to one side, and her hands loosened their grip. Without a sound, the young woman fell off the rope. There was a dull thud. The body disappeared, and did not surface again. The two policemen threw out the rope again. A girl pulled herself up, let go, and then stood up once again in the water. She felt clearly that she was standing on the bodies of drowned people. She shivered with horror. Terrified, with death staring her in the face, she clutched the rope convulsively. It was slowly drawn up. Her wet clothes hampered her rescuers. They pulled with all their might and wound the rope around the railing of the staircase in order to have their hands free to catch the girl. A strong arm clutched at her hair and pulled her up. At the same moment, someone cut off her clothes and lifebelt with a sharp knife and removed them from her body. They fell into the water with a smack. The girl lay naked and unconscious on the slanting upper deck. A policeman threw a blanket over her. She was put inside a boat which took her to the jetty where she was left lying until she recovered consciousness by herself.

So long as a human being sees a tiny patch of sky, a glimmer of light, hope keeps him alive. He draws strength to fight from the tiniest ray of light. In the "Patria"'s dormitories, however, where light no longer penetrated and where not even the smallest patch of sky could be seen, death claimed victim after victim. All the furnishings, the last belongings of the poor unfortunates which had been stowed away in suitcases and rucksacks, eddied wildly around in the rising water. The electric light no longer functioned. People were thrown down by the force of the water as it streamed into the cabin. Pieces of wood and iron fell upon their heads in the darkness. The death cries did not penetrate through the side of the ship. The gurgling of water choked every cry for help. There was, moreover, hardly anyone there who could have called. The "Patria"'s side had touched bottom. The water in the dormitories no longer roared; it lay as quietly as in a bathtub. At the bottom of the tub, bodies lay intertwined. In this gloom of death and horror, a young woman still kept herself afloat. A child drifted past her body in the darkness and touched her. A soft child's voice called out "Mother." The woman did not have any children. She wanted to live for the sake of this strange child, to take care of it, to be a mother to it. She herself was still very young. She tried to catch hold of the weeping child but could not find it. She heard the desperate cry a few more times, but could do nothing in the dark. After hours spent in terror, the woman was carried out of the room, half paralyzed. She was scratched all over. The skin hung in shreds from her hands. She alone had survived — the child could no longer be found.

A man could not be persuaded to leave the hull which projected half-way out of the water. He did not weep he had no more tears left. He had lost nine members of his family. The police had to remove him from the hull by force.

The wife of a pharmacist lay in her cabin, paralyzed in both feet, at the time of the explosion. Her husband could have saved himself. He was right next ot the ship's hospital, and it would have been easy for him to reach the ropes and climb across to dry land. He fought his way through the crowd of people pushing upwards from the hull, and jumped down the stairs. He went knowingly to his death. A tradesman from Berlin had succeeded in smuggling a few valuable pieces of jewelry through the Nazi frontier controls. He had hoped that he would thus be able to put his young wife, who was suffering from consumption, into a sanatorium. He helped the gravely-ill woman to catch hold of the rope-ladder which hung down into the sea from the high railing. The ladder swung to and fro as she slowly climbed down. Her husband looked on while she was taken on board a lifeboat. Then he went back into the ship in order to retrieve his briefcase with the jewelry. He was never seen again.

A young British policeman stood imperiously at the top of the staircase leading to the bridge. He threw down a long rope, lost his balance, toppled over and knocked his head against a concrete cornice. In those frightful moments of terror, people were still locked inside the ship's prison. They could not open the heavy door from the inside. The water had already risen to their armpits. They rattled the door and shouted. They clung desperately to the narrowly-barred windows. A Palestine Police sergeant finally hurried over to them, unlocked the door and helped the prisoners out. They jumped into the sea, and the sergeant followed. They swam to the jetty and safety.

Three young brothers jumped overboard after the explosion. In the chaos, they lost sight of one another. Too many people were swimming around them. Pieces of wood and suitcases were drifting in the water. How were the three to find one another under such conditions? The youngest of the brothers kept close to the ship. He was a good swimmer. He whistled a signal which the brothers had known from their earliest childhood. The whistle was returned from a short distance away. One of the other brothers was holding onto a board. They found one another. Again and again, they pursed their lips, which were burning from the sea water, in order to give the signal. The answer came faintly back. They swam in the direction from which the signal had been answered until they finally found the third brother who had been swimming near a boat but had refused to be picked up. Only when he saw his brothers coming towards him did he climb into the boat and then helped his brothers aboard.

A fishing boat steered as fast as it could towards a pink silk shirt which was being tossed about on the waves like a balloon. Muscular arms reached out for it. The shirt belonged to a man lying face downwards in the water who was on the point of drowning. The fishermen attempted to save the man's life. They only gave up the struggle when they noticed that blood was welling out of a wound at the back of his head.

***

An elegant car drove from Jerusalem down the winding road through the Judean hills. It turned off by the Arab cemetery at

Ramleh. At Lod, it drove past the airport and Wilhelma, the German Templar settlement where Germans were still living who were hoping for Hitler's victory and in the meantime were inciting their Arab workers against the Jews. The car stopped for a moment to let a small caravan of camels pass, and the British policeman at the crossroads near Wilhelma saw a high-ranking officer sitting in the back of the car next to a correctly-dressed, clean-shaven gentleman. The chauffeur of the car, as well as the guide in the front seat, were uniformed police officials. Their blue, flat-peaked caps bore the intertwined letters "P" of the Palestine Police. The sentry at the crossroads saluted. The car continued on its way, not unduly fast as it was in no hurry. Behind Petach-Tikva it reached the main road from Tel Aviv to Haifa. The car avoided the Jewish settlement area around Tel Aviv and accelerated, driving through the coastal plain which had been planted with orange-tree orchards by the Jews. Towards ten a.m., it passed the police station next to the wine-growing colony of Zichron Ya'akov, which had been founded by Baron Rothschild. From this concrete fortress onwards, the road to Haifa passed through Arab territory, and was very sparsely frequented at that hour. The picturesque lower slopes of the Carmel reached almost to the road. On the seaward side lay the fertile narrow Cabara strip which only a few years earlier had still been a malaria-infested swamp. The men in the car conversed about the excavations in the old Roman war-port of Caesaria, which lay behind the pale yellow sand dunes protecting the area from the sea.

The car was in no hurry, for the deportation of the "Patria" had been fixed for two o'clock. There was thus still plenty of time to sign the necessary documents in Haifa and to supervise the deportation process.

A truck came out of a lane into the main road. The chauffeur of the elegant car thought that he would be able to pass the truck; he had the right of way according to the law as he was on the main road. He felt a slight jolt. There was a grinding of metal and he stopped. The two men in the back of the car and the guide got out and looked at the damage. The car had a puncture and could not continue the journey. The Arab truck driver climbed down from his seat. He bore the police officials' curses with oriental indifference. He pretended not to understand English. The policemen took down his car number and asked to see his driving license.

The man's name was Hassan Ahmed Mustafa, and he lived in the Arab village of Anabta. His identity card, which was dog-eared and dirty, bore the same name. The officials noted all this down exactly, and then let the man drive on.

They hoped to reach Haifa with the next passing car. The silly accident had not caused too much difficulty. When the men reached Haifa after a lengthy delay, the rescue teams were already at work on the "Patria." They carried the patients out of the ship's hospital. Two men took Albert Wachsmann onto a stretcher into a boat. Lea Adler, who was quite exhausted, kept watch beside him.

When the Nablus police station summoned Hassan Ahmed Mustafa for a hearing, they ascertained that the real person of that name had been dead for months.

***

The people who had saved themselves by climbing onto the narrow cement jetty shivered in their wet clothes. Many were almost naked. A cold wind blew from the sea. Those with injuries dragged themselves across the boulders and tried to climb the escarpment high above them. The salt water burned their scratches and cuts. A mother ran half distracted along the jetty, holding a small child in her arms. She screamed that the child was dead.

A British soldier — one of a group who had been detailed to help transport the wounded Jews — put his rifle down on the ground, took the motionless child from the woman and began to rub it near the heart. The child opened its eyes. The soldier covered it with his sweater in order to keep it warm. Minutes passed before it dawned upon the traumatized woman that her child had been saved.

A young girl began laughing hysterically. Men searched desperately for their wives. Children called for their mothers. A man who had crawled through a porthole in order to save himself had a long cut which reached from his hip bone half-way down his thigh. A medical orderly who was surrounded by people in need of help was at his wits' end. Many, far too many survivors, were demanding treatment for their injuries. Someone took a bottle of iodine from his tray and poured some of it into the man's wound. The latter roared with pain. The doctors and nurses, who were themselves bruised and ready to collapse from exhaustion, helped the

235

injured. They had neither medicines nor instruments, but their presence alone and their unflagging sense of duty, even a temporary bandage, had a soothing effect.

People still swam from the "Patria" to the jetty, although the rescue teams were already at work on board.

A boy of scarcely sixteen had saved the blue and white flag. He held it above his head while he swam to the jetty so that it should not get wet.

A textile merchant from Prague had picked up his playing cards in the panic. That was the only article he saved.

An Arab fishing boat pulled two men out of the water. It put them down on a boulder and turned back towards the ship.

Eliezer Hirsch helped an old man ashore. He did not yet know of the death of his wife.

Kerner watched as Eliezer climbed up the jetty with the old man whom he had saved, but he avoided him and disappeared into the crowd. He did not want to be the first to tell him the news of his wife's death. In the crowd, Erwin met Mrs. Wachsmann and her small daughter. Both of them were completely soaked. Mrs. Wachsmann already knew that her husband had been rescued.

British soldiers and policemen had taken up positions at all the exits from the port. They tried to assemble all the survivors of the shipwreck into one group in order to be able to escort them to the port at the same time. They politely requested the survivors to congregate on the sandy shore. The first ambulances arrived. Among them were two with a red Star of David.

Those with severe injuries were carried inside the ambulances on stretchers. A policeman sat beside every driver. Slowly, the ambulances drove away.

The British gradually succeeded in persuading people to leave the jetty. They let the exhausted survivors rest on the damp sand and stood beside them, waiting patiently.

They distributed all the cigarettes which they had. A Jewish policeman from the Palestine Police asked the survivors if a Mrs. Goldberg from Breslau had been on the ship. No one could tell him.

Kronberger sat by himself a few yards away from the crowd and looked across at the "Patria." Kerner went up to him and spoke to him. Kronberger got up very slowly.

He had not seen his family during the entire episode, and

had asked about them for the first time. No one knew anything, however.

"A great many people were brought in lifeboats directly to the harbor. Only a minority made their way to the jetty. I'm sure your family is already safe," said Kerner.

Kronberger looked again at the hull projecting out of the water. For a long time he could not tear himself away.

The sun slowly began to set. It was apparently already long after midday. Kerner's watch showed nine thirty, and did not move. He ascertained from the people standing near him that everyone's watch had stopped due to the sea-water exposure.

Finally Kronberger turned away from the sea. "We have suffered a terrible misfortune," he said. He looked around him and continued with a sigh: "This little crowd of battered people — are they the only survivors from the 'Patria'?"

"I saw ships full of people sailing directly towards the harbor," said Kerner, but his voice was weary.

"Take a few people who still have some strength left and organize the survivors into marching order. We don't want to be driven like a flock of sheep. Make this wretched remnant of our convoy regain a little of its self-control."

A beaten army was led away to the prison camp. They maintained their composure even in those terrible moments. Kerner dragged himself back to his fellow convoy members. Everyone stood up. Women and children walked in the middle of the procession. Kronberger walked in the first row next to Captain Grossfeld, the most senior officer in the reserve among the passengers. Next to him went Eliezer Hirsch who had found a few young people to help transport the wounded. The procession moved painfully through the sand. The survivors' clothing hung in tatters on their lean bodies. A few women were wrapped in blankets which had been thrown to them by the policemen. Blood seeped through the temporary dressings; the wounded hobbled along, leaning on pieces of wood which had drifted ashore from the "Patria." An elderly religious man was carried by four men on a stretcher. He had just enough strength to raise his head, but there was a glimmer of light in his eyes. He encouraged his tired bearers.

"Children, we're home! Home in Eretz Israel!" he repeated.

His grandchild, a small, delicate boy with reddish-gold sidelocks, walked behind the stretcher. From time to time, he bent

237

down. He was picking up shells.

The procession was flanked by British soldiers and policemen. They walked a short distance behind, stopping when the first row halted in order to wait for the wounded people who were laboriously making their way forward.

Some Arabs stood crowded behind a barbed-wire fence which separated the harbor from an oriental-looking housing quarter. They called out something, but no one understood what they were saying. A few oranges flew over the fence. They fell in the sand and rolled to the feet of the exhausted survivors. The procession stopped for a moment as the survivors thought that the stones were being thrown at them. The policemen tried to drive the Arabs away, but to no avail as the Arab children continued to press their noses against the wire fence, following the procession curiously with their eyes. The survivors had already reached the port depot. A few yards away from them stood a squad of blue-uniformed policemen with white ambulances behind them. Kronberger raised his right arm and signalled to the procession to halt.

He beckoned to Eliezer Hirsch who was standing nearby. "Tell the convoy members that I request that everyone keeps himself under control for the last few steps."

Eliezer Hirsch went back and said a few words to the men. Their bowed shoulders straightened. The last rows joined up again with the procession.

Kronberger looked round at the people and then walked with military erectness past the waiting policemen. The entire procession followed him men and women with their heads held high and their lips pressed tightly together, who did not so much as glance at their surroundings.

They passed between the rows of policemen and went into a granary.

The large warehouse was full of people. Women covered in blankets or still in their torn clothes rushed towards the new arrivals. Married couples who were finally reunited fell crying into one another's arms.

Mothers embraced their children and kissed them. They felt their bodies to check that they had not been injured. Reunited families looked for somewhere to sit down on the piled-up sacks of grain.

Many people asked desperately about their relatives. They searched the emergency hospital behind a wooden partition which was full of wounded people. A woman swooned beside the stretcher on which her seriously wounded husband was lying. She was laid on a blanket spread out on the floor. A nurse came to look after her. All the stretchers and beds were occupied. Those with slight injuries lay or sat on benches. A girl not yet out of her teens with a red Star of David on her nurse's cap disinfected wounds.

Four long wooden tables stood in the middle of the warehouse. Jewish women in white aprons, Englishwomen in close-fitting costumes, Protestant priests, elderly, extremely correctly-dressed gentlemen and a Catholic clergyman distributed sandwiches, tea, cigarettes, chocolate and oranges to the survivors. Police officers went in and out. The Czechoslovakian consul and his wife, together with a major from the military mission, tried to assist the citizens of their Nazi-occupied country. They represented the Czechoslovakian government-in-exile, which ruled in London with its president, Dr. Benes, and which still considered the Jews who had just been saved as natives of Czechoslovakia with full civil rights. The consul was a Jew.

After nineteen months, Captain Grossfeld once again saw an officer in uniform with the escutcheon of the Bohemian lion on his buttons. He went up to the major and saluted. While the major spoke to him, a police officer approached. The consul intercepted him with a few polite questions. Kronberger had found his son. There was no trace of his wife and small daughter. He held the boy by the hand. The child wept. Kronberger stared straight ahead of him. No one said anything to him.

A man had lost his wife and six children. Of his entire family, only a brother-in-law had remained alive. The two men squatted behind the wooden wall of the emergency hospital. Tears ran down the faces of the men and women standing next to them. No one spoke — what could one say?

There could be no comfort. Eliezer Hirsch asked desperately if anyone had seen Magda. No one could give him any information. The only person to have seen her was Erwin Kerner, but he now lay alone with his eyes closed behind some sacks of grain. He did not want to see anyone, not to be seen himself. He hid his face in his hands and wept.

At about eight o'clock, the British began to remove the survivors. A long row of buses stood outside the warehouse. Those whose relatives had survived went onto the bus with them. There were not enough buses to take everyone away, so some people had to wait until the buses returned.

Kerner joined the last group. He came out slowly from behind the sacks and stood in line with the others. Just in front of him stood Mrs. Wachsmann and her child. Kerner spoke to her and stroked the little girl's damp hair.

"My husband has already been driven off in an ambulance," said Mrs. Wachsmann.

"Where to?" asked Kerner.

"I don't know. The main thing for me is that he's been saved. Do you by any chance know where they're taking us? People say that we're going to be interned. What have we done wrong?"

"We have always known that the British would arrest us if we were caught. According to their laws, we have entered the country illegally, and the punishment for that is imprisonment," explained Kerner.

"Even for the survivors of a shipwreck, who have barely escaped with their lives?" asked Mrs. Wachsmann.

One bus after another drove off. Now it was the last group's turn to embark. Kerner held tight with both hands as he hoisted himself up inside the bus. Every step hurt him. He sat down behind the driver. Mrs. Wachsmann sat behind him. Kerner reserved the window seat next to him for the child.

A tall, blond English soldier waited in front of the bus until all the seats had been taken.

The driver was a Jew. Kerner asked him if they were going to be taken to Acco.

"No, to the Atlit camp," the driver replied.

"What's that?" asked Kerner.

"Much better than Acco," answered the driver. The soldier came inside the bus and the man at the wheel refused to say anymore. The bus advanced a few yards, joined the column of vehicles in front of it and waited.

The blond Englishman offered cigarettes. Most of the passengers were smokers but they refused. They did not want to accept anything from the British. The soldier seemed to notice their refusal, or understood a few words of the conversation. He seemed somewhat hurt. He asked Erwin, whom he took to be the father of the Wachsmanns' little girl, if she would be permitted to accept chocolate. Kerner was already on the point of answering in the negative when one of the passengers advised him to accept the chocolate for the little girl, as it would be important for a delicate child to eat some nourishing food.

The blond soldier handed the child a large slab of chocolate and gave her a friendly smile.

"Well, say thank you!" said her mother.

The little girl thanked the donor almost inaudibly, and did not deign to look at him.

The column began to move.

The streets were empty. The curfew was still in effect. A long column of vehicles transported the last survivors of the "Patria" to the Atlit concentration camp. The convoy was led by an armored police car. The headlights of the buses, which were darkened with blue glass due to the danger of bombing, slowly passed by the last houses in the city. Men and women stood by their dimly-lit windows. They had seen the "Patria" sinking from their balconies. They, too, had relatives in Europe who had no prospect of escaping. The convoy's dimmed headlights moved slowly along the wet asphalt road. After a few miles, the procession turned off the main road from Haifa to Tel Aviv. A dark lane led towards the sea. A narrow sickle-moon rose above the palm trees which lined the road on either side.

The gate of the concentration camp was wide open. Policemen with high, black, lambskin caps — Calpaks — formed a cordon. The camp's main street was lit up. On either side of the street, which was enclosed by a strong barbed-wire fence, were wooden barracks. Two searchlights flashed at brief intervals from the watch towers. The convoy members were led from the buses into a warehouse. They went over in groups of five to long tables where an English sergeant from the Palestine Police had two blankets, shoes, cutlery, and clothing distributed to each prisoner. He entered the names of the arrivals, as well as the articles which had been given to them, in a large account book, asked the prisoners to sign, and then dispatched them through a second door. Three hundred Jews from the Bulgarian "Libertad" convoy were interned in the camp. The camp commander had given them permission to look after the "Patria" passengers on their arrival in Atlit. They did so with a love and consideration that made the survivors feel far better. Kerner was one of the last to climb out of the bus. The gates of the camp clanged shut behind him, with a sound of finality.

241

Chapter Twenty

At two p.m. on November 27, 1960, a light grey taxi passed the Zichron Ya'akov police station. The broad asphalt road was wet from the first rain which had fallen after a very dry summer. The car slowed down. The rain stopped after they had turned off onto the road to Atlit. The taxi drove faster again.

"Do you know at which entrance we should turn in?" asked Dr. Bieber.

"We'll stop where we see a crowd of people. Everyone is sure to come," Kerner replied.

When they reached the cemetery, the service had already begun. They went over to the memorial to the people who had died on the "Patria." Two hundred forty graves were laid out in long rows. The flowers exuded a delicate scent after the rain. The two men walked slowly forward. Friends greeted them. They no longer recognized many of the people there. Albert Wachsmann came up to them.

"I knew you'd come," he said.

The venerable Chief Rabbi of Haifa gave the memorial address.

"In this hour, the free people of Israel remember all those who died while coming illegally on Aliyah:

"We remember especially the 257 passengers on the 'Patria' who lost their lives in the harbor of their homeland; the 1160 Jews who were murdered by the Nazis in Kladovo on their way to freedom; the 430 passengers who died on the 'Mafkura'; the 769 men, women and children on the 'Struma'; the 230 passengers on the 'Salvadore' who were drowned; and the 124 members of the 'Atlantic' convoy who died in British internment camps on the malaria-infested island of Mauritius."

***

While the memorial service was taking place in the cemetery, a boat sailed to within a few yards of the wreck of the "Patria." A wreath with the national flag was raised on board. The boat's crew honored those whose grave would forever remain the hull of the "Patria."